1985 Supplement

PROPERTY

EDITORIAL ADVISORY BOARD

Little, Brown and Company
Law Book Division

A. James Casner, *Chairman*
Austin Wakeman Scott Professor of Law, Emeritus
Harvard University

Francis A. Allen
Edson R. Sunderland Professor of Law
University of Michigan

Clark Byse
Byrne Professor of Administrative Law, Emeritus
Harvard University

Thomas Ehrlich
Provost and Professor of Law
University of Pennsylvania

Richard A. Epstein
James Parker Hall Professor of Law
University of Chicago

E. Allan Farnsworth
Alfred McCormack Professor of Law
Columbia University

Geoffrey C. Hazard, Jr.
Nathan Baker Professor of Law
Yale University

Bernard Wolfman
Fessenden Professor of Law
Harvard University

1985 Supplement
PROPERTY

Jesse Dukeminier
Professor of Law
University of California
Los Angeles

James E. Krier
Professor of Law
University of Michigan

Little, Brown and Company   *Boston and Toronto*

Copyright © 1985 by Jesse Dukeminier and James E. Krier

All rights reserved. No part of this book may be reproduced in any form or by any electronic or mechanical means including information storage and retrieval systems without permission in writing from the publisher, except by a reviewer who may quote brief passages in a review.

Library of Congress Catalog Card No. 80-84030

ISBN 0-316-19516-2

Third Printing

CCP

*Published simultaneously in Canada
by Little, Brown & Company (Canada) Limited*

PRINTED IN THE UNITED STATES OF AMERICA

Contents

Table of Cases   *ix*
Preface   *xiii*
Acknowledgments   *xv*

PART 1. AN INTRODUCTION TO SOME FUNDAMENTALS   1

Chapter One. Acquisition of Property Other than by Voluntary Transfer   2

A. Ownership and Possession: The Law of Finders   2
B. The Rule of Capture   3
C. Acquisition of Water Rights   4
D. Adverse Possession   4
    Note: Adverse Possession and the Common Law Method   6

PART 2. THE SYSTEM OF ESTATES   9

Chapter Two. The Leasehold Estates: Tradition, Tension, and Change in Landlord-Tenant Law   10

A. The Leasehold Estates   10
B. The Lease   11
C. Selection of Tenants   11
    Stewart, Landlords' Verdict: Lawyers as Tenants Have Little Appeal   12
E. Assignments and Subleases   15
    Funk v. Funk   *15*
F. Tenant's Duties; Landlord's Rights and Remedies   20
G. Landlord's Duties; Tenant's Rights and Remedies   21

	Note: Landlord's Tort Liability — Abandoning the Conventional View	21
	Problem	21
	Problem	24
H.	Government Support of Housing	25

Chapter Three. Possessory Estates (Leaseholds Aside) — 27

B.	The Fee Simple	27
	Mahrenholz v. County Board of School Trustees	27
	Questions	35
D.	The Life Estate	35
	White v. Brown	35
F.	Cooperatives and Condominiums	40
	Laguna Royale Owners Assn. v. Darger	40
	Questions	50
	Franklin v. Spadaforo	50
	Ellickson, Cities and Homeowners Associations	54

Chapter Four. Future Interests — 59

B.	Future Interests in the Transferor	59
D.	The Trust	59
	Sullivan v. Burkin	59
E.	Rules Furthering Marketability	66
	Brown v. Independent Baptist Church of Woburn	66
	Notes and Questions	68

Chapter Five. Co-Ownership and Marital Interests — 69

A.	Common Law Concurrent Interests	69
	Allen v. Batchelder	70
B.	Marital Interests	74
	Wenig, The Marital Property Act	75

PART 3. VOLUNTARY TRANSFER OF PROPERTY: HEREIN MOSTLY SALES OF LAND — 79

Chapter Six. Transfer by Sale and by Gift — 80

A.	The Land Transactions Industry	80

Contents

B.	The Contract of Sale	81
	Reed v. King	*81*

Chapter Seven. Methods of Title Assurance — 87

B.	Title Insurance	87
	L. Smirlock Realty Corp. v. Title Guaranty Co.	*87*

PART 4. MORE ON VOLUNTARY AND INVOLUNTARY TRANSFER: CONTROL OF LAND USE THROUGH "PRIVATE" AND "PUBLIC" MEANS — 97

Chapter Eight. Nuisances Private and Public — 98

A.	An Introduction to the Substantive Law	98
	Note: Solar Energy and the Law of Nuisance	98
	Prah v. Maretti	*98*
	Note	111
	Friendswood Development Co. v. Smith-Southwest Industries	*111*
	Notes and Questions	127
B.	Remedies (and More on the Substantive Law)	128

Chapter Nine. Private Land-Use Arrangements: A Comparative Study of Servitudes — 131

A.	An Overview of Servitudes	131
B.	Creation of Servitudes	131
E.	Termination of Servitudes	132
	Crane Neck Association, Inc. v. New York City/Long Island County	*132*
	Questions	137

Chapter Ten. Eminent Domain and the Implicit Taking Problem — 139

B.	The Public-Use Puzzle	139
	Hawaii Housing Authority v. Midkiff	*139*
	Note: Recent (Extreme) Instances of "Public Use"	146
	Poletown Neighborhood Council v. City of Detroit	146
	City of Oakland v. Oakland Raiders	150

vii

	C.	Measuring Just Compensation	154
		United States v. 50 Acres of Land	*154*
	D.	Explicit and Implicit Takings	160
		Loretto v. Teleprompter Manhattan CATV Corp.	*160*
		Notes and Questions	178
		Note: What is a "Physical Invasion"?	180
		Fresh Pond Shopping Center, Inc. v. Acheson	180
		Nash v. City of Santa Monica	183
		Gregory v. City of San Juan Capistrano	186
		San Diego Gas and Electric Co. v. San Diego	*187*
		Notes and Questions	195

Chapter Eleven. Zoning Processes, Practices, and Problems — 197

	B.	The Nonconforming Use	197
	C.	Achieving Flexibility in Zoning	197
	D.	The Objectives of Zoning (Legitimate and Otherwise)	198
		Metromedia, Inc. v. San Diego	*198*
		Notes	209
		Southern Burlington County NAACP v. Township of Mount Laurel [Mount Laurel II]	*213*
		Notes and Questions	234

Table of Cases

Italics indicate principal cases.
All references are to Supplement page numbers.

Acton v. Blundell, 127
Ailes v. Decatur County Area Planning Commn., 197
Allen v. Batchelder, 70

Berman v. Parker, 146
Boudreau v. General Elec. Co., 22
Brown v. Independent Baptist Church of Woburn, 66, 68
Burrows v. City of Keene, 195
Burt, Charles E., Inc. v. Seven Grand Corp., 21

Charles E. Burt, Inc. v. Seven Grand Corp., 21
City of New York v. Rodriguez, 25
City of Oakland v. Oakland Raiders, 150
City of Seattle, In re, 150
Crane Neck Association, Inc. v. New York City/Long Island County, 132

Elwes v. Brigg Gas Co., 2

Fasano v. Board of County Commrs., 197
Fidelity First Federal Sav. & Loan Assn. v. de la Cuesta, 80
Franklin v. Spadaforo, 50
Fresh Pond Shopping Center, Inc. v. Acheson, 180
Fresh Pond Shopping Center, Inc. v. Rent Control Bd., 180
Friendswood Dev. Co. v. Smith-Southwest Industries, 111, 127
Funk v. Funk, 15

Graham v. Estuary Props., Inc., 160
Granat v. Keasler, 186
Gray v. Crotts, 70
Gregory v. City of San Juan Capistrano, 186

Halet v. Wend Inv. Co., 11
Hamilton Bank v. Williamson County Regional Planning Commn., 195
Harms v. Sprague, 69
Hawaii Hous. Auth. v. Midkiff, 139, 146
Henry v. Kennedy, 70
Hernandez v. City of Lafayette, 196
Hubbard v. Curtiss, 6

In re City of Seattle, 150
In re Pruner's Estate, 68

Just v. Marinette County, 160

Kaiser Aetna v. United States, 178
Kent v. Humphries, 21
Kerwin v. Donaghy, 59

Laguna Royale Owners Assn. v. Darger, 40
Langbrook Props., Ltd. v. Surrey County Council, 127
Loretto v. Teleprompter Manhattan CATV Corp., 160, 178, 180
L. Smirlock Realty Corp. v. Title Guar. Co., 87

McAvoy v. Medina, 7
Mahrenholz v. County Bd. of School Trustees (417 N.E. 2d), 27
Mahrenholz v. County Bd. of School Trustees (466 N.E. 2d), 35
Martino v. Santa Clara Valley Water Dist., 195
Members of City Council of Los Angeles v. Taxpayers for Vincent, 209
Metromedia, Inc. v. City of San Diego (32 Cal. 3d), 209
Metromedia, Inc. v. San Diego (453 U.S.), 198, 209
Minonk State Bank v. Grassman, 69
Mountain States Legal Found. v. Clark, 3

Nash v. City of Santa Monica, 183
National Shawmut Bank v. Cumming, 59

Oak's Oil Service, Inc. v. Massachusetts Bay Transp. Auth., 59
Olwell v. Clark, 70

Pagelsdorf v. Safeco Ins. Co. of America, 24
Park West Management Corp. v. Mitchell, 24
Paset v. Old Orchard Bank & Trust Co., 7
Philpot v. Field, 10
Poletown Neighborhood Council v. City of Detroit, 146

Table of Cases

Prah v. Maretti, 98, 128
Pruner's Estate, In re, 68
PruneYard Shopping Center v. Robins, 178, 179

Reed v. King, 81
Rice v. Boston & Worcester R.R., 59
Riddle v. Harmon, 69
Rippley v. City of Lincoln, 195

San Diego Gas & Elec. Co. v. San Diego, 187, 195, 196
Sargent v. Ross, 24
Schad v. Mount Ephraim, 212
S.D.G. v. Inventory Control Co., 10
Simon v. Solomon, 22
Smirlock, L., Realty Corp. v. Title Guar. Co., 87
Southern Burlington County NAACP v. Township of Mount Laurel [*Mount Laurel I*], 212, 234
Southern Burlington County NAACP v. Township of Mount Laurel [*Mount Laurel II*], 212, *213,* 234
Spur Feeding Co. v. Superior Court, 129
Stevan v. Brown, 21
Sullivan v. Burkin, 59

United States v. 50 Acres of Land, 154
United States v. 564.54 Acres of Land, 154

Vance v. Universal Amusement Co., 128

White v. Brown, 35
Wilson v. Interlake Steel Co., 98

Young v. American Mini Theatres, 212

Zimmerman v. Moore, 22
Zinn v. State, 195

Preface

It would be surprising for the law of property to undergo significant change in a few short years; property doctrine is, after all, notable for its stability. The fact remains, however, that since publication of the coursebook in 1981 there have been important developments, and not just in the more volatile "public law" areas such as zoning or eminent domain. The last two areas have, to be sure, generated perhaps the most provocative material — in eminent domain, for example, the Supreme Court's decisions in *Midkiff* and *Loretto* (the latter really only endorsing some rather old, and perhaps odd, law) and Justice Brennan's dissent (or should one call it the majority opinion?) in the *San Diego* case; in zoning, the Court's decision in *Metromedia* and the decision of the New Jersey Supreme Court in *Mount Laurel II*.

These and other developments in eminent domain and zoning are reported in Chapters 10 and 11 of this supplement. More traditional (or stable, or "private") areas of property have also experienced some alteration, however. Prah v. Maretti announces a cause of action in nuisance (Chapter 8) for solar obstruction; Sullivan v. Burkin makes new law in the area of trusts (Chapter 4); and so on. Each chapter of the book has had to contend with new events and new ideas — including contributions in the scholarly literature — of varying significance. We have tried to provide a thorough but judicious account.

Footnotes in this supplement take the number of the preceding footnote in the coursebook and add an alphabetical postscript, except in those instances where the new footnote follows the final footnote of a given chapter in the book. As always, we are grateful to our secretaries, our research assistants — Megan Dorsey especially — and our editors at Little, Brown for their kind and efficient assistance.

Jesse Dukeminier
James E. Krier

March 1985

Acknowledgments

The authors acknowledge the permissions kindly granted to reproduce excerpts from the materials indicated below.

Ellickson, Cities and Homeowners Associations, 130 University of Pennsylvania Law Review 1519 (1982). Reprinted by permission.
Helmholz, Adverse Possession and Subjective Intent, 61 Washington University Law Quarterly 331 (1983). Reprinted by permission.
Rose, The *Mount Laurel II* Decision: Is It Based on Wishful Thinking?, 12 Real Estate Law Journal 115 (1983). Reprinted by permission of Warren, Gorham & Lamont, 210 South Street, Boston, Massachusetts 02111. All rights reserved.
Stewart, Landlords' Verdict: Lawyers as Tenants Have Little Appeal, Wall Street Journal, Jan. 23, 1984. Reprinted by permission of the Wall Street Journal, © Dow Jones & Co., Inc. 1984. All rights reserved.
Wenig, The Marital Property Act, 12 Probate and Property 9 (summer 1983). Probate and Property is a publication of the American Bar Association section on Real Property, Probate & Trust Law. Reprinted by permission.
Williams, The Requirement of Beneficial Use as a Cause of Waste in Water Resources Development, 23 Natural Resources Journal 7 (1983). Reprinted with permission.

1985 Supplement
PROPERTY

Part 1
An Introduction to Some Fundamentals

Chapter One
Acquisition of Property Other than by Voluntary Transfer

A. OWNERSHIP AND POSSESSION: THE LAW OF FINDERS

Page 24. After the end of the first full paragraph, add:

The English common law of treasure trove has been criticized for giving insufficient attention to the government's interest in protecting antiquities. See Palmer, Treasure Trove and the Protection of Antiquities, 44 Mod. L. Rev. 178, 180 (1981), noting a number of "extraordinary deficiencies" that make the law of treasure trove "incapable of responding satisfactorily to the challenge of modern amateur and commercial archaeology." Two of these "deficiencies" have already been mentioned: Treasure trove does not apply to items — however antiquarian, precious, or interesting — made of base metal or of nonmetallic materials (such as the prehistoric ship in *Elwes*), nor to items deemed abandoned. It also does not apply to items whose owners (or successors) can be traced — imagine, for instance, gold objects hidden by someone with remote but still identifiable descendants surviving — or to items erected as monuments (since they were not hidden). Needless to say, in the United States the law of treasure trove affords even less protection to antiquities. For a comparative treatment of the English and American law, see Krys, Treasure Trove under Anglo-American Law, 11 Anglo-Amer. L. Rev. 214 (1982).

Page 32. Add the following to footnote 13:

The *Fordham Law Review* comment was recently considered at length and generally approved in Helmholz, Equitable Division and the Law of Finders, 52 Fordham L. Rev. 313 (1983). The author of the earlier *Fordham* comment concluded that the distinction between lost and mislaid items fails to serve its intended purpose, and Professor Helmholz appears to agree. Why, do you suppose? Helmholz disagrees, however, with the contention that the finder and the owner of the locus should *always* share equally in found property (absent the appearance of the true owner) — in some instances (which?), he argues, the finder should get all, and in others (which?) the locus owner. — Eds.

B. THE RULE OF CAPTURE

Page 41. Add the following new paragraph to Problem 6:

In Mountain States Legal Foundation v. Clark, 740 F.2d 792 (10th Cir. 1984), the owners of grazing lands sought compensation from the United States government for damages sustained when herds of wild horses subject to control by the government under the Wild Free-Roaming Horses and Burros Act, 16 U.S.C. §1331 (1982), roamed and foraged on their lands. The court, against a vigorous dissent, reversed a trial court order granting summary judgment to the government, and remanded the case for trial. The court said:

> The horses generally, and especially those with identifiable characteristics of particular breeds, cannot be classified as "wild animals" in an attempt to compare them or the Act to other statutes relating to wild birds and wild animals. . . .
>
> Since the Government has assumed jurisdiction over the horses under the Act it has thereby taken the exclusive and complete control of the horses and also the duty to manage them. As to control, the Act and Regulations permit no one else to move the horses no matter where they are. No one else can manage the horses. Landowners cannot move them from their land. . . .
>
> It is this complete and exclusive control which makes the Act unique. It cannot be compared, as we have stated, with statutes which relate to wild animals or birds. [740 F.2d at 794]

Page 41. Add the following references to Note 7:

T. Lund, American Wildlife Law (1980); M. Bean, The Evolution of National Wildlife Law (rev. ed. 1983); Wildlife and America (H. Brokaw ed. 1983); J. Tober, Who Owns the Wildlife? The Political Economy of Conservation in Nineteenth Century America (1981).

Page 53. Add the following references to footnote 16:

A.M. Polinsky, An Introduction to Law and Economics (1983); C. Goetz, Cases and Materials on Law and Economics (1984).

C. ACQUISITION OF WATER RIGHTS

Page 72. After the block of indented material that concludes Note 4, add:

5. See Williams, The Requirement of Beneficial Use as a Cause of Waste in Water Resources Development, 23 Nat. Resources J. 7 (1983):

> The doctrine of prior appropriation is a rule of capture. Under the doctrine, one may acquire a property right in water only by applying it to a "beneficial use," and in no state does reservation of water for future use qualify as a beneficial use. Moreover, with a few special exceptions (for instream uses such as recreation), one must also divert the water. As a result, anyone anticipating a surge of future demand and higher prices for water rights can exploit that insight only by investing in diversion works. Such projects are likely to be premature or economically unjustifiable regardless of their timing. To the extent that premature or otherwise uneconomic investment occurs, the beneficial use requirement — ironically — causes waste.[28a] If this requirement of prior appropriation law is applied to nonrenewable groundwater, an additional waste — premature consumption of the water itself — may result.
>
> Similar waste would result from unmitigated application of the rule of capture to oil and gas reserves — the other great resources to which it nominally applies. All the major oil and gas states, however, have adopted conservation legislation aimed at curing the problem. It is thus curious that neither legislative action nor even scholarly discussion has focused on this defect of prior appropriation law.[28b]

D. ADVERSE POSSESSION

Page 97. After the second full paragraph, add:

A recent study of adverse possession cases decided since 1966 — Helmholz, Adverse Possession and Subjective Intent, 61 Wash. U.L.Q. 331, 356-358 (1983) — concludes as follows:

> If the cases decided during the recent eighteen year period adequately represent the state of the law enforced in American courts, the question may fairly be asked whether good faith should be considered a prerequisite for the acquisition of title by adverse possession. Good faith was a requirement in the Roman law, and remains so in modern civil law systems, so that there would be nothing in-

---

[28a]. I use the term waste in an economic sense: "Waste is a preventable loss the value of which exceeds the cost of avoidance." *See* S. McDonald, Petroleum Conservation in the United States 129 (1971).

[28b]. The great exception is C. Meyers & R. Posner, Market Transfers of Water Rights: Toward an Improved Market in Water Resources 39-43 (National Water Commission Legal Study No. 4, 1971).

herently unreasonable or unworkable about adopting it openly. Adopting such a requirement would also be in line with the express provisions of a number of recent statutory enactments in the area. In addition, many of the cases come so close to requiring good faith, apparently stopping short of doing so in express terms only because of the weight of contrary statements found in the standard treatises, that considering good faith a prerequisite would seem to make sense.

On the other hand, the question of what would be gained by expressly requiring good faith in adverse possession cases may also fairly be asked. The likely answer is that very little would be gained and that something good might be lost. In a great many adverse possession cases, there is simply no evidence of the possessor's intent, nothing to show one way or another whether he honestly thought the property belonged to him. The possessor may be dead at the time of litigation. Even if he is alive, no one can read his secret thoughts. Were the law to require proof of his good faith, decision of such cases would inevitably call for even more speculative explorations of probable states of mind than is currently possible. Such explorations are not to be wished for. As things stand now, cases can be handled relatively easily. Hostility and "claim of right" can be, and are, judged by external manifestations of dominion. We should only be encouraging speculation, and even perjury, if the law were to require opening up the question of intent in all cases.

It is another matter, however, where there is actual evidence of the intent of the possessor, or where the evidence suggests very strongly that he knew that he was trespassing at the time he began using the land in dispute. Where such evidence exists, and the recent cases show that it does more often than might be thought, courts do take it into account. The elasticity of the terms "hostility" and "claim of right" allows them to do so. They regularly award title to the good faith trespasser, where they will not award it to the trespasser who knows what he is doing at the time he enters the land in dispute. Perhaps that is all that can be said.

If so, this survey nevertheless provides a salutary lesson for those who, like the present writer, presume to comment upon the law of property. We write about human beings. Though a reasonable preference for an objective view of adverse possession militates in favor of a pure possession and an "availability of ejectment" test, if we consequently describe that test as the law, or even as the dominant rule, we underestimate the complexity of the matter. Judges and juries decide the cases. They do take "subjective factors" into account when these can be proved or inferred from the evidence. And they do regularly prefer the claims of an honest man over those of a dishonest man. If that results in more litigation than there ought to be, because it opens up questions of subjective intent, then perhaps we must simply accept the result as a fact of life. At least such a description of the state of the law seems preferable to the pretense that it is pure possession and the accrual of a cause of action in ejectment which determine the outcome in adverse possession cases.

Page 99.   Add the following to footnote 44:

Kalo, The Doctrine of Color of Title in North Carolina, 13 N.C. Cent. L.J. 123, 124 (1982), argues that color of title, commonly regarded as an outdated historical curiosity, is in fact of contemporary value as a means of curing the title defects accompanying the "tremendous upsurge in real estate development" and the mobility of the modern American family — conditions that "have led to the proliferation of title transactions. . . . Each time that title to land changes hands, the likelihood increases that some defect may occur. . . ."

Page 100. After Problem 3, add the following new problem:

4. *O*, believing he owns certain vacant land, lot 13, conveys it to *A* by a deed describing adjacent vacant land, lot 12. The actual owner of lot 13 is *X*. *A* enters lot 13. Is the doctrine of color of title working in her behalf? See Hubbard v. Curtiss, 684 P.2d 842 (Alaska 1984).

Page 112. Before "3. Adverse Possession against the Government," add:

NOTE: ADVERSE POSSESSION AND THE COMMON LAW METHOD

Recall Ballantine's remark (at page 85 of the main text) that "the great purpose" of adverse possession is "to quiet all titles which are openly and consistently asserted," with little if any regard for the merits or demerits of the landowner or the possessor. Surely Ballantine makes matters too simple. The bona fides of possessors *do* matter to some courts (including some courts that say otherwise; see Note 4 on pages 95-97 of the main text and the excerpt from the essay by Professor Helmholz on pages 4-5 of this supplement); the negligence of landowners who "sleep upon their rights" *is* relevant, a point made clear by the disability provisions that excuse owner inaction in appropriate circumstances (see pages 110-111 of the main text).

Adverse possession cases are relatively easy when the considerations underlying the doctrine all cut in the same direction — when, for example, the owner is dormant and the possessor earnest, or when the possessor is an ill-motivated and secretive trespasser and the owner an attentive guardian of his holdings. Adverse possession cases are difficult when, on a particular set of facts, underlying policies come into conflict, when there is good reason to punish the owner but *not* to reward the possessor (the case, say, of an owner dispossessed for the statutory period by a series of trespassers, none of them in privity with the others, each of them holding for a time short of the statutory period — see pages 108-109 of the main text), or vice versa (an example would be, again, the case of the disabled landowner). One could imagine a way to resolve the clash of policies presented in cases like these: In a case of the first type, we could say that the owner loses the land, but not to the adverse possessor; rather, the land (or an equivalent value) is put

Acquisition of Property Other than by Voluntary Transfer

into a "bank." Then, in a case of the second type, the adverse possessor would be awarded land or an equivalent value, but not as against the owner; rather, the award would be drawn from the bank. To so proceed, however, would not be the common law method. Generally, it appears, common law courts neglect to separate out the individual components of a controversy and to resolve each as it deserves without regard to the others. Adverse possession, as we have seen, provides some examples. So does the law of finders, where we see courts (in a case like *McAvoy* at page 20 of the main text) failing to distinguish between *custody* of the found item now and *ownership* of the found item — perhaps as against all but the true owner, perhaps as against the world — eventually. (Compare the *Paset* case at page 26 of the main text and consider the notion of equitable sharing introduced in footnote 13 on page 32 of the main text and discussed more fully at pages 2-3 of this supplement. Does equitable sharing have a place in the law of adverse possession?)

Perhaps you can think of other illustrations of the common law method discussed above. Is it sensible?

Page 129. After Note 2, add:

3. England and some countries on the Continent recognize the doctrine of market overt, according to which a bona fide purchaser may acquire good title from a thief, so long as the sale in question takes places in an open public market. Though market overt is not recognized in the United States, it nevertheless provides opportunities for the laundering of stolen objects. A thief steals a painting from Georgia O'Keeffe, takes it to Europe and sells it in a public market to an innocent American tourist who then returns home with the item. Under conventional conflict-of-laws principles, the law of the place of sale may well govern this transaction. If so, the tourist will have acquired a good title. The problem has not gone unnoticed in the art world (nor, we presume, the underworld).

Part 2
The System of Estates

Chapter Two

The Leasehold Estates: Tradition, Tension, and Change in Landlord-Tenant Law

A. THE LEASEHOLD ESTATES

Page 136. After Problem 2, add:

2a. *T*, a month-to-month tenant, notified *L* on November 16, 1984, that she would vacate as of November 30, 1984. *T* subsequently vacated on that date and paid no further rent to *L*. *L*, after reasonable efforts, finally relet the premises in question beginning April 1, 1985. The jurisdiction in question has no statute prescribing the method of terminating a month-to-month tenancy. *L* sues *T* for unpaid rent for the months of December 1984 and January through March 1985. What result? See S.D.G. v. Inventory Control Co., 178 N.J. Super. 411, 429 A.2d 394 (1981).

Page 136. After Problem 4, add:

Compare with Problems 3 and 4 above the decision in Philpot v. Field, 633 S.W.2d 546 (Tex. Civ. App. 1982), involving a lease to *T* for a term of 20 years and so long thereafter as *T* used the premises for particular purposes. Thereafter the premises were used continuously by *T* for the particular purposes. *L*, sometime after the expiration of the 20 year term, wished to terminate the lease. *L* argued that because the lease had an uncertain term, it was a tenancy at will terminable by either party once the 20 years expired. The court held otherwise, saying (633 S.W.2d at 548):

> Although there is no definite ending date after the 20 year term, that date is tied to the cessation of the use of the land for certain definitely ascertainable purposes. Common sense, logic and the trend in the law supports this decision. It appears that the parties intended to create a perpetual right to lease the land. When the parties' intent is made clear, courts should enforce the agreement as written, even though perpetual rights are not favored. . . .

No legitimate reason exists for us to hold that the parties cannot freely and intelligently lease land for so long as a certain definite use is made of the land. Although [T] can terminate this lease when he desires by his voluntary choice, this lease does not create a tenancy at will terminable at the will of either party.

B. THE LEASE

Page 143. Add the following new footnote to the end of the carryover paragraph:

10a. For recent criticism of the new emphasis on contract theory in landlord-tenant law, arguing that it is largely unnecessary and, in some instances, less conducive to reform than the traditional view of a lease as a conveyance, see Humbach, The Common-Law Conception of Leasing: Mitigation, Habitability, and Dependence of Covenants, 60 Wash. U.L.Q. 1213 (1983). And see, in a related vein, Chase, The Property-Contract Theme in Landlord and Tenant Law: A Critical Commentary on Schoshinski's American Law of Landlord and Tenant, 13 Rutgers L.J. 189 (1982).

C. SELECTION OF TENANTS

Page 151. At the end of line 3, add:

See also Rice, Judicial Enforcement of Fair Housing Laws: An Analysis of Some Unexamined Problems that the Fair Housing Amendments Act of 1983 Would Eliminate, 27 Howard L.J. 227 (1984); Lamb, Congress, the Courts, and Civil Rights: The Fair Housing Act of 1968 Revisited, 27 Vill. L. Rev. 1115 (1982).

Page 166. At the end of Note 1, add:

On discrimination against families in rental housing, see Note, Why Johnny Can't Rent — An Examination of Laws Prohibiting Discrimination against Families in Rental Housing, 94 Harv. L. Rev. 1829 (1981); Comment, Apartment for Rent: Adults Only; No Children Allowed, 15 Cal. W.L. Rev. 219 (1979); Annot., 30 A.L.R.4th 1187 (1984). In Halet v. Wend Investment Co., 672 F.2d 1305 (9th Cir. 1982), plaintiff challenged an adults-only rental policy on the ground that it violated his right to live with his family. The court held that plaintiff had standing to proceed with his suit under the Fair Housing Act (see page 148 of the main text), the Fourteenth Amendment, and §1983 of the Civil Rights Act of 1866, 42 U.S.C. §1983 (1982). The case is noted at 28 St. Louis U.L.J. 1085 (1984); 23 Santa Clara L. Rev. 965 (1983).

Page 168. At the bottom of the page, insert:

STEWART, LANDLORDS' VERDICT: LAWYERS AS TENANTS HAVE LITTLE APPEAL
Wall St. J., Jan. 23, 1984, at 1

In most U.S. cities, a landlord can't reject a tenant on the basis of race, color or creed. In some cities, he can't reject one on the basis of sexual inclination, either. But if he wants to reject a *lawyer* as a tenant, that may be perfectly legal — and is certainly understandable.

Just ask Sandra Greer about Paul Chessin. Even with a midwinter tan, the 45-year-old Mrs. Greer turns pale at the mere mention of his name. "Oh my God," she moans, clutching her throat. "I divorced two husbands and I'd take either of them over Chessin. I just want him out of my life."

Mr. Chessin, 30, is a lawyer. The very day he moved into a Manhattan apartment building managed by Mrs. Greer, he threatened to sue her over the paint job. They soon became combatants in six different lawsuits and administrative proceedings. Among Mr. Chessin's complaints: a missing soap-dish tile and a monthly rent overcharge later determined to be 66 cents.

Mrs. Greer tried a variety of defensive tactics. First she gave Mr. Chessin whatever he wanted — two months' free rent, for example, and a brand-new soap dish. Then she ignored him. But when he bought a new refrigerator and deducted its price from his rent, she decided to fight back in court.

Then her troubles really began.

CLASHES IN WASHINGTON

Lawyer-tenants are making life difficult for landlords in various parts of the country, but they seem to be particularly troublesome in New York and Washington, presumably because those cities attract so many lawyers. Not all lawyer-tenants are so litigious, but landlords have heard enough horror stories to make them wary, says Lawrence Stand, accounts manager for J.I. Sopher Real Estate, the largest rental agency in New York. Mr. Stand represents the owners of 25 apartment buildings, and they categorically refuse to rent to lawyers, he says.

Often, lawyer-tenants go to court for what seem to be trivial reasons. Arthur Zabarkes, who supervises tenant litigation for Church Management Corp., which manages luxury apartment houses in Manhattan, says he is currently in litigation with lawyer-tenants over inadequate putty around a windowpane, a stain on a porcelain sink and a loose doorknob. "Lawyer-tenants are the worst," he says.

Norman Peck, one of the owners of the building Mr. Chessin moved into, says that lawyer-tenants are one of the reasons he is converting all his apartment houses into cooperatives. "The landlord can't win," he says. He cites a building of his where a lawyer-tenant filed a complaint charging that the replacement of elevator men with new automatic elevators and a doorman was a "diminution of services." The city's conciliation and appeals board, which hears rent complaints, agreed — and rolled back all rents in the building by 10%.

VACANCIES AND CHOOSINESS

No wonder, then, that some landlords in New York City, where an extremely low vacancy rate lets them be choosy about their tenants, are turning down lawyers flatly. In Washington, housing isn't so tight, says James Sweeney, sales manager in the Georgetown office of Dale Denton Real Estate, so landlords generally aren't able to indulge their preference for nonlawyers.

In Chicago, John Nagy, a senior vice president of Downs-Mohl, a property-management and brokerage firm, says that he has had problems with lawyer-tenants, who "can make life very difficult." But he reports only isolated instances of landlords who refuse to rent to lawyers. He attributes the low refusal rate to the absence of rent-control regulations in Chicago; rent-control provisions are the grounds for many suits.

Once lawyers in heavily regulated housing markets like New York City decide they want to embroil their landlords in legal proceedings, they have a plethora of statutes and regulations to choose from. Besides rent-control and rent-stabilization laws, the New York City housing-maintenance code alone mentions 180 specific violations, ranging from heating requirements in public hallways to cracks in the plaster. There are so many other applicable statutes and regulations that Howard Malatzky, deputy general counsel for the city's Department of Housing Preservation and Development, says he can't name them all.

But you don't have to be a lawyer to sue about these things. Why is it that lawyer-tenants sue more often than anyone else? For one thing, they have confidence, frequently justified, in their ability to win. For another, their costs of suing are generally low because most of them do their own legal work. Mr. Chessin, for example, says he spent "hundreds" of hours of his own time on his various cases against Mrs. Greer, and enlisted the help of a colleague in his law firm as well.

Young lawyers sometimes sue landlords "to get trial experience," says Mr. Sweeney, the Washington real-estate man. "They treat it like a classroom project." he says. And some lawyers, says Mr. Zabarkes of New York's Church Management, are simply nit-pickers by nature.

DISCRIMINATION RULING

In New York, at least, a landlord's right not to rent to such nit-pickers has been established. Six years ago, a lawyer who had been turned down for the apartment she wanted went to court and argued that discrimination against lawyers was as bad as discrimination on the basis of race, color or creed. She lost.

The decision was handed down in State Supreme Court — a lower court in New York — by Justice Edward J. Greenfield. He noted that the managing agent candidly admitted that "rather than a lawyer attuned to her legal rights, he would have preferred a person who was likely to be less informed and more passive." The justice ruled that "there is nothing illegal in a landlord discriminating against lawyers as a group, or trying to keep out of his building intelligent persons, aware of their rights, who may give him trouble in the future."

In all fairness to lawyers, it should be noted that in high-rent Beverly Hills, Calif., lawyer-tenants actually seem to be in demand, demonstrating once again that all things are relative. Says Beverly Hills real estate broker Peter Bruni: "Rock stars are my problem."

FROM BAD TO WORSE

Back in New York, Mrs. Greer's courtroom showdown with Mr. Chessin went from bad to worse. After the refrigerator incident, she sued to evict him, claiming that she had received one of his rent checks a month late. He promptly countersued for damages. He accused her of retaliatory eviction and harassment.

Last November, a New York City Civil Court judge ruled in Mr. Chessin's favor. He conceded that Mr. Chessin was "a thorn in her side" but concluded that Mrs. Greer had fabricated the late-payment charge in a desperate attempt to get rid of her bothersome tenant. Mr. Chessin was awarded $750 in damages, $10,000 in punitive damages, and attorney's fees still to be determined.

Because of the ruling, which is being appealed, Mr. Peck fired Mrs. Greer as managing agent for the building. She figures that will cost her $100,000 in lost commissions. Mr. Peck, who is a co-defendant, and Mrs. Greer are still on good terms, but he figured that his co-op conversion plan would fare better if he could state in it that he had dismissed her after a court found her in the wrong.

Nor is Mrs. Greer's ordeal over. She is still involved in appeals of other decisions in Chessin cases. And Mr. Chessin is trying to have her and Mr. Peck expelled from the rent stabilization association, a group that New York landlords pretty much have to belong to if they want to avoid stricter rent control.

HAPPY IN DENVER

Meanwhile, Mr. Chessin has left New York for the comparatively unregulated city of Denver. There, he says, he had "no problems whatsoever" with his rental apartment and recently purchased and moved into a con-

The Leasehold Estates

dominium unit. But he is in no mood to let bygones be bygones. "I feel complete outrage," he says, "at the injustices I suffered at the hands of Sandra Greer."

Mrs. Greer is about ready to throw in the towel. Mr. Chessin "ground me down, wore me out and beat me," she concedes. "It isn't just lawyers I'm afraid of now. It's everyone. I insist on meeting every prospective tenant personally. I try to get a gut feeling about whether they'll sue me. If you knew the heartache that Chessin caused me —" She pauses but then confesses a certain admiration for her tenacious adversary:

"I must say I'd hire him as my lawyer."

E. ASSIGNMENTS AND SUBLEASES

Page 182. At the end of Problem 2(d) add:

For criticism of the different legal consequences attending subleases and assignments, see Jaccard, The Scope of Liability Between Landlord and Subtenant, 16 Colum. J.L. & Soc. Prob. 365 (1981), recommending "that L and ST be given the same rights against each other as landlords and assignees presently enjoy. . . ."

Page 184. Before *Ringwood Associates,* insert:

FUNK v. FUNK
Supreme Court of Idaho, 1981
102 Idaho 521, 633 P.2d 586

SHEPARD, J. The appellant-lessors correctly argue that the traditional majority position is that unless the lease provides that the lessors' consent shall not be unreasonably withheld, a provision against assignment or subletting without the lessors' consent authorizes the lessor to arbitrarily withhold consent for any reason or for no reason. . . .

We find, however, an increasing number of jurisdictions departing from that traditional position and an increasing volume of authority that the consent of a lessor may not be *unreasonably* withheld. As stated in [Homa-Goff Interiors, Inc. v. Cowden, 350 So.2d 1035, 1037 (Ala. 1977),] "[the majority] rule, however, has been under steady attack in several states in the past twenty years; and this for the reason that, in recent times, the necessity of reasonable alienation of commercial building space has become paramount in our ever-increasing urban society." . . .

We deem the principal enunciated in the minority position to be based on more solid policy rationale than is the traditional orthodox majority's position. A landlord may and should be concerned about the personal qualities of a proposed subtenant. A landlord should be able to reject a proposed subtenant when such rejection reflects a concern for the legitimate interest of the landlord, such as assurances of rent receipt, proper care of the property and in many cases the use of the property by the subtenant in a manner reasonably consistent with the usage of the original lessee. Such concerns by the landlord should result in the upholding of a withholding of consent by a landlord. However, no desirable public policy is served by upholding a landlord's arbitrary refusal of consent merely because of whim or caprice or where, as here, it is apparent that the refusal to consent was withheld for purely financial reasons and that the landlord wanted the lessees to enter into an entirely new lease agreement with substantial increased financial benefits to the landlord. If the lessor is allowed to arbitrarily refuse consent to a sublease for what is in effect no reason at all, such would virtually nullify the right of a lessee to sublet. The imposition of a reasonableness standard also gives greater credence to the doctrine that restraints on alienation of leased property are looked upon with disfavor and are strictly construed against the lessor. . . .

The burden of proving that the landlord's conduct is unreasonable rests upon the party challenging that conduct. . . . A standard of reasonableness has been applied in cases which have *implied* a reasonable standard as well as those cases in which the lease contained express langauage that consent could not be unreasonably withheld. . . .

In the instant case, the proper standard by which to review the lessors' refusal to consent to the proposed sublease is one of a reasonable person in the position of a landlord owning and leasing commercial farm land. Criteria to be utilized in application of that standard would include, but would not necessarily be limited to, assurances of proper farming practices and financial responsibility. In the instant case the record discloses no contentions by the landlord of the absence of these or any other criteria and hence we hold that the arbitrary refusal of the appellant-lessors in the instant case to grant their consent to the sublease was unreasonable. . . .

BAKES, C.J., dissenting: I must dissent from the majority's decision to rewrite the lease provision in question. The lessee's right to assign or sublease the premises was unambiguous and unconditional in its requirement that the lessor consent. For the members of this Court to inject a new requirement that "the consent of the lessor may not be unreasonably withheld" is in effect to say that this Court may at any time disregard the intentions of the parties as expressed in their unambiguous agreement and rewrite the contract because a majority of this Court is of the opinion that it should be altered. The action of the majority constitutes not only a severe encroachment upon the right of persons to freely contract and to maintain control over their own property, but is also a serious intrusion into the province of the legislature.

In support of its action, the majority adopts a minority rule which it implies is the trend of the future. However, the majority's own citations manifest no such trend. Clearly, in the last year jurisdictions have split on the issue. Compare B & R Oil Co., Inc. v. Ray's Mobile Homes, Inc., 422 A.2d 1267 (Vt.1980) (permitting arbitrary refusal of consent) with Warmack v. Merchants Nat. Bank of Fort Smith, 612 S.W.2d 733 (Ark.1981) (prohibiting unreasonable withholding of consent). The majority cites only three states which have adopted the majority rule. However, there are at least five other recent cases not cited by the majority which in some manner either recognize the continuing validity or apply the majority rule. Carleno v. Vollmert Tire Co., 36 Colo. App. 446, 540 P.2d 1149, 1151 (1975); Robinson v. Weitz, 171 Conn. 545, 370 A.2d 1066, 1068 (1976); Kruger v. Page Management Co., 105 Misc. 2d 14, 432 N.Y.S.2d 295, 300 (1980) (recognizing rule absent applicability of statute governing residential leases); Herlou Card Shop, Inc. v. Prudential Ins. Co. of America, 73 A.D.2d 562, 422 N.Y.S.2d 708 (1979). See also Dutch Inns of America, Inc. v. United Virginia Leasing Corp., 134 Ga. App. 525, 215 S.E.2d 290, 291 (1975); Moritz v. S & H Shopping Centers, 197 Neb. 206, 247 N.W.2d 454, 456 (1976) (both cases applying the rule that lessee has no authority to assign the lease without consent of the lessor, but not addressing issue of unreasonable withholding of consent). Including the majority's citation to Food Pantry v. Waikiki Business Plaza, Inc., 58 Hawaii 606, 575 P.2d 869 (1978), it appears that even in recent years the majority rule of allowing freedom in contracting continues to far outdistance the minority view.

More important than numbers, however, are the reasons behind the rules. The majority opinion states that "the minority position [is] based on more solid policy rationale than is the traditional orthodox majority's position," and that "no desirable public policy is served by upholding a landlord's arbitrary refusal to consent." I disagree. Upholding contracts and deeds voluntarily entered into between two parties is certainly a "desirable public policy." We said so unanimously in Mollendorf v. Derry, 95 Idaho 1, 501 P.2d 199 (1972). "The policy of the law is not to defeat a grantor's intent." 95 Idaho at 3, 501 P.2d 199.

The rationale behind the majority rule is supported by several basic concepts of property law.

> The reasons expressed in support of this rule are that, since the lessor has exercised a personal choice in the selection of a tenant for a definite term and has expressly provided that no substitute shall be acceptable without his written consent, no obligation rests upon him to look to anyone but the lessee for his rent . . . ; that a lease is a conveyance of an interest in real property and, when a lessor has delivered the premises to his lessee, the latter is bound to him by privity of estate as well as by privity of contract . . . ; that a lessor's right to reenter the premises upon lessee's default or abandonment thereof is at the lessor's option and not the lessee's . . . ; and that a lessee's unilateral action in abandoning leased

premises, *unless accepted by his lessor,* does not terminate the lease or forfeit the estate conveyed thereby, nor the lessee's right to use and possess the leased premises and, by the same token, his obligation to pay the rent due therefor.

Gruman v. Investors Diversified Services, 247 Minn. 502, 78 N.W.2d 377, 380 (1956) (citations omitted, emphasis in original). The reasons given in the *Gruman* case are supported by the fundamental principle that the owner of property may transfer as much or as little control over his property as he sees fit. Freedom of ownership and control over one's own property forms the very basis of our social system. If that is to change, the proper forum for such changes is the legislature and not this Court.

The unsettling nature of the majority opinion is magnified when one realizes that the effect of the decision is to potentially subject every denial of consent to litigation and approval by a judge. Rather than the lessor being sure of his right to control his property by retaining an unrestricted right to deny consent to assign or sublease, by its decision today this Court has destroyed that right and vested in the courts the power to determine what the lessor *should have intended* and award control of the property based upon that determination. Certainly, as evidenced by this case, the parties will rarely agree on what is reasonable under particular circumstances. Is there any assurance that judges will be unified in their opinions on what is reasonable? The only assurance to be gained by the rule adopted by the majority today is that the parties' attempt to write their lease to avoid litigation will be frustrated. Had the parties wished or bargained to place a question mark on the lessor's right to withhold consent, they would have provided in the agreement that consent would not be arbitrarily or unreasonably withheld. See Annot., 54 A.L.R.3d 681 (1973). This Court should not foist that uncertainty off on them.

It is not clear from the majority opinion whether lessors in the future will have the right to contract for "an absolute right to withhold consent." The Restatement (Second) of Property, §15.2, and Warmack v. Merchants Nat. Bank of Fort Smith, supra, the most recent case cited by the majority in support of its position, both so provide when they state: "The landlord's consent to an alienation by the tenant cannot be withheld unreasonably, unless a freely negotiated provision in the lease gives the landlord an absolute right to withhold consent." The broad language of the majority opinion suggests that even that provision would violate its "public policy," The Court's decision today will no doubt disrupt, dislocate and confuse thousands of existing contractual leasehold relationships which have provisions limiting the right to assign the lessee's interest.

When a court injects a new requirement that "the consent of the lessor may not be unreasonably withheld," as the majority has done in this case, it not only constitutes an interference with the right of persons to freely con-

The Leasehold Estates — Page 192

tract, but also interferes with the traditional rules for conveyancing real property. If, as the majority holds, it is against public policy for a lessor to provide in his lease that the lessee cannot assign his interest without the lessor's consent which may be denied for any reasons the lessor may give, including those which the majority concludes are arbitrary, the effect of such a rule is to modify the nature of the estate conveyed by the lessor. One wonders what the majority of this Court will do when faced with the conveyance of a fee conditional, the condition being an event which the majority might conclude is arbitrary or unreasonable. As an example, it is not uncommon for a benefactor to convey real property to a city in fee conditional, the condition being that the property be used perpetually for a park to be named after the benefactor, e.g., In re Hart's Estate, 151 Cal. App. 271, 311 P.2d 605 (1957), and in the event that any part of the park is not used for that purpose then the property reverts to the heirs of the benefactor. If this Court, as it has done today, can modify the conditions of a grant of a lease, then it is only a short step to stating that it can also modify the terms of a grant of a fee conditional estate. The decision of the Court today will have a tremendously unsettling effect not only upon the conveyancing of real property but also upon the execution of contracts in this state. It is for this reason that the court in Gruman v. Investors Diversified Services, *supra*, in deciding to adhere to the majority rule, stated:

> [We] are motivated by the fact that the language of the assignment provision is clear and unambiguous and that many leases now in effect covering a substantial amount of real property and creating valuable property rights were carefully prepared by competent counsel in reliance upon the majority viewpoint. It would seem clear from the language adopted in all such cases that the lessors therein are entitled to place full reliance upon the responsibility of their respective lessees for the rentals they have contracted to pay. Should a lessee desire the right to assign or sublet to a suitable tenant, a clause might readily be inserted in the lease similar to those now included in many leases to the effect that the lessor's written consent to the assignment or subletting of the leased premises should not be unreasonably withheld. There being no clause in the present lease to such effect, we are compelled to give its terms their full force and effect as have the courts of a majority of other jurisdictions.

78 N.W.2d at 381-82.

I would vote to carry out the contract as the parties negotiated it, and not as the majority of this Court thinks they should have negotiated it.

Page 192. Delete the first paragraph of Note 1, and substitute:

1. As we shall see in Chapters 3 and 4, courts generally disfavor restraints on the alienation (transfer) of freehold interests in land, presumably because such restraints may promote inefficiency by interfering with the

movement of land resources to their highest valued use (as measured by willingness to pay). In the case of nonfreeholds, the judicial reaction has been generally different, as Jacobs v. Klawans suggests. The case represents the majority view, though Funk v. Funk indicates a contrary trend. See also Levin, Withholding Consent to Assignment: The Changing Rights of the Commercial Landlord, 30 DePaul L. Rev. 109 (1980); Comment, The Approval Clause in a Lease: Toward a Standard of Reasonableness, 17 U.S.F.L. Rev. 681 (1983); Annot., 21 A.L.R.4th 188 (1983). The Restatement would deny a landlord the right to withhold consent unreasonably "unless a freely negotiated provision in the lease gives the landlord an absolute right to withhold consent." 2 Restatement (Second) of Property §15.2 (1977). What position would you take?

F. TENANT'S DUTIES; LANDLORD'S RIGHTS AND REMEDIES

Page 202. At the end of the last paragraph, add:

On fair return, see Note, Rethinking Rent Control: An Analysis of "Fair Return," 12 Rutgers L.J. 617 (1981). For a full overview of current rent control law (and how to cope with it), see Baar, Guidelines for Drafting Rent Control Laws: Lessons of a Decade, 35 Rutgers L. Rev. 723 (1983). The Baar essay discusses, among a host of other issues, rent-control provisions that constrain an owner's freedom to remove rental units from the market (whether through conversion to condominiums and cooperatives — see pages 396-406 of the main text — or through demolition). 35 Rutgers L. Rev. at 835-840. On demolition controls in particular, see pages 180-186 of this supplement. The pros and cons of rent controls and conversion controls are considered in Symposium, Redistribution of Income Through Regulation in Housing, 32 Emory L.J. 691 (1983), and Berger, The New Residential Tenancy Law — Are Landlords Public Utilities?, 60 Neb. L. Rev. 707 (1981).

Page 247. At the end of Note 2, add:

See generally Weissenberger, The Landlord's Duty to Mitigate Damages on the Tenant's Abandonment: A Survey of Old Law and New Trends, 53 Temp. L.Q. 1 (1980).

Page 250. At the end of Note 2, add:

For a recent overview of a landlord's remedies against an abandoning tenant, including anticipatory breach (or repudiation), see Love, Landlord's Remedies When the Tenant Abandons: Property, Contract, and Leases, 30 Kan. L. Rev. 533 (1982).

The Leasehold Estates   Page 283

G. LANDLORD'S DUTIES; TENANT'S RIGHTS AND REMEDIES

Page 262. After Problem 4, add:

NOTE: LANDLORD'S TORT LIABILITY — ABANDONING THE CONVENTIONAL VIEW

Understand that the foregoing materials illustrate the *conventional* law of landlord's tort liability. Although it is probably still the majority view that a landlord is not liable to tenants for injuries resulting from defective premises (subject to the exceptions examined in Jordan v. Savage and the foregoing problems), this conventional outlook appears to be changing. One aspect of the larger body of reforms presently underway in the law of landlord and tenant, see pages 283-316 of the main text, is a move in the direction of abandoning the general rule of nonliability in favor of one imposing a duty on landlords to maintain the leased premises. See pages 307-308 of the main text. On the conventional tort law and the new developments, see Browder, The Taming of a Duty — The Tort Liability of Landlords, 81 Mich. L. Rev. 99 (1982).

Page 282. In line 16, before "In any event . . .," add:

For a recent decision to this effect, see Stevan v. Brown, 54 Md. App. 235, 458 A.2d 466 (1983). *Stevan* implies that certain actions (or inactions) of the landlord may breach the implied covenant of quiet enjoyment, yet fall short of constructive eviction.[56a] Under such circumstances, it appears that the *only* remedy available to the tenant (with the exception, perhaps, of equitable or declaratory relief; see the discussion of the *Burt* case below) would be the damage remedy endorsed by the court.

Page 283. Insert the following before "3. Reforms and Implications":

PROBLEM

T is a tenant at will of *L*. *L* causes a nuisance that interferes with *T*'s business on the leased premises. *T* vacates and subsequently sues on a theory of constructive eviction, claiming damages resulting from *L*'s actions. What problem arises on such facts? Cf. Kent v. Humphries, 303 N.C. 675, 281 S.E.2d 43 (1981).

56a. See 54 Md. App. at 247, 458 A.2d at 473: "Even if the problems with the Tower Building complained of by tenants are found not to support a claim of constructive eviction, they may constitute a breach of the covenant of quiet enjoyment."

Page 302. At the end of the first paragraph of Note 4, add:

Greenfield & Margolies, An Implied Warranty of Fitness in Nonresidential Leases, 45 Albany L. Rev. 855 (1981); McCloskely, Commercial Leases: Behind the Green Door, 12 Pac. L.J. 1067 (1981); Note, Landlord-Tenant — Should a Warranty of Fitness be Implied in Commercial Leases?, 13 Rutgers L.J. 91 (1981).

Should the implied warranty of habitability apply to landlords who are not regularly in the business of renting property? See Boudreau v. General Electric Co., 2 Hawaii App. 10, 625 P.2d 384 (1982) (yes); Zimmerman v. Moore, 441 N.E.2d 690 (Ind. App. 1982) (no); Mallor, The Implied Warranty of Habitability and the "Non-Merchant" Landlord, 22 Duq. L. Rev. 637 (1984).

Page 305. At the end of the carryover paragraph, add:

See also Simon v. Solomon, 385 Mass. 91, 95-97, 431 N.E.2d 556, 561-562 (1982), where a tenant who suffered through 30 incidents of water and sewage flowing into her apartment from an adjoining basement successfully claimed damages of $35,000 for reckless infliction of emotional distress. The court said:

> ... Our decisions in recent years have firmly established that a plaintiff may recover for emotional distress inflicted recklessly or intentionally. Agis v. Howard Johnson Co., 371 Mass. 140, 355 N.E.2d 315 (1976); George v. Jordan Marsh Co., 359 Mass. 244, 268 N.E.2d 915 (1971). See Restatement (Second) of Torts §46 (1965). In *Agis*, we listed four elements necessary to a recovery on this theory. The plaintiff must show "(1) that the actor intended to inflict emotional distress or that he knew or should have known that emotional distress was the likely result of his conduct; ... (2) that the conduct was 'extreme and outrageous' ... ; (3) that the actions of the defendant were the cause of the plaintiff's distress; ... and (4) that the emotional distress sustained by the plaintiff was 'severe'...." *Agis*, *supra* 371 Mass. at 144-145, 355 N.E.2d 315. If each of these elements is proven, the plaintiff can recover for purely emotional suffering unaccompanied by physical injury. *Id.*
>
> Gem does not seriously challenge the finding of the jury that Solomon suffered severe emotional distress as a result of the floods in her apartment. Instead, Gem stresses that Solomon did not identify a specific "defect" in the apartment building that Gem, as landlord, should have repaired. On this basis Gem argues that it did not act recklessly, did not engage in outrageous conduct, and did not cause Solomon's floods.
>
> The central thrust of Gem's contentions appears to be that its conduct was not the proximate cause of Solomon's injuries — that it was not legally responsible for her misfortune. As Gem points out, the source of the floods was not clear.

The water appears to have entered Solomon's apartment primarily from an adjoining basement area. Two waste stacks, admittedly very old, extended from roof to basement collecting waste from the bathrooms, and on occasion may have backed up through a drain in the basement. Gem's plumber, however, testified that the plumbing system and stacks were in good repair and complied with State plumbing regulations. He also stated that backups in the waste stacks were probably caused by objects that other tenants had introduced through the toilets or roof vents. On the basis of this uncontroverted testimony, Gem argues that it acted reasonably in its plumbing maintenance and therefore was not responsible for the flooding.

Gem's legal responsibility, however, depends on the duties it owed to Solomon, and Gem's arguments concerning plumbing misstate the scope of a landlord's duty to its tenants. We have held that every landlord that rents residential property warrants to its tenants that the premises will be delivered and maintained in a habitable condition. Boston Hous. Auth. v. Hemingway, 363 Mass. 184, 293 N.E.2d 831 (1973). At a minimum, this warranty imposes on the landlord a duty to keep the dwelling in conformity with the State Sanitary Code. *Id.* at 200 n.16, 293 N.E.2d 831. Crowell v. McCaffrey, 377 Mass. 443, 451, 386 N.E.2d 1256 (1979). See also Hemingway, *supra* 363 Mass. at 215-219, 293 N.E.2d 831 (Quirico, J., concurring in part and dissenting in part). A landlord's breach of this duty abates the tenant's obligation to pay rent, even when the landlord is not at fault and has no reasonable opportunity to make repairs. Berman & Sons v. Jefferson, 379 Mass. 196, 396 N.E.2d 981 (1979). Further, a landlord that fails to maintain a habitable dwelling for its tenant is liable for resulting personal injuries, at least when the landlord has failed to exercise reasonable care in maintenance. *Crowell, supra* 377 Mass. at 450-451, 386 N.E.2d 1256.

There was evidence at trial that the wall between Solomon's apartment and the adjoining basement area was extremely porous. There was also testimony suggesting that Gem may have considered cementing the wall to prevent floods, but never carried out this plan. The jury could reasonably conclude that Gem's failure to do so caused Solomon's injuries — that but for Gem's inaction, no floods would have occurred. . . .

Having recognized that an inference was warranted that Gem failed in its duty to prevent the flooding, we find ample evidence in the record from which the jury could conclude that the remaining elements of an action for reckless infliction of emotional distress — recklessness, outrageous conduct, and severe emotional distress — were present. . . . Solomon testified that she had repeatedly complained to Gem of floods. She stated that Gem on each occasion sent a cleanup crew to pump out the water, but never took permanent action. The jury, if they believed this testimony, could find that Gem knew or should have known that unless it fixed the porous wall flooding would occur, and that floods of sewage water were very likely to cause emotional harm. . . . The jury could also find that Gem had displayed, over a long and repetitious course, such a pattern of indifference that its conduct was outrageous, "beyond all possible bounds of decency."

Page 307. Before "Note: Tort Implications of the Implied Warranty of Habitability," insert:

PROBLEM

L owns a high-rise apartment building. L's entire maintenance and janitorial staff goes on strike for two weeks. The building's incinerators are inoperative as a consequence of the strike; tenants must take their garbage to the curb in paper bags supplied by L. City sanitation workers refuse to cross the striking employees' picket lines. Trash piles up to the height of the building's first-floor windows. The garbage exudes noxious odors and results in a declaration of a health emergency by the city. Routine maintenance and extermination service is not performed during the strike, and rats and vermin become a problem. Has L breached the implied warranty of habitability? See Park West Management Corp. v. Mitchell, 47 N.Y.2d 316, 391 N.E.2d 1288, 418 N.Y.S.2d 310, *cert. denied,* 444 U.S. 992 (1979).

Page 307. At the end of the second paragraph of "Note: Tort Implications of the Implied Warranty of Habitability," add:

For a discussion of the arguments for and against the strict liability position, see Browder, The Taming of a Duty — The Tort Liability of Landlords, 81 Mich. L. Rev. 99, 118-122, 135-141 (1982). See also Mallor, The Implied Warranty of Habitability and the "Non-Merchant" Landlord, 22 Duq. L. Rev. 637, 650-654 (1984). On the tort implications of the warranty of habitability generally, see Davis & DeLaTorre, A Fresh Look at Premises Liability as Affected by the Warranty of Habitability, 59 Wash. L. Rev. 141 (1984) (noting "intimations of strict liability").

Page 308. At the end of the carryover paragraph, add:

See generally Moore, The Landlord's Liability to His Tenants for Injuries Criminally Inflicted by Third Persons, 17 Akron L. Rev. 395 (1984); Selvin, Landlord Tort Liability for Criminal Attacks on Tenants: Developments Since *Kline,* 9 Real Est. L.J. 311 (1981); Comment, The Landlord's Duty in New York to Protect His Tenants against Criminal Intrusions, 45 Albany L. Rev. 988 (1981); Comment, Landlord Liability for the Criminal Acts of Third Parties: Recent Developments in Connecticut, 14 Conn. L. Rev. 843 (1982).

Page 308. At the end of the page, add:

To the same effect as Sargent v. Ross, see Pagelsdorf v. Safeco Ins. Co. of America, 91 Wis. 2d 734, 284 N.W.2d 55 (1979), noted in 54 Marq. L. Rev. 563 (1981).

Page 325. At the end of Note 1, add:

More recent surveys of landlord-tenant reforms and their implications include Rabin, The Revolution in Residential Landlord Tenant Law: Causes and Consequences, together with commentary, all appearing as Symposium, 69 Cornell L. Rev. 517 (1984); Glendon, The Transformation of American Landlord-Tenant Law, 23 B.C.L. Rev. 503 (1982); Berger, The New Residential Tenancy Law — Are Landlords Public Utilities?, 60 Neb. L. Rev. 707 (1981). For a comparative treatment, see Tiplady, Recent Developments in the Law of Landlord and Tenant: The American Experience, 44 Mod. L. Rev. 1 (1981).

H. GOVERNMENT SUPPORT OF HOUSING

Page 333. At the end of the second line, add:

On housing allowances, see two recent studies: Do Housing Allowances Work? (K. Bradbury & A. Downs eds. 1981); Housing Vouchers for the Poor: Lessons from a National Experiment (R. Struyk & M. Bendick, Jr., eds. 1981).

Page 340. At the end of Note 3, add:

In City of New York v. Rodriguez, 117 Misc. 2d 986, 461 N.Y.S.2d 149 (Sup. Ct. App. Term 1983), noted in 50 Brooklyn L. Rev. 1103 (1984), the court held that breach of the warranty of habitability may be asserted by a tenant against the city as landlord in a suit by the city for unpaid rent.

> While we are sympathetic with the City's plight in having to assume responsibility for [dilapidated] properties . . . , we perceive no logic in requiring tenants of City-owned property to pay rent for services not received while recognizing the right of tenants of privately owned properties to abate their rents under identical circumstances. Nor is the claim by the City that it is not in the business of making a profit from these premises persuasive. [The legislation in question] affords no exemption to not-for-profit entities, and indeed this court only recently held that cooperative corporations, which clearly do not operate for profit, are obligated by the warranty of habitability. . . . [117 Misc. 2d at 990, 461 N.Y.S.2d at 152]

Page 349. At the end of Note 2, add:

On tenant selection generally in governmentally assisted housing, see Comment, Public Housing: Choosing among Families in Need of Housing, 77 NW. U.L. Rev. 700 (1982).

Chapter Three
Possessory Estates (Leaseholds Aside)

B. THE FEE SIMPLE

Page 371. Insert the following after "Problem":

MAHRENHOLZ v. COUNTY BOARD OF SCHOOL TRUSTEES
Illinois Appellate Court, 1981
93 Ill. App. 3d 366, 417 N.E.2d 138

JONES, J. This case involves an action to quiet title to real property located in Lawrence County, Illinois. Its resolution depends on the judicial construction of language in a conveyance of that property. The case is before us on the pleadings, plaintiffs' third amended complaint having been dismissed by a final order. The pertinent facts are taken from the pleadings.

On March 18, 1941, W.E. and Jennie Hutton executed a warranty deed in which they conveyed certain land, to be known here as the Hutton School grounds, to the Trustees of School District No. 1, the predecessors of the defendants in this action. The deed provided that "this land to be used for school purpose only; otherwise to revert to Grantors herein." W. E. Hutton died intestate on July 18, 1951, and Jennie Hutton died intestate on February 18, 1969. The Huttons left as their only legal heir their son Harry E. Hutton.

The property conveyed by the Huttons became the site of the Hutton School. Community Unit School District No. 20 succeeded to the grantee of the deed and held classes in the building constructed upon the land until May 30, 1973. After that date, children were transported to classes held at other facilities operated by the District. The District has used the property since then for storage purposes only.

Earl and Madeline Jacqmain executed a warranty deed on October 9, 1959, conveying to the plaintiffs over 390 acres of land in Lawrence County and which included the 40 acre tract from which the Hutton School grounds were taken. [The Jacqmains acquired this land from W. E. and Jennie Hutton in July, 1941, by a deed that excepted from the conveyance the tract conveyed to the school trustees on March 18, 1941.] The deed from the Jacqmains to the plaintiffs excepted the Hutton School grounds, but purported to convey the disputed future interest, with the following language:

> Also, except the following tract of land which was on the 18th day of March, 1951, by the said grantors [sic] conveyed to the Trustees of Schools of District No. One (1) of the Town of Allison, in the County of Lawrence and State of Illinois, and described as follows:
>
> [legal description]
>
> and containing one and one-half (1½) acres, more or less; Reversionary interest to Grantees. . . .

On May 7, 1977, Harry E. Hutton, son and sole heir of W. E. and Jennie Hutton, conveyed to the plaintiffs all of his interest in the Hutton School land. This document was filed in the recorder's office of Lawrence County on September 7, 1977. On September 6, 1977, Harry Hutton disclaimed his interest in the property in favor of the defendants. The disclaimer was in the form of a written document entitled "Disclaimer and Release." It contained the legal description of the Hutton School grounds and recited that Harry E. Hutton disclaimed and released any possibility of reverter or right of entry for condition broken, or other similar interest, in favor of the County Board of School Trustees for Lawrence County, Illinois, successor to the Trustees of School District No. 1 of Lawrence County, Illinois. The document further recited that it was made for the purpose of releasing and extinguishing any right Harry E. Hutton may have had in the "interest retained by W. E. Hutton and Jennie Hutton . . . in that deed to the Trustees of School District No. 1, Lawrence County, Illinois dated March 18, 1941, and filed on the same date. . . ." The disclaimer was filed in the recorder's office of Lawrence County on October 4, 1977.

The plaintiffs filed a complaint in the circuit court of Lawrence County . . . in which they sought to quiet title to the school property in themselves. . . . This complaint recited the interests acquired from the Jacqmains and from Harry Hutton. On March 21, 1979, the trial court entered an order dismissing this complaint. In the order the court found that the

> [W]arranty deed dated March 18, 1941, from W. E. Hutton and Jennie Hutton to the Trustees of School District No. 1, conveying land here concerned, created a fee simple subject to a condition subsequent followed by the right of entry for condition broken, rather than a determinable fee followed by a possibility of reverter.

Plaintiffs have perfected an appeal to this court.

The basic issue presented by this appeal is whether the trial court correctly concluded that the plaintiffs could not have acquired any interest in the school property from the Jacqmains or from Harry Hutton. Resolution of this issue must turn upon the legal interpretation of the language contained in the March 18, 1941, deed from W. E. and Jennie Hutton to the Trustees of School District No. 1: "this land to be used for school purpose only; otherwise to revert to Grantors herein." In addition to the legal effect of this language we must consider the alienability of the interest created and the effect of subsequent deeds.

The parties appear to be in agreement that the 1941 deed from the Huttons conveyed a defeasible fee simple estate to the grantee, and gave rise to a future interest in the grantors, (See Restatement of the Law, Property, sec. 153), and that it did not convey a fee simple absolute, subject to a covenant. The fact that provision was made for forfeiture of the estate conveyed should the land cease to be used for school purposes suggests that this view is correct. Dunne v. Minsor (1924), 312 Ill. 333, 143 N.E. 842; Newton v. Village of Glen Ellyn (1940), 374 Ill. 50, 27 N.E.2d 821. Restatement of the Law, Property, secs. 44, 45.

The future interest remaining in this grantor or his estate can only be a possibility of reverter or a right of re-entry for condition broken. As neither interest may be transferred by will or by inter vivos conveyance (Ill. Rev. Stat., ch. 30, par. 37b), and as the land was being used for school purposes in 1959 when the Jacqmains transferred their interest in the school property to the plaintiffs, the trial court correctly ruled that the plaintiffs could not have acquired any interest in that property from the Jacqmains by the deed of October 9, 1959.

Consequently this court must determine whether the plaintiffs could have acquired an interest in the Hutton School grounds from Harry Hutton. The resolution of this issue depends on the construction of the language of the 1941 deed of the Huttons to the school district. As urged by the defendants and as the trial court found, that deed conveyed a fee simple subject to a condition subsequent followed by a right of re-entry for condition broken. As argued by the plaintiffs, on the other hand, the deed conveyed a fee simple determinable followed by a possibility of reverter. In either case, the grantor and his heirs retain an interest in the property which may become possessory if the condition is broken. We emphasize here that although sec. 1 of An Act relating to Rights of Entry or Reentry for breach of condition subsequent and possibilities of reverter effective July 21, 1947 (Ill. Rev. Stat., ch. 30, par. 37b) provides that rights of re-entry for condition broken and possibilities of reverter are neither alienable or devisable, they are inheritable. (Deverick v. Bline (1950), 404 Ill. 302, 89 N.E.2d 43). The type of interest held governs the mode of reinvestment with title if reinvestment is to occur. If the grantor had a possibility of reverter, he or his heirs become the owner of the property by operation of law as soon as the condition is broken. If he has a right of re-entry for condition broken, he or his heirs become the owner of the property only after they act to re-take the property.

It is alleged, and we must accept, that classes were last held in the Hutton School in 1973. Harry Hutton, sole heir of the grantors, did not act to legally retake the premises but instead conveyed his interest in that land to the plaintiffs in 1977. If Harry Hutton had only a naked right of re-entry for condition broken, then he could not be the owner of that property until he had legally re-entered the land. Since he took no steps for a legal re-entry, he had only a right of re-entry in 1977, and that right cannot be conveyed inter vivos. On the other hand, if Harry Hutton had a possibility of reverter in the property, then he owned the school property as soon as it ceased to be used for school purposes. Therefore, assuming (1) that cessation of classes constitutes "abandonment of school purposes" on the land, (2) that the conveyance from Harry Hutton to the plaintiffs was legally correct, and (3) that the conveyance was not pre-empted by Hutton's disclaimer in favor of the school district, the plaintiffs could have acquired an interest in the Hutton School grounds if Harry Hutton had inherited a possibility of reverter from his parents.

The difference between a fee simple determinable (or, determinable fee) and a fee simple subject to a condition subsequent, is solely a matter of judicial interpretation of the words of a grant.

. . .[T]he Huttons would have created a fee simple determinable if they had allowed the school district to retain the property *so long as* or *while* it was used for school purposes, or *until* it ceased to be so used. Similarly, a fee simple subject to a condition subsequent would have arisen had the Huttons given the land *upon condition that* or *provided that* it be used for school purposes. In the 1941 deed, though the Huttons gave the land "to be used for school purpose only, otherwise to revert to Grantors herein," no words of temporal limitation, or terms of express condition, were used in the grant.

The plaintiffs argue that the word "only" should be construed as a limitation rather than a condition. The defendants respond that where ambiguous language is used in a deed, the courts of Illinois have expressed a constructional preference for a fee simple subject to a condition subsequent. (Storke v. Penn Mutual Life Ins. Co. (1954), 390 Ill. 619, 61 N.E.2d 552.) Both sides refer us to cases involving deeds which contain language analogous to the 1941 grant in this case.

We believe that a close analysis of the wording of the original grant shows that the grantors intended to create a fee simple determinable followed by a possibility of reverter. Here, the use of the word "only" immediately following the grant "for school purpose" demonstrates that the Huttons wanted to give the land to the school district only as long as it was needed and no longer. The language "this land to be used for school purpose only" is an example of a grant which contains a limitation within the granting clause. It suggests a limited grant, rather than a full grant subject to a condition, and thus, both theoretically and linguistically, gives rise to a fee simple determinable.

The second relevant clause furnishes plaintiffs' position with additional support. It cannot be argued that the phrase "otherwise to revert to grantors herein" is inconsistent with a fee simple subject to a condition subsequent. Nor does the word "revert" automatically create a possibility of reverter. But, in combination with the preceding phrase, the provisions by which possession is returned to the grantors seem to trigger a mandatory return rather than a permissive return because it is not stated that the grantor "may" re-enter the land. See City of Urbana v. Solo Cup Co. (4th Dist. 1979), 66 Ill. App. 3d 45, 22 Ill. Dec. 786, 383 N.E.2d 262.

The terms used in the 1941 deed, although imprecise, were designed to allow the property to be used for a single purpose, namely, for "school purpose." The Huttons intended to have the land back if it were ever used otherwise. Upon a grant of exclusive use followed by an express provision for reverter when that use ceases, courts and commentators have agreed that a fee simple determinable, rather than a fee simple subject to a condition subsequent, is created. (1 Simes and Smith, The Law of Future Interests (2nd ed. 1956) sec. 286 n. 58.) Our own research has uncovered cases from other jurisdictions and sources in which language very similar to that in the Hutton deed has been held to create a fee simple determinable:

> A conveyance "for the use, intent and purpose of a site for a School House [and] whenever the said School District removes the School House from said tract of land or whenever said School House ceases to be used as the Public School House . . . then the said Trust shall cease and determine and the said land shall revert to the grantor and his heirs" [Consolidated School District v. Walter (1954, 243 Minn. 159, 66 N.W.2d 881, 882.]

> [I]t being absolutely understood that when said land ceases to be used for school purposes it is to revert to the above grantor, his heirs. [U.S. v. 1119.15 Acres of Land, (E.D. Ill.1942), 44 F. Supp. 449.]

> That I, S. S. Gray (Widower), for and in consideration of the sum of Donation to Wheeler School District to be used by said Wheeler Special School District for school and church purposes and to revert to me should school and church be discontinued or moved. [Williams v. Kirby School District (Ark. 1944), 181 S.W.2d 488, 490.]

> It is understood and agreed that if the above described land is abandoned by the said second parties and not used for school purposes then the above described land reverts to the party of the first part. [School District No. 6 v. Russell (1964), 156 Colo. 75, 396 P.2d 929, 930.]

[T]o B and C [trustees of a school district] and their heirs and successors for school purposes and to revert to the grantor when it ceases to be so used. [Restatement of Property, sec. 44, comment 1, illustration V (1936).]

Thus, authority from this state and others indicates that the grant in the Hutton deed did in fact create a fee simple determinable. We are not persuaded by the cases cited by the defendants for the terms of conveyance in those cases distinguish them from the facts presented here....

The deed in Sherman v. Town of Jefferson (1916), 274 Ill. 294, 113 N.E. 624, stated,

This conveyance is made, understood and agreed by and between the parties hereto upon the express condition the premises conveyed shall be occupied, used and enjoyed for town purposes only, and upon ceasing to be so used and enjoyed by the said party of the second part, in whole or in any part thereof, the conveyance above becomes and remains absolutely void and of no longer force, effect or obligation as against the said party of the first part, his heirs and assigns.

274 Ill. 294, 295, 113 N.E. 624, 625. This conveyance may be distinguished from the Hutton deed because the reversion clause in *Sherman* provided that the grant would, upon breach of condition, be void only against the grantor. This unusual language is merely another way to state that the grantee may retain possession until the grantor re-enters the property.

The estate created in Latham v. Illinois Central Railroad Co. (1912), 253 Ill. 93, 97 N.E. 254, was held to be a fee simple subject to a condition subsequent. Land was conveyed to a railroad in return for the railroad's agreement to erect and maintain a passenger depot and a freight depot on the premises. The deed was made to the grantee, "their successors and assigns forever, for the uses and purposes hereinafter mentioned and for NONE other." Those purposes were limited to "railroad purposes only." The deed provided "that in case of non-user of said premises so conveyed for the uses and purposes aforesaid, that then and in that case the title to said premises shall revert back to [the grantors], their heirs, executors, administrators and assigns." The property was granted to the railroad to have and hold forever, "subject, nevertheless, to all the conditions, covenants, agreements and limitations in this deed expressed." The estate in *Latham* may be distinguished from that created here in that the former was a grant "forever" which was subjected to certain use restrictions while the Hutton deed gave the property to the school district only as long as it could use it.

In Northwestern University v. Wesley Memorial Hospital (1919), 290 Ill. 205, 125 N.E. 13, a conveyance was "made upon the express condition that said Wesley Hospital, the grantee herein, shall erect a hospital building on said lot . . . and that on the failure of said Wesley Hospital to carry out these conditions the title shall revert to Northwestern University." This language cannot be interpreted as creating anything but a fee simple subject to a condition subsequent, and the court so held.

The defendants also direct our attention to the case of McElvain v. Dorris (1921), 298 Ill. 377, 131 N.E. 608. There, land was sold subject to the following condition: "This tract of land is to be used for mill purposes, and if not used for mill purposes the title reverts back to the former owner." When the mill was abandoned, the heirs of the grantor brought suit in ejectment and were successful. The Supreme Court of Illinois did not mention the possibility that the quoted words could have created a fee simple determinable but instead stated,

> Annexed to the grant there was a condition subsequent, by a breach of which there would be a right of re-entry by the grantor or her heirs at law. [Citations.] A breach of the condition in such a case does not, of itself, determine the estate, but an entry, or some act equivalent thereto, is necessary to revest the estate, and bringing a suit in ejectment is equivalent to such re-entry.

298 Ill. at 379, 131 N.E. 608. It is urged by the defendants that McElvain v. Dorris stands for the proposition that the quoted language in the deed creates a fee simple subject to a condition subsequent. We must agree with the defendants that the grant in *McElvain* is strikingly similar to that in this case. However, the opinion in *McElvain* is ambiguous in several respects. First, that portion of the opinion which states that "Annexed to the grant there was a condition subsequent . . ." may refer to the provision quoted above, or it may refer to another provision not reproduced in that opinion. Second, even if the court's reference is to the quoted language, the holding may reflect only the court's acceptance of the parties' construction of the grant. (A similar procedure was followed in Trustees of Schools v. Batdorf (1955), 6 Ill. 2d 486, 130 N.E.2d 111, as noted by defendants.) After all, as an action in ejectment was brought in *McElvain,* the difference between a fee simple determinable and a fee simple subject to a condition subsequent would have no practical effect and the court did not discuss it.

To the extent that *McElvain* holds that the quoted language establishes a fee simple subject to a condition subsequent, it is contrary to the weight of Illinois and American authority. A more appropriate case with which to resolve the problem presented here is North v. Graham (1908), 235 Ill. 178, 85 N.E. 267. Land was conveyed to trustees of a church under a deed which stated that "said tract of land above described to revert to the party of the first part whenever it ceases to be used or occupied for a meeting house or church." Following an extended discussion of determinable fees, the court concluded that such an estate is legal in Illinois and that the language of the deed did in fact create that estate.

North v. Graham, like this case, falls somewhere between those cases in which appears the classic language used to create a fee simple determinable and that used to create a fee simple subject to a condition subsequent. The language used classically to create a fee simple determinable is "so long as it is used for . . . ," as may be seen in Blackert v. Dugosh (1957), 12 Ill. 2d 171, 145 N.E.2d 606; Carlsen v. Carter (1941), 377 Ill. 484, 36 N.E.2d 740; Pure Oil Co. v. Miller-McFarland Drilling Co. (1941), 376 Ill. 486, 34 N.E.2d 854; Regular Predestinarian Baptist Church of Pleasant Grove v. Parker (1940), 373 Ill. 607, 27 N.E.2d 522; Dees v. Cheuvronts (1909), 240 Ill. 486, 88 N.E. 1011; Danaj v. Anest (2nd Dist. 1979), 77 Ill. App. 3d 533, 33 Ill. Dec. 19, 396 N.E.2d 95.

The language used typically to create a fee simple subject to a condition subsequent is, variously, "provided it be used for . . . ," O'Donnell v. Robson (1909), 239 Ill. 634, 88 N.E. 175; "that in case of breach of these covenants . . . said premises shall immediately revert . . . ," Storke v. Penn Mutual Life Ins. Co. (1945), 390 Ill. 619, 61 N.E.2d 552; "and, if this agreement is broken, said land shall revert . . . ," Wakefield v. Van Tassel (1903), 202 Ill. 41, 66 N.E. 830, *writ of error dismissed*, 192 U.S. 601, 24 S. Ct. 850, 48 L. Ed. 583; "in the event the [grantee] shall fail to perform . . . all the above requirements and conditions, all the lands . . . shall revert . . . ," Gray v. Chicago, Milw. and St. Paul Rwy. Co. (1901), 189 Ill. 400, 59 N.E. 950.

Although the word "whenever" is used in the North v. Graham deed, it is not found in a granting clause, but in a reverter clause. The court found this slightly unorthodox construction sufficient to create a fee simple determinable, and we believe that the word "only" placed in the granting clause of the Hutton deed brings this case under the rule of North v. Graham.

We hold, therefore, that the 1941 deed from W. E. and Jennie Hutton to the Trustees of School District No. 1 created a fee simple determinable in the Trustees followed by a possibility of reverter in the Huttons and their heirs. Accordingly, the trial court erred in dismissing plaintiffs' . . . complaint which followed its holding that the plaintiffs could not have acquired any interest in the Hutton School property from Harry Hutton. We must therefore reverse and remand this cause to the trial court for further proceedings.

We refrain from deciding the following issues: (1) whether the 1977 conveyance from Harry Hutton was legally sufficient to pass his interest in the school property to the plaintiffs, (2) whether Harry Hutton effectively disclaimed his interest in the property in favor of the defendants by virtue of his 1977 disclaimer, and (3) whether the defendants have ceased to use the Hutton School grounds for "school purposes." . . .

Reversed and remanded.

On remand to the trial court, the school district alleged that it had not ceased to use the Hutton School property for school purposes. The school

Possessory Estates   Page 385

district moved for summary judgment upon the affidavits of the superintendent and assistant superintendent of the school district that the school district continued to use the Hutton School property for storage of school equipment. In opposing the school district's motion, the plaintiffs filed an affidavit that the items stored in the school were junk. The trial court granted the school district's motion for summary judgment. On appeal, the appellate court reversed. It held that "school purpose" includes other use than holding classes, but that the conflicting affidavits raised an issue of material fact as to whether the Hutton School property was being used for "school purpose." Therefore, it was improper for the trial court to grant summary judgment. Mahrenholz v. County Board of School Trustees 466 N.E.2d 322 (Ill. App. Ct. 1984).

QUESTIONS

In Illinois, by statute neither a possibility of reverter nor a right of entry can be transferred by deed or will. Is this a good idea? Suppose that the Huttons had attempted to convey to the Jacqmains the possibility of reverter together with the 40 acres of land adjacent to the school tract. From the viewpoint of public policy would it be better to have the possibility of reverter in the owner of the adjacent tract or in the heirs of the original grantors?

D. THE LIFE ESTATE

Page 385.   Insert the following before "Problems":

WHITE v. BROWN
Supreme Court of Tennessee, 1977
559 S.W.2d 938

BROCK, J. This is a suit for the construction of a will. The Chancellor held that the will passed a life estate, but not the remainder, in certain realty, leaving the remainder to pass by inheritance to the testatrix's heirs at law. The Court of Appeals affirmed.

Mrs. Jessie Lide died on February 15, 1973, leaving a holographic will which, in its entirety, reads as follows:

April 19, 1972

I, Jessie Lide, being in sound mind declare this to be my last will and testament. I appoint my niece Sandra White Perry to be the executrix of my estate. I wish Evelyn White to have my home to live in and <u>not</u> to be <u>sold</u>.

I also leave my personal property to Sandra White Perry. My house is not to be sold.

Jessie Lide
(Underscoring by testatrix).

Mrs. Lide was a widow and had no children. Although she had nine brothers and sisters, only two sisters residing in Ohio survived her. These two sisters quitclaimed any interest they might have in the residence to Mrs. White. The nieces and nephews of the testatrix, her heirs at law, are defendants in this action.

Mrs. White, her husband, who was the testatrix's brother, and her daughter, Sandra White Perry, lived with Mrs. Lide as a family for some twenty-five years. After Sandra married in 1969 and Mrs. White's husband died in 1971, Evelyn White continued to live with Mrs. Lide until Mrs. Lide's death in 1973 at age 88.

Mrs. White, joined by her daughter as executrix, filed this action to obtain construction of the will, alleging that she is vested with a fee simple title to the home. The defendants contend that the will conveyed only a life estate to Mrs. White, leaving the remainder to go to them under our laws of intestate succession. The Chancellor held that the will unambiguously conveyed only a life interest in the home to Mrs. White and refused to consider extrinsic evidence concerning Mrs. Lide's relationship with her surviving relatives. Due to the debilitated condition of the property and in accordance with the desire of all parties, the Chancellor ordered the property sold with the proceeds distributed in designated shares among the beneficiaries.

I

Our cases have repeatedly acknowledged that the intention of the testator is to be ascertained from the language of the entire instrument when read in the light of surrounding circumstances. . . . But, the practical difficulty in this case, as in so many other cases involving wills drafted by lay persons, is that the words chosen by the testatrix are not specific enough to clearly state her intent. Thus, in our opinion, it is not clear whether Mrs. Lide intended to convey a life estate in the home to Mrs. White, leaving the remainder interest to descend by operation of law, or a fee interest with a restraint on alienation. Moreover, the will might even be read as conveying a fee interest subject to a condition subsequent (Mrs. White's failure to live in the home).

In such ambiguous cases it is obvious that rules of construction, always yielding to the cardinal rule of the testator's intent, must be employed as auxiliary aids in the courts' endeavor to ascertain the testator's intent.

In 1851 our General Assembly enacted two such statutes of construction, thereby creating a statutory presumption against partial intestacy.

Chapter 33 of the Public Acts of 1851 (now codified as T.C.A. §§64-101 and 64-501) reversed the common law presumption that a life estate was intended unless the intent to pass a fee simple was clearly expressed in the instrument. T.C.A. §64-501 provides: "Every grant or devise of real estate, or any interest therein, shall pass all the estate or interest of the grantor or devisor, unless the intent to pass a less estate or interest shall appear by express terms, or be necessarily implied in the terms of the instrument."

Chapter 180, Section 2 of the Public Acts of 1851 (now codified as T.C.A. §32-301) was specifically directed to the operation of a devise. In relevant part, T.C.A. §32-301 provides: "A will ... shall convey all the real estate belonging to [the testator] or in which he had any interest at his decease, unless a contrary intention appear by its words and context."

Thus, under our law, unless the "words and context" of Mrs. Lide's will clearly evidence her intention to convey only a life estate to Mrs. White, the will should be construed as passing the home to Mrs. White in fee. "'If the expression in the will is doubtful, the doubt is resolved against the limitation and in favor of the absolute estate.'" Meacham v. Graham, 98 Tenn. 190, 206, 39 S.W. 12, 15 (1897) (quoting Washbon v. Cope, 144 N.Y. 287, 39 N.E. 388); Weiss v. Broadway Nat'l Bank, 204 Tenn. 563, 322 S.W.2d 427 (1959); Cannon v. Cannon, 182 Tenn. 1, 184 S.W.2d 35 (1945).

Several of our cases demonstrate the effect of these statutory presumptions against intestacy by construing language which might seem to convey an estate for life, without provision for a gift over after the termination of such life estate, as passing a fee simple instead. In Green v. Young, 163 Tenn. 16, 40 S.W.2d 793 (1931), the testatrix's disposition of all of her property to her husband "to be used by him for his support and comfort during his life" was held to pass a fee estate. Similarly, in Williams v. Williams, 167 Tenn. 26, 65 S.W.2d 561 (1933), the testator's devise of real property to his children "for and during their natural lives" without provision for a gift over was held to convey a fee. And, in Webb v. Webb, 53 Tenn. App. 609, 385 S.W.2d 295 (1964), a devise of personal property to the testator's wife "for her maintenance, support and comfort, for the full period of her natural life" with complete powers of alienation but without provision for the remainder passed absolute title to the widow.

II

Thus, if the sole question for our determination were whether the will's conveyance of the home to Mrs. White "to live in" gave her a life interest or a fee in the home, a conclusion favoring the absolute estate would be clearly required. The question, however, is complicated somewhat by the caveat contained in the will that the home is "not to be sold" — a restriction conflicting with the free alienation of property, one of the most significant incidents of fee ownership. We must determine, therefore, whether Mrs.

Lide's will, when taken as a whole, clearly evidences her intent to convey only a life estate in her home to Mrs. White.

Under ordinary circumstances a person makes a will to dispose of his or her entire estate. If, therefore, a will is susceptible of two constructions, by one of which the testator disposes of the whole of his estate and by the other of which he disposes of only a part of his estate, dying intestate as to the remainder, this Court has always preferred that construction which disposes of the whole of the testator's estate if that construction is reasonable and consistent with the general scope and provisions of the will. See Ledbetter v. Ledbetter, 188 Tenn. 44, 216 S.W.2d 718 (1949); Cannon v. Cannon, *supra*; Williams v. Williams, *supra*; Jarnagin v. Conway, 21 Tenn. 50 (1840); 4 Page, Wills §30.14 (3d ed. 1961). A construction which results in partial intestacy will not be adopted unless such intention clearly appears. Bedford v. Bedford, 38 Tenn. App. 370, 274 S.W.2d 528 (1954); Martin v. Hale, 167 Tenn. 438, 71 S.W.2d 211 (1934). It has been said that the courts will prefer any reasonable construction or any construction which does not do violence to a testator's language, to a construction which results in partial intestacy. *Ledbetter, supra.*

The intent to create a fee simple or other absolute interest and, at the same time to impose a restraint upon its alienation can be clearly expressed. If the testator specifically declares that he devises land to A "in fee simple" or to A "and his heirs" but that A shall not have the power to alienate the land, there is but one tenable construction, viz., the testator's intent is to impose a restraint upon a fee simple. To construe such language to create a life estate would conflict with the express specification of a fee simple as well as with the presumption of intent to make a complete testamentary disposition of all of a testator's property. By extension, as noted by Professor Casner in his treatise on the law of real property:

> Since it is now generally presumed that a conveyor intends to transfer his whole interest in the property, it may be reasonable to adopt the same construction, [conveyance of a fee simple] even in the absence of words of inheritance, if there is no language that can be construed to create a remainder.

6 American Law of Property §26.58 (A. J. Casner ed. 1952).

In our opinion, testatrix's apparent testamentary restraint on the alienation of the home devised to Mrs. White does not evidence such a clear intent to pass only a life estate as is sufficient to overcome the law's strong presumption that a fee simple interest was conveyed.

Accordingly, we conclude that Mrs. Lide's will passed a fee simple absolute in the home to Mrs. White. Her attempted restraint on alienation must be declared void as inconsistent with the incidents and nature of the estate devised and contrary to public policy. Nashville C & S.L. Ry. v. Bell, 162 Tenn. 661, 39 S.W.2d 1026 (1931).

The decrees of the Court of Appeals and the trial court are reversed and the cause is remanded to the chancery court for such further proceedings as may be necessary, consistent with this opinion. Costs are taxed against appellees.

COOPER and FONES, J. J., concur.

HARBISON, J., dissents.

HENRY, C.J., joins in dissent.

HARBISON, J., dissenting.

With deference to the views of the majority, and recognizing the principles of law contained in the majority opinion, I am unable to agree that the language of the will of Mrs. Lide did or was intended to convey a fee simple interest in her residence to her sister-in-law, Mrs. Evelyn White.

The testatrix expressed the wish that Mrs. White was "to have my home to live in and *not* to be *sold*". The emphasis is that of the testatrix, and her desire that Mrs. White was not to have an unlimited estate in the property was reiterated in the last sentence of the will, to wit: "My house is not to be sold."

The testatrix appointed her niece, Mrs. Perry, executrix and made an outright bequest to her of all personal property.

The will does not seem to me to be particularly ambiguous, and like the Chancellor and the Court of Appeals, I am of the opinion that the testatrix gave Mrs. White a life estate only, and that upon the death of Mrs. White the remainder will pass to the heirs at law of the testatrix. . . .

In the present case the testatrix knew how to make an outright gift, if desired. She left all of her personal property to her niece without restraint or limitation. As to her sister-in-law, however, she merely wished the latter have her house "to live in", and expressly withheld from her any power of sale.

The majority opinion holds that the testatrix violated a rule of law by attempting to restrict the power of the donee to dispose of the real estate. Only by thus striking a portion of the will, and holding it inoperative, is the conclusion reached that an unlimited estate resulted.

In my opinion, this interpretation conflicts more greatly with the apparent intention of the testatrix than did the conclusion of the courts below, limiting the gift to Mrs. White to a life estate. I have serious doubt that the testatrix intended to create any illegal restraint on alienation or to violate any other rules of law. It seems to me that she rather emphatically intended to provide that her sister-in-law was not to be able to sell the house during the lifetime of the latter — a result which is both legal and consistent with the creation of a life estate.

In my opinion the judgment of the courts below was correct and I would affirm.

I am authorized to state that Chief Justice HENRY joins in this opinion.

F. COOPERATIVES AND CONDOMINIUMS

Page 405. After the first paragraph, insert:

LAGUNA ROYALE OWNERS ASSN. v. DARGER
California Court of Appeal, 1981
119 Cal. App. 3d 670, 174 Cal. Rptr. 136

KAUFMAN, A.J. Defendants Stanford P. Darger and Darlene B. Darger (the Dargers) were the owners of a leasehold condominium in Laguna Royale, a 78-unit community apartment complex on the ocean front in South Laguna Beach. The Dargers purported to assign three one-quarter undivided interests in the property to three other couples: Wendell P. Paxton and Daila D. Paxton, Keith I. Gustaveson and Elsie Gustaveson, and Keith C. Brown and Geneva B. Brown (collectively the other defendants) without the approval of Laguna Royale Owners Association (Association). Association instituted this action to obtain a declaration that the assignments from the Dargers to defendants were invalid because they were made in violation of a provision of the instrument by which the Dargers acquired the property, prohibiting assignment or transfer of interests in the property without the consent and approval of Association's predecessor in interest. Following trial to the court judgment was rendered in favor of Association invalidating the assignments from the Dargers to the other defendants. Defendants appeal.

FACTS

The Laguna Royale development is built on land leased by the developer from the landowner in a 99-year ground lease executed in 1961. As the units were completed, the developer sold each one by executing a Subassignment and Occupancy Agreement with the purchaser. This document conveyed an undivided $1/78$ interest in the leasehold estate for a term of 99 years, a right to exclusive use of a designated unit and one or more garage spaces and a right to joint use of common areas and facilities; it also contained certain restrictions. The restriction pertinent to this action is paragraph 7, which provides in relevant part: "7. Subassignee [the purchaser] shall not assign or otherwise transfer this agreement, . . . nor shall subassignee sublet . . . without the consent and approval of Lessee. . . ."

Upon the sale of all units and completion of the project, the developer entered into an "Assignment Agreement" with the Association, transferring and assigning to the Association all the developer's rights, powers and duties under the Subassignment and Occupancy Agreements, including inter alia the "right to approve or disapprove assignments or transfers of interests in Laguna Royale pursuant to Paragraph 7 of the Subassignment and Occupancy Agreements."

Possessory Estates   **Page 405**

In 1965, Ramona G. Sutton acquired unit 41, consisting of some 3,000 square feet, by a Subassignment and Occupancy Agreement with the developer. In 1973 the Dargers purchased unit 41 from the executrix of Mrs. Sutton's estate. As owner of a unit in the project, the Dargers automatically became members of the Association and were bound by the Association's by-laws.

The Dargers reside in Salt Lake City, Utah, where Mr. Darger became a vice president of a large banking chain not long after the Dargers acquired their unit at Laguna Royale. The responsibilities of Mr. Darger's new position made it difficult for them to get away, and they attempted unsuccessfully to lease their unit through real estate agents in Laguna Beach. On October 30, 1973, Mr. Darger wrote to Mr. Yount, then chairman of the board of governors of the Association, in which he stated in part:

> It has been suggested that we might sell shares in our apartment to two or three other couples here. These associates would be aware of the restrictions regarding children under 16 living there, as well as the restrictions regarding pets, and would submit themselves to the regular investigation of the Board given prospective purchasers and lessees. I would expect that the apartment will remain vacant most of the time, as now, and not more than one of the families will occupy the apartment at one time. . . .

[After several letters between the Dargers and the association, the association in 1976 refused consent to transfer of the Dargers' unit in undivided shares to four couples.]

By a letter from its attorney to the Dargers dated March 16, 1976, Association advised the Dargers that it would not consent to the requested transfer. It was denied that written and verbal approvals had been given the Dargers in the past, and it was stated in relevant part:

> The reason the Association will not consent to your requested transfer is that the Board feels it is obligated to protect and preserve the private single family residential character of Laguna Royale, together with the use and quiet enjoyment of all apartment owners of their respective apartments and the common facilities, taking into consideration the close community living circumstances of Laguna Royale. [¶] The Board feels strongly about its power of consent to assignments and other transfers of leasehold interests and considers the protection and preservation of that power to be critical in maintaining the character of Laguna Royale for the benefit of all owners as a whole. A four family ownership of a single apartment, with the guests of each owner potentially involved, would compound the use of the apartment and common facilities well beyond the normal and usual private single family residential character to the detriment of other owners and would frustrate effective controls over general security, guest occupants and rule compliance, as has been the case in the past. [¶] Provision 7 of the Subassignment and Occupancy Agreement, under which all apartment leasehold interests are

41

held, requires the unqualified consent to any transfer. Provision 10 of said agreement provides for the termination of the leasehold interest in the event of a violation of Provision 7, or other breach. . . . [¶] No apartments in Laguna Royale are held by multiple families in the manner that you have requested. In any event, any consents given by the Association to transfers in the past cannot be regarded as setting any precedent or in any way limiting or impairing the power of the Association to refuse its consent to any present or future transfer. In this regard, the language of Provision 7 of the Subassignment and Occupancy Agreement provides that consent given to any particular transfer shall not operate as a waiver for any other transfer.

After consultation with legal counsel the Dargers proceeded nevertheless, and on June 11 they executed instruments purporting to assign undivided one-fourth interests in the property to themselves and the other three couples. The instruments were recorded on June 30, and on July 3, 1976, the Dargers informed Association by letter of the transfers inclosing on Association's forms a separate "Request For Approval Of Sale Or Lease" and financial statement prepared and executed by each of the other couples. These papers show that the other defendants all reside in Salt Lake City, Utah. Each executed request form contains a warranty by the purchaser that if the application is approved no child under 16 years of age "will make residency at this property" and an agreement that the purchaser "will abide by and conform to the terms and conditions of the master lease, . . . all amendments described in the Subassignment and Occupancy Agreement . . . and the By-Laws of the Laguna Royale Owners . . . Association."

After unsuccessfully demanding that the other defendants retransfer their purported interests to the Dargers, the Association filed this action.

At trial the testimony confirmed that no more than one family of defendants used the property at a time and, although the matter was not examined in detail, answers to questions by one or more defendants indicated that 13-week periods had been agreed upon for exclusive use by each of the four families. It was also indicated that for substantial periods during the year, no use at all was being made of the unit. The evidence also showed that a number of Laguna Royale units were owned by several unrelated persons, but that in each case the owners used the unit "as a family."

No formal findings were made. However, in its notice of intended decision the court stated in relevant part:

> The Court . . . finds that the plaintiff association acted reasonably in refusing to grant consent to the proposed transfer by Darger to the other defendants. Plaintiff is entitled to a declaration that the assignments by Darger to the other defendants are invalid. Plaintiff is awarded attorney fees in the amount of $2500.

Judgment was entered accordingly.

CONTENTIONS, ISSUES AND DISCUSSION

Defendants contend paragraph 7 of the Subassignment and Occupancy Agreement prohibiting assignments or transfers without the consent of Association is invalid because it is in violation of their constitutional rights to associate with persons of their choosing (U.S. Const., 1st amend.; Cal. Const., art. I, §1), [and] because it constitutes an unlawful restraint on alienation (Civ. Code, §711). . . . Failing those, defendants contend finally that if by its finding that Association acted reasonably in refusing to approve the transfers, the court meant to indicate that Association had the duty to act reasonably in withholding consent and did so, that determination is not supported by substantial evidence and is contrary to law.

Association contends that the prohibition against transfer or assignment without its consent is not invalid on any of the bases urged by defendants. It argues primarily that its right to withhold approval or consent is absolute, that in exercising its power it is not required to adhere to a standard of reasonableness but may withhold approval or consent for any reason or for no reason at all. Secondarily, it argues that the evidence supports the finding it acted reasonably in disapproving the transfers to the other defendants.

We reject Association's contention that its right to give or withhold approval or consent is absolute. We likewise reject defendants' contention that the claimed right to approve or disapprove transfers is an invalid restraint on alienation because it is repugnant to the conveyance of a fee. We hold that in exercising its power to approve or disapprove transfers or assignments Association must act reasonably, exercising its power in a fair and nondiscriminatory manner and withholding approval only for a reason or reasons rationally related to the protection, preservation and proper operation of the property and the purposes of Association as set forth in its governing instruments. We hold that the restriction on transfer contained in paragraph 7 of the Subassignment and Occupancy Agreement (hereafter simply paragraph 7), thus limited, does not violate defendants' constitutional rights of association and is not invalid as an unreasonable restraint on alienation. However, we conclude that in view of the present provisions of Association's bylaws, its refusal to consent to the transfers to defendants was unreasonable as a matter of law. Accordingly, we reverse the judgment with directions to enter judgment for defendants. . . .

As indicated, the initial positions of the parties are at opposite extremes. Association contends that the Subassignment and Occupancy Agreement constitutes a sublease and that under the law applicable to leasehold interests, when a lease contains a provision permitting subletting only upon consent of the lessor, the lessor is under no obligation to give consent and, in fact, may withhold consent arbitrarily. . . . Defendants on the other hand contend that the Subassignment and Occupancy Agreement conveys, in essence, a fee,[37] and that under California law when a fee simple interest is granted, any restriction on the subsequent conveyance of the grantee's interest contained in the original grant is repugnant to the interest conveyed and is therefore void. . . .

We reject the extreme contentions of both parties; the rules of law they propose, borrowed from the law of landlord and tenant developed during the feudal period in English history (see Green v. Superior Court (1974) 10 Cal. 3d 616, 622, 111 Cal. Rptr. 704, 517 P.2d 1168), are entirely inappropriate tools for use in affecting an accommodation of the competing interests involved in the use and transfer of a condominium. Even assuming the continued vitality of the rule that a lessor may arbitrarily withhold consent to a sublease (but see Note, Effect of Leasehold Provision Requiring the Lessor's Consent to Assignment (1970) 21 Hast. L.J. 516), there is little or no similarity in the relationship between a condominium owner and his fellow owners and that between lessor and lessee or sublessor and sublessee. Even when the right to the underlying land is no more than an undivided interest in a ground lease or sublease, ownership of a condominium constitutes a statutorily recognized estate in real property (see Civ. Code, §783), and in our society the right freely to use and dispose of one's property is a valued and protected right. (U.S. Const., amends. 5 and 14; Cal. Const., art. I, §7, subd. (a); see 5 Witkin, Summary of Cal. Law (8th ed. 1974) Constitutional Law, §273, p.3563.) Ownership and use of condominiums is an increasingly significant form of "home ownership" which has evolved in recent years to meet the desire of our people to own their own dwelling place, in the face of heavy concentrations of population in urban areas, the limited availability of housing, and, thus, the impossibly inflated cost of individual homes in such areas.

On the other hand condominium living involves a certain closeness to and with one's neighbors, and, as stated in Hidden Harbour Estates, Inc. v. Norman (Fla. App.1975) 309 So. 2d 180, 181-182:

> [I]nherent in the condominium concept is the principle that to promote the health, happiness, and peace of mind of the majority of the unit owners since they are living in such close proximity and using facilities in common, each unit owner must give up a certain degree of freedom of choice which he might otherwise enjoy in separate, privately owned property.

---

37. It is unclear to us how the Subassignment and Occupancy Agreement could convey a fee interest when the entire interest in the land underlying the development is only a 99-year ground lease. It would appear that defendants' argument more appropriately ought to be that once consent was given pursuant to the Subassignment and Occupancy Agreement to the transfer from the estate of Romona Sutton to the Dargers, the rule in Dumpor's Case (1578), 76 Eng. Rep. 110, became applicable and that thereafter no consent to any further assignment was required. (See Witkin, Summary of Cal. Law (8th ed. 1973) Real Property, §491, at 2170).

(See also White Egret Condominium v. Franklin (Fla. 1979) 379 So.2d 346, 350; Seagate Condominium Association, Inc. v. Duffy (Fla. App.1976) 330 So. 2d 484, 486.) Thus, it is essential to successful condominium living and the maintenance of the value of these increasingly significant property interests that the owners as a group have the authority to regulate reasonably the use and alienation of the condominiums.

Happily, there is no impediment to our adoption of such a rule; indeed, the existing law suggests such a rule. In the only California appellate decision of which we are aware dealing with the problem of restraints on alienation of a condominium, Ritchey v. Villa Nueva Condominium Assn. (1978), 81 Cal. App.3d 688, 695, 146 Cal. Rptr. 716, the court upheld as a reasonable restriction on an owner's right to sell his unit to families with children, a duly adopted amendment to the condominium bylaws restricting occupancy to persons 18 years and over.[38] And, of course, Civil Code section 1355 pertaining to condominiums expressly authorizes the recordation of a declaration of project restrictions and subsequent amendments thereto, "which restrictions shall be enforceable equitable servitudes where reasonable, and shall inure to and bind all owners of condominiums in the project."

. . . The day has long since passed when the rule in California was that all restraints on alienation were unlawful under the statute; it is now the settled law in this jurisdiction that only unreasonable restraints on alienation are invalid. . . .

Nor does the right of Association reasonably to approve or disapprove the assignment or transfer of the Dargers' ownership interest violate defendants' constitutional right to associate freely with persons of their choosing. Preliminarily, there is considerable doubt of whether the actions of Association constitute state action so as to bring into play the constitutional guarantees. (Cf. Moose Lodge No. 107 v. Irvis (1972) 407 U.S. 163, 173, 92 S. Ct. 1965, 1971, 32 L. Ed. 2d 627, 637; Newby v. Alto Riviera Apartments (1976) 60 Cal. App. 3d 288, 293-295, 131 Cal. Rptr. 547; see generally 5 Witkin, Summary of Cal. Law (8th ed. 1974) Constitutional Law, §338, pp. 3631-3632.) In any event, however, the constitutionally guaranteed freedom of association, like most other constitutionally protected rights, is not absolute but is subject to reasonable restriction in the interests of the general welfare. (Village of Belle Terre v. Boraas (1974) 416 U.S. 1, 9, 94 S. Ct. 1536, 1541, 39 L. Ed. 2d 797, 804; White Egret Condominium v. Franklin, *supra*, 379 So. 2d at pp. 349-351.) Moreover, it may be persuasively argued

---

38. In O'Connor v. Village Green Owners Assn., 33 Cal. 3d 790, 191 Cal. Rptr. 320, 662 P.2d 427 (1983), the California Supreme Court held void, as in violation of the Unruh Civil Rights Act, a restriction in a condominium agreement limiting residency to persons over the age of 18 years. Thus the *Ritchey* case does not represent current California law. — Eds.

that if any constitutional right is at issue it is the due process right of an owner of property to use and dispose of it as he chooses. . . . And, of course, property rights are subject to reasonable regulation to promote the general welfare. . . . Finally, any determination of the validity or invalidity of Association's right to approve or disapprove assignments or transfers of the Dargers' interest will of necessity impinge upon someone's constitutional freedom of association. A determination that the power granted the Association is invalid would adversely affect the constitutional right of association of the remaining owners at least as much as a contrary determination would affect the same right of the Dargers. (Cf. Presbytery of Riverside v. Community Church of Palm Springs (1979) 89 Cal. App. 3d 910, 925, 152 Cal. Rptr. 854.)

Having concluded that a reasonable restriction on the right of alienation of a condominium is lawful, we must now determine whether Association's refusal to approve the transfer of the Dargers' interest to the other defendants was reasonable in the circumstances of the case at bench. The criteria for testing the reasonableness of an exercise of such a power by an owners' association are (1) whether the reason for withholding approval is rationally related to the protection, preservation or proper operation of the property and the purposes of the Association as set forth in its governing instruments and (2) whether the power was exercised in a fair and nondiscriminatory manner. . . . Another consideration might be the nature and severity of the consequences of application of the restriction (e.g., transfer declared void, estate forfeited, action for damages). . . .

As to the last observation, a potential problem in the case at bench was avoided by the nature of the relief granted in the court below. Although in its complaint Association asserted a right to terminate the Dargers' ownership interest because of their assignments without Board approval and although there is some reference in the briefs to a "forfeiture," the judgment of the trial court simply invalidated the transfers to the other defendants, leaving the Dargers as the owners of the unit as they were at the outset. If Association's disapproval of the transfers was otherwise reasonable, we would find nothing unreasonable in the invalidation of the transfers.

To determine whether or not Association's disapproval of the transfers to the other defendants was reasonable it is necessary to isolate the reason or reasons approval was withheld. Aside from the assertion that it had the power to withhold approval arbitrarily, essentially three reasons were given by the Association for its refusal to approve the transfers: (1) the multiple ownership of undivided interests; (2) the use the defendants proposed to make of the unit would violate a bylaw restricting use of all apartments to "single family residential use"; and (3) the use proposed would be inconsistent with "the private single family residential character of Laguna Royale, together with the use and quiet enjoyment of all apartment owners of their respective apartments and the common facilities, taking into consideration the close community living circumstances of Laguna Royale." As to (3) Association asserted:

> A four family ownership of a single apartment, with the guests of each owner potentially involved, would compound the use of the apartment and common facilities well beyond the normal and usual private single family residential character to the detriment of other owners and would frustrate effective controls over general security, guest occupants and rule compliance. . . .

We examine each of these reasons in light of the indicia of reasonableness referred to above.

Insofar as approval was withheld based on multiple ownership alone, Association's action was clearly unreasonable. In the first place, multiple ownership has no necessary connection to intensive use. Twenty, yea a hundred, persons could own undivided interests in a condominium for investment purposes and lease the condominium on a long-term basis to a single occupant whose use of the premises would probably be less intense in every respect than that considered "normal and usual." Secondly, the Association bylaws specifically contemplate multiple ownership; in Section 7 of Article III, dealing with voting at meetings, it is stated:

> Where there is more than one record owner of a unit, any or all of the record owners may attend [the meeting] but only one vote will be permitted for said unit. In the event of disagreement among the record owners of a unit, the vote for that unit shall be cast by a majority of the record owners.[39]

Finally, the evidence is uncontroverted that a number of units are owned by several unrelated persons. Although those owners at the time of trial used their units "as a family," there is nothing in the governing instruments as they presently exist that would prevent them from changing the character of their use.

We turn to the assertion that the use of the premises proposed by defendants would be in violation of section 1 of article VIII of the bylaws which provides: "All apartment unit uses are restricted and limited to single family residential use and shall not be used or occupied for any other purpose" and paragraph 4 of the Subassignment and Occupation Agreement which

---

39. In a thought-provoking article, Cities and Homeowner Associations, 130 U. Pa. L. Rev. 1519, 1543 (1982), Professor Robert Ellickson compares the city and the private homeowners association, which is a form of private government. He points out that the one-resident/one-vote constitutional rule applicable to cities is not followed in homeowners associations. Homeowner associations are usually required by statute to follow a one-vote-per-unit-rule, as in the Laguna Royale Owners Association. Absentee owners can vote in a homeowners association, but not in a city. Why these differences? Is it because the constitutional rule advances redistributive goals, which are not desired by condominium members? Or because the one-vote-per-unit is easier to administer? — Eds.

provides: "The premises covered hereby shall be used solely for residential purposes...." The term "single family residential use" is not otherwise defined, and if there is any ambiguity or uncertainty in the meaning of the term it must be resolved most favorably to free alienation. (Randol v. Scott (1895) 110 Cal. 590, 595-596, 42 P. 976; Burns v. McGraw (1946) 75 Cal. App. 2d 481, 485-486, 171 P.2d 148; Riley v. Stoves (1974) 22 Ariz. App. 223, 526 P.2d 747, 749.) Actually, there is no evidence that defendants proposed to use the property other than for single family residential purposes. It is uncontroverted that they planned to and did use the property one family at a time for residential purposes. Thus, the proposed use was not in violation of the restriction to single family residential use.[40] (White Egret Condominium v. Franklin, *supra*, 379 So. 2d at p.352).

The reasonableness of Association's disapproval of the transfers from the Dargers to the other defendants must stand or fall in the final analysis on the third reason offered by the Association for its action: the prospect that defendants' proposed use of the apartment and common facilities would be so greatly in excess of that considered "usual and normal" as to be inconsistent with the quiet enjoyment of the premises by the other occupants and the maintenance of security.[41]

There can be no doubt that the reason given is rationally related to the proper operation of the property and the purposes of the Association as set forth in its governing instruments. The bylaws provide that "[t]he purpose of the Association is to manage and maintain the community apartment project ... on a non-profit basis for the benefit of all owners of Laguna Royale." By subdivision (M)(6) of section 2 of Article V of the bylaws the Board is empowered to "prescribe reasonable regulations pertaining to ... [r]egulating the purchase and/or lease of an apartment to a buyer or sublessee who has no children under 16 years of age that will occupy the apartment temporarily or full time as a resident." This power is said by the bylaws to be given the Board in recognition of "the prime importance of both security and quiet enjoyment of the Apartments owned by each member, and of the common recreational areas...."

The difficulty with upholding the Association's disapproval of the transfers by the Dargers to the other defendants is twofold. First, no evidence

---

40. In the trial court counsel for Association argued that "single family residential use" meant the same thing as "single family residential" customarily found in zoning ordinances, typically in connection with the zoning designation R-1. We cannot conceive a decision that the ownership of a private dwelling in an R-1 zone by four families to be used by each family 13 weeks each with no use being made by more than one family at any time would be a use in violation of the R-1 zoning....

41. It is probable that this was the principal reason Association refused to approve the transfers. Defendants' proposed use of the unit has been characterized from time to time during these proceedings as "time sharing."

was introduced to establish that the intensity or nature of the use proposed by defendants would in fact be inconsistent with the peaceful enjoyment of the premises by the other occupants or impair security. We may take judicial notice as a matter of common knowledge that the use of a single apartment by four families for 13 weeks each during the year would create some problems not presented by the use of a single, permanent resident family. The moving in and out would, of course, be more frequent, and it might be that some temporary residents would not be as considerate of their fellow occupants as more permanent residents. However, we are not prepared to take judicial notice that the consecutive use of unit 41 by these four families, one at a time, would be so intense or disruptive as to interfere substantially with the peaceful enjoyment of the premises by the other occupants or the maintenance of building security.

Secondly, and most persuasive, a provision of the bylaws, subdivision (A) of section 1 of article VIII, provides:

> Residential use and purpose, as used herein and as referred to in the lease, sub-assignment and occupancy agreement pertaining to and affecting each apartment unit in LAGUNA ROYALE shall be and is hereby deemed to exclude and prohibit the rental of any apartment unit for a period of time of less than ninety (90) days, as it is deemed and agreed that rentals of apartment units for less than ninety (90) day periods of time are contrary to the close community apartment character of LAGUNA ROYALE; interfere with and complicate the orderly administration and process of the security system and program and maintenance program of LAGUNA ROYALE, and interfere with the orderly management and administration of the common areas and facilities of LAGUNA ROYALE. Accordingly, no owner shall rent an apartment unit for a period of time of less than ninety (90) days.

The point is self-evident: under the present bylaws the Dargers could effect the same *use* of the property as is proposed by defendants by simply leasing to each couple for a period of 90 days each year.

Under these circumstances we are constrained to hold that Board's refusal to approve the transfers to the other defendants on the basis of the prospect of intensified use was unreasonable as a matter of law. . . .

DISPOSITION

The judgment is reversed with directions to the trial court to enter judgment for the defendants.

McDaniel, J., concurs.

Gardner, P.J., dissenting.

I dissent.

Stripped to its essentials, this is a case in which the other owners of a condominium are attempting to stop the owner of one unit from embarking on a time sharing enterprise. The majority properly conclude that the owners as a group have the authority to regulate reasonably the use and alienation of the units. The majority then conclude that the Board's refusal to approve this transfer was unreasonable as a matter of law. To the contrary, I would find it to be entirely reasonable and would affirm the judgment of the trial court.

The use of a unit on a time sharing basis is inconsistent with the quiet enjoyment of the premises by the other occupants. Time sharing is a remarkable gimmick. P. T. Barnum would have loved it. It ordinarily brings enormous profits to the seller and in this case would bring chaos to the other residents. Here we have only four occupants but if this transfer is permitted there is nothing to stop a more greedy occupant of a unit from conveying to 52 or 365 other occupants.

If as an occupant of a condominium I must anticipate that my neighbors are going to change with clocklike regularity I might just as well move into a hotel — and get room service.

QUESTIONS

Suppose that one of the couples in the Dargers' unit finds the other couples do not keep the unit as clean as the couple desires. What are the couple's remedies? See pages 503-511 of the main text.

Suppose that one of the couples does not pay a quarter share of the maintenance charges. What rights has the association against the defaulting couple and against the other three couples? See pages 1033-1044 of the main text.

FRANKLIN v. SPADAFORO

Supreme Judicial Court of Massachusetts, 1983
388 Mass. 764, 447 N.E.2d 1244

NOLAN, J. The issue here is whether a trust by-law adopted by the defendants, trustees of the Melrose Towers Condominium Trust (trust), limiting to two the number of units in the Melrose Towers Condominium (condominium) which may be owned by any one person or entity, represents an unreasonable restraint on alienation or operates to deny the plaintiffs equal protection of the laws or due process of law. The case was submitted to a judge of the Superior Court on a statement of agreed facts. The judge entered a judgment declaring that the bylaw was "valid and not unconstitutional." The plaintiffs appealed to the Appeals Court, and we transferred the case here on our own motion. We affirm.

Possessory Estates

The facts are as follows. On September 25, 1980, the trustees voted to amend the by-laws of the trust to restrict to two the number of condominium units which could be owned by any one person or entity. The amendment was duly recorded in the Registry of Deeds. In adopting the amendment, the trustees acted pursuant to the applicable by-law and with the written consent of condominium unit owners holding 80.45% of the beneficial interest under the trust.

On the date of the amendment, the plaintiff George J. Franklin, Jr., owned six units in the condominium complex. On October 17, 1980, Franklin, as buyer, executed a purchase and sale agreement with the plaintiffs, Daniel and Florence A. Clarke, as sellers, for the purchase of a condominium unit owned by the Clarkes. As required by the Master Deed, the Clarkes then informed the trustees of the pending sale so that the trustees might exercise their right of first refusal. Thereafter, the trustees notified the Clarkes that the sale was in violation of the by-law amendment. Franklin and the Clarkes then brought this action in the Superior Court for declaratory relief from the by-law amendment. After the action was filed, the Clarkes sold the unit to Franklin on April 16, 1981. In his judgment upholding the validity of the by-law amendment, the judge also declared that 'the Clarke-Franklin deed . . . is null and void."

I. Restraint on Alienation

Reasonable restraints on alienation may be enforced. Dunham v. Ware Savs. Bank, 384 Mass. 63, —, Mass. Adv. Sh. (1981) 1607, 1611, 423 N.E.2d 998, and authorities cited. The following factors, if found, tend to support a conclusion that the restraint is reasonable:

> 1. the one imposing the restraint has some interest in land which he is seeking to protect by the enforcement of the restraint; 2. the restraint is limited in duration; 3. the enforcement of the restraint accomplishes a worthwhile purpose; 4. the type of conveyances prohibited are ones not likely to be employed to any substantial degree by the one restrained; 5. the number of persons to whom alienation is prohibited is small. . . .

Restatement of Property §406 comment i (1944). None of these factors is determinative, nor is the list exhaustive. Each case must be examined in light of all the circumstances. *Id.* However, we think that consideration of these factors in the context of the condominium housing arrangement, see G.L. c.183A, is sufficient to demonstrate the reasonableness of the restraint here at issue. . . .

. . . The plaintiffs do not challenge the judge's finding that the "declared purpose" of the amendment was to encourage "maximum occupancy by resident owners.". . . They do assert that there was no evidence to support the judge's further conclusions that "[i]mplicit in this purpose is the desire to impart a degree of continuity of residence, inhibit transiency and safeguard the value of investment" and that enforcement of rules and regulations against tenants is more difficult than with resident owners. The plaintiffs ask us to take judicial notice of the current high mortgage interest rates and the limited stock of rental housing units in Melrose and the surrounding area. They argue that these factors preclude any finding that tenants in the relatively stable community of Melrose would be more transient or less responsible than owners in such a community. Leaving aside the question of the appropriateness of our taking judicial notice of these conditions, and assuming that we did take such notice, the plaintiffs would not prevail. To the extent that the by-law would promote owner occupancy, we cannot conclude on this record that such an objective is against public policy or in itself not worthwhile. Indeed, we agree with the trial judge that a "desire to impart a degree of continuity of residence, inhibit transiency and safeguard the value of investment" is implicit within the by-law amendment and its "declared purpose," and we think that such objectives are proper. Those who live in condominiums must be willing to give up a certain degree of personal choice in order to promote the welfare of the majority of the owners. See Hidden Harbour Estates, Inc. v. Norman, 309 So. 2d 180, 181-182 (Fla. Dist. Ct. App. 1975).

On this point, the plaintiffs also contend that the by-laws themselves belie the purpose of the amendment because the by-laws would not prohibit a person who owns two units from leasing either or both of them. However, the amendment may also be construed as a compromise between the desire of the majority of unit owners to maintain the residential character of the condominium and the right of a person owning one or two units to use his property as he desires. As so construed, the amendment is a reasonable means of achieving the majority's proper goal. . . . By way of comparison, we consider the restriction here no more onerous than the restriction upheld by the court in Seagate Condominium Ass'n v. Duffy, 330 So. 2d 484 (Fla. Dist. Ct. App. 1976). That restriction, by banning leasing except for limited times in special circumstances, effectively required the owner to occupy the unit.

II. The Constitutional Challenges

The plaintiffs here contend that the amendment has denied them equal protection of the laws and due process of law under the Fourteenth Amendment to the United States Constitution and arts. 1 and 10 of the Massachusetts Declaration of Rights. Specifically, they allege that Franklin has been "effectively denied his right to own property," and that both Franklin and the Clarkes have been denied "their constitutional rights to dispose of their property as they see fit."

The judge found that there was no State action sufficient to trigger the constitutional guarantees claimed. Because we conclude that the amendment did not deprive the plaintiffs of any constitutional rights, we may assume, without deciding, that the amendment represents State action. See Johnson v. Keith, 368 Mass. 316, 321-322, 331 N.E.2d 879 (1975) (condominium by-laws, because amendable and compliance required, resemble municipal by-laws more than private deed restrictions). But see Laguna Royale Owners Ass'n v. Darger, 119 Cal. App. 3d 670, 683, 174 Cal. Rptr. 136 (1981) (expressing doubt whether actions of condominium association constituted "state action").

There can be no doubt that the Fourteenth Amendment to the United States Constitution and the analogous provisions of our State Constitution safeguard the rights of property owners to use and enjoy their property. However, the rights are not absolute; they may be made subject to reasonable regulations designed to promote general welfare.... In the present case, we are not concerned with an unqualified right of the plaintiffs to buy or sell property. Rather, we are concerned with their rights to buy and sell property within the condominium. As unit owners, they are by statute subject to the terms of the condominium's by-laws. G.L. c.183A, §4(3). Since the plaintiffs' decisions to purchase units within the condominium were no doubt voluntary, any restrictions imposed on the plaintiffs' right to buy or sell property within the condominium are, for this reason, essentially self-imposed.

> [T]he restriction is not a zoning ordinance adopted under the police power but rather a mutual agreement entered into by all condominium apartment owners of the complex. With this type of land use restriction, an individual can choose at the time of purchase whether to sign an agreement with these restrictions or limitations.

White Egret Condominium, Inc. v. Franklin, 379 So. 2d 346, 350 (Fla. 1979). In addition, and as noted previously, G.L. c.183A, §§8(g) & 11(e), contemplate that restrictions may be imposed on the uses that may be made of units. In these circumstances, we do not view the amendment as impinging on fundamental rights of the plaintiffs. See White Egret Condominium, Inc., *supra*. Therefore, the amendment's limitation to two of the number of units a person may own does not set up a classification scheme requiring "strict scrutiny." . . .

We have previously likened condominium trust by-laws to municipal by-laws. Johnson v. Keith, 368 Mass. 316, 322, 331 N.E.2d 879 (1975). We think that the test employed in determining the constitutional validity of municipal by-laws affecting economic relations is appropriate to the present inquiry, especially given our assumption that the amendment represents State action. Accordingly, we hold that, "[i]f a [by-law amendment] serves a legitimate purpose, and if the means the [condominium association] adopted are rationally related to the achievement of that purpose, the [amendment] will withstand constitutional challenge." Shell Oil Co. v. Revere, 383 Mass. 682, —, Mass. Adv. Sh. (1981) 1285, 1289, 421 N.E.2d 1181.

We have previously analyzed the legitimacy of the by-law's purpose, and we have held that limitation of ownership to two units represents a reasonable adjustment between the rights of unit owners to use their property and the desire of the owners of a majority of the beneficial interest to attempt to create a residential atmosphere within the condominium development. We think it sufficiently clear from the discussion of those matters that the amendment meets the test of validity we announce today.[42] We hold, therefore, that the by-law amendment did not deprive the plaintiffs of their rights to due process and equal protection.

Judgment affirmed.

ELLICKSON, CITIES AND HOMEOWNERS ASSOCIATIONS
130 U. Pa. L. Rev. 1519, 1526-1530 (1982)

II. Judicial Review of Public and Private Regulations

Both cities and homeowners associations regulate the conduct of residents. Both may have rules requiring that dogs be kept on leashes, that residential structures be built in a Colonial style, or that external noise from social gatherings cease at 8:00 p.m. Nevertheless, courts rightly use different standards in reviewing the substantive validity of public and private rules.

In the case of public rules, the basic federal constitutional constraints arise from the due process and equal protection clauses of the fourteenth amendment. More often than not, the constitutional issue is whether the contested regulation is rationally related to a legitimate state interest. In the hands of most state and federal courts, this test now usually proves undemanding.

Because the fourteenth amendment only applies when state action is present, one might expect even greater judicial deference to the substantive validity of private regulations. In fact, however, courts are more vigorous in their examination of the validity of certain types of private regulations. Pre-

___

42. We might also add that the Legislature's choice to require compliance with the by-laws furthers a permissible legislative goal. "Enforcement . . . fosters condominium development by attracting buyers seeking a stable, planned environment [and] also protects the contractual interests . . . of buyers who purchase their units in reliance on the existence of a restrictive scheme and who may pay a premium to obtain restrictions." Note, Judicial Review of Condominium Rulemaking, 94 Harv. L. Rev. 647, 653 (1980).

vailing common-law and statutory rules ask courts to scrutinize the "reasonableness" of private regulations. This active judicial review is inappropriate when the provisions contained in an association's original governing documents are at issue, but it is fully appropriate when litigants challenge amendments to those documents.

A. JUDICIAL REVIEW OF THE "CONSTITUTION" OF A PRIVATE ASSOCIATION

The initial members of a homeowners association, by their voluntary acts of joining, unanimously consent to the provisions in the association's original governing documents.... [T]his unanimous ratification elevates those documents to the legal status of a private "constitution." ...

In most instances, familiar principles of contract law justify strict judicial enforcement of the provisions of a private constitution. Strict enforcement protects members' reliance interests. By allowing the establishment of, and subsequently protecting the integrity of, diverse types of private residential communities, courts can provide genuine choice among a range of stable living arrangements. . . .

External legal norms of course constrain the contracting process, and in some instances should lead to the judicial invalidation of offensive "constitutional" provisions, such as those that would regulate the racial characteristics of association members.[43] Nevertheless, because original membership in an association is more voluntary than original membership in a city, an association's constitution should be allowed to contain substantive restrictions not permissible in a city charter. For example, if a group of orthodox Jews set up a condominium and stipulated by original covenant that males were required to wear yarmulkes in common areas on holy days, a court should enforce that original covenant in deference to the unanimous wishes of the original members.[44] An identical "public" regulation would, of course, violate the first amendment's ban on the establishment of religion, and perhaps a number of other constitutional guarantees.

The pattern of judicial decisions tends to honor the suggested principle of greater private associational autonomy. Although the Supreme Court has recently held that age is not a suspect classification, lower courts perceive municipal zoning by age as posing serious constitutional questions. By contrast, homeowners-association regulations that limit the age of dwelling

---

43. See e.g., Shelley v. Kraemer, 334 U.S. 1 (1948) (judicial enforcement of racially discriminatory covenants would violate the equal protection clause).

44. But see Taormina Theosophical Community, Inc. v. Silver, 140 Cal. App. 3d 964, 190 Cal. Rptr. 38 (1983). Taormina Philosophical Community, Inc., established a retirement community for Theosophists. A covenant limiting occupancy to members of the Theosophical Society who were 50 years of age or over was held unreasonable and unenforceable because (a) it limited the number of possible buyers to a small number, and (b) it operated like a religious restriction even though Theosophy is not a religion but a comparative study of religions aimed at achieving the universal brotherhood of man. — Eds.

occupants have tended to survive legal challenge. As a second example, private associations have successfully defended design controls (dealing with exterior paint colors and so on) whose public counterparts would make city attorneys squirm.

In sum, as a Florida appellate court has perceived, the "reasonableness" standard that courts apply to an association's post-formation actions should not apply to provisions of the association's original constitution:

> [The original] restrictions are clothed with a very strong presumption of validity which arises from the fact that each individual unit owner purchases his unit knowing of and accepting the restrictions to be imposed. . . . [A]lthough case law has applied the word "reasonable" to determine whether such restrictions are valid, this is not the appropriate test, and to the extent that our decisions have been interpreted otherwise, we disagree. Indeed, a use restriction *in a declaration of condominium* may have a certain degree of unreasonableness to it, and yet withstand attack in the courts. If it were otherwise, a unit owner could not rely on the restrictions found in the declaration of condominium, since such restrictions would be in a potential condition of continuous flux.[45]

B. Judicial Review of a Private Association's Actions to Implement Its "Constitution"

When courts are asked to rule on the validity of an association's actions to flesh out and apply its original constitution, they currently apply the previously mentioned test of "reasonableness." The association's governing documents or a state statute may call for application of the reasonableness standard; if not, courts imply the standard as a matter of law into the original constitution. The reasonableness standard applies to several types of association actions. It constrains all administrative actions — for example, an association's decision to expel a member, to veto the transfer of a membership, or to deny approval of architectural plans. In addition, it constrains the substance of all "legislation" that an association adopts by procedures less cumbersome than the association's procedures for a constitutional amendment. "Legislation" would include, for example, house rules that a board of directors might adopt under an express grant of authority in the original declaration.

"Reasonable," the most ubiquitous legal adjective, is not self-defining. In reviewing an association's legislative or adminstrative decisions, many judges have viewed the "reasonableness" standard as entitling them to undertake an independent cost-benefit analysis of the decision under review and to invalidate association decisions that are not cost-justified by general societal standards. This variant of reasonableness review ignores the contractarian underpinnings of the private association. As some courts have

---

45. Hidden Harbour Estates, Inc. v. Basso, 393 So. 2d 637, 640 (Fla. Dist. Ct. App. 1981) (emphasis in original).

Possessory Estates

recognized, respect for private ordering requires a court applying the reasonableness standard to comb the association's original documents to find the association's collective purposes, and then to determine whether the association's actions have been consonant with those purposes. To illustrate, the reasonableness of a board rule banning alcoholic beverages from the swimming pool area cannot be determined in the abstract for all associations. So long as the rule at issue does not violate fundamental external norms that constrain the contracting process, the rule's validity should not be tested according to external values, for example, the precise package of values that would constrain a comparable action by a public organization. Rather, the validity of the rule should be judged according to the enacting association's own original purposes.

Page 406. At the end of line 3, add:

See also pages 20 and 183-186 of this supplement.

Chapter Four
Future Interests

B. FUTURE INTERESTS IN THE TRANSFEROR

Page 413. Insert the following after the second paragraph:

Oak's Oil Service, Inc. v. Massachusetts Bay Transportation Authority, 15 Mass. App. 593, 447 N.E.2d 27, *appeal denied*, 389 Mass. 1103 (1983), held that a 1954 Massachusetts statute had the effect of making rights of entry alienable. Thus Rice v. Boston & Worcester Railroad Corp. is no longer the law in Massachusetts. The rule of the case may still be followed in other states, however.

D. THE TRUST

Page 445. National Shawmut Bank v. Cumming is no longer good law in Massachusetts. Delete the case and substitute the following, which prospectively overrules Kerwin v. Donaghy:

SULLIVAN v. BURKIN

Supreme Judicial Court of Massachusetts, 1984
390 Mass. 864, 460 N.E.2d 572

WILKINS, J. Mary A. Sullivan, the widow of Ernest G. Sullivan, has exercised her right, under G.L. c.191, §15, to take a share of her husband's estate. By this action, she seeks a determination that assets held in an inter vivos trust created by her husband during the marriage should be considered as part of the estate in determining that share. A judge of the Probate Court for the county of Suffolk rejected the widow's claim and entered judgment dismissing the complaint. The widow appealed, and, on July 12, 1983, a panel of the Appeals Court reported the case to this court.

In September, 1973, Ernest G. Sullivan executed a deed of trust under which he transferred real estate to himself as sole trustee. The net income of the trust was payable to him during his life and the trustee was instructed to pay to him all or such part of the principal of the trust estate as he might request in writing from time to time. He retained the right to revoke the trust at any time. On his death, the successor trustee is directed to pay the principal and any undistributed income equally to the defendants, George F. Cronin, Sr., and Harold J. Cronin, if they should survive him, which they did. There were no witnesses to the execution of the deed of trust, but the husband acknowledged his signatures before a notary public, separately, as donor and as trustee.

The husband died on April 27, 1981, while still trustee of the inter vivos trust. He left a will in which he stated that he "intentionally neglected to make any provision for my wife, Mary A. Sullivan and my grandson, Mark Sullivan." He directed that, after the payment of debts, expenses, and all estate taxes levied by reason of his death, the residue of his estate should be paid over to the trustee of the inter vivos trust. The defendants George F. Cronin, Sr., and Harold J. Cronin were named coexecutors of the will. The defendant Burkin is successor trustee of the inter vivos trust. On October 21, 1981, the wife filed a claim, pursuant to G.L. c.191, §15, for a portion of the estate.[34a]

Although it does not appear in the record, the parties state in their briefs that Ernest G. Sullivan and Mary A. Sullivan had been separated for many years. We do know that in 1962 the wife obtained a court order providing for her temporary support. No final action was taken in that proceeding.

34a. As relevant to this case, G.L. c.191, §15, as appearing in St.1964, c.288, §1, provides:

"The surviving husband or wife of a deceased person . . . within six months after the probate of the will of such deceased, may file in the registry of probate a writing signed by him or by her . . . claiming such portion of the estate of the deceased as he or she is given the right to claim under this section, and if the deceased left issue, he or she shall thereupon take one third of the personal and one third of the real property; . . . except that . . . if he or she would thus take real and personal property to an amount exceeding twenty-five thousand dollars in value, he or she shall receive, in addition to that amount, only the income during his or her life of the excess of his or her share of such estate above that amount, the personal property to be held in trust and the real property vested in him or her for life, from the death of the deceased. . . . If the real and personal property of the deceased which the surviving husband or wife takes under the foregoing provisions exceeds twenty-five thousand dollars in value, and the surviving husband or wife is to take only twenty-five thousand dollars absolutely, the twenty-five thousand dollars, above given absolutely, shall be paid out of that part of the personal property in which the husband or wife is interested; and if such part is insufficient the deficiency shall, upon the petition of any person interested, be paid from the sale or mortgage in fee, in the manner provided for the payment of debts or legacies, of that part of the real property in which he or she is interested."

The record provides no information about the value of any property owned by the husband at his death or about the value of any assets held in the inter vivos trust. At oral argument, we were advised that the husband owned personal property worth approximately $15,000 at his death and that the only asset in the trust was a house in Boston which was sold after the husband's death for approximately $85,000.

As presented in the complaint, and perhaps as presented to the motion judge, the wife's claim was simply that the inter vivos trust was an invalid testamentary disposition and that the trust assets "constitute assets of the estate" of Ernest G. Sullivan. There is no suggestion that the wife argued initially that, even if the trust were not testamentary, she had a special claim as a widow asserting her rights under G.L. c.191, §15. If the wife is correct that the trust was an ineffective testamentary disposition, the trust assets would be part of the husband's probate estate. In that event, we would not have to consider any special consequences of the wife's election under G.L. c.191, §15, or, in the words of the Appeals Court, "the present vitality" of Kerwin v. Donaghy, 317 Mass. 559, 572, 59 N.E.2d 299 (1945).

We conclude, however, that the trust was not testamentary in character and that the husband effectively created a valid inter vivos trust. Thus, whether the issue was initially involved in this case, we are now presented with the question (which the executors will have to resolve ultimately, in any event) whether the assets of the inter vivos trust are to be considered in determining the "portion of the estate of the deceased" (G.L. c.191, §15) in which Mary A. Sullivan has rights. We conclude that, in this case, we should adhere to the principles expressed in Kerwin v. Donaghy, *supra,* that deny the surviving spouse any claim against the assets of a valid inter vivos trust created by the deceased spouse, even where the deceased spouse alone retained substantial rights and powers under the trust instrument. For the future, however, as to any inter vivos trust created or amended after the date of this opinion, we announce that the estate of a decedent, for the purposes of G.L. c.191, §15, shall include the value of assets held in an inter vivos trust created by the deceased spouse as to which the deceased spouse alone retained the power during his or her life to direct the disposition of those trust assets for his or her benefit, as, for example, by the exercise of a power of appointment or by revocation of the trust. Such a power would be a general power of appointment for Federal estate tax purposes (I.R.C. §2041(b)(1) [1983]) and a "general power" as defined in the Restatement (Second) of Property §11.4(1) (Tent. Draft No. 5, 1982).

We consider first whether the inter vivos trust was invalid because it was testamentary. A trust with remainder interests given to others on the settlor's death is not invalid as a testamentary disposition simply because the settlor retained a broad power to modify or revoke the trust, the right to receive income, and the right to invade principal during his life. Ascher v. Cohen, 333 Mass. 397, 400, 131 N.E.2d 198 (1956); Leahy v. Old Colony Trust Co., 326 Mass. 49, 51, 93 N.E.2d 238 (1950); Kerwin v. Donaghy, 317 Mass. 559, 567, 59 N.E.2d 299 (1945); National Shawmut Bank v. Joy, 315 Mass. 457, 473-475, 53 N.E.2d 113 (1944); Kelley v. Snow, 185 Mass. 288, 298-299, 70 N.E. 89 (1904). The fact that the settlor of such a trust is the sole trustee does not make the trust testamentary. In National Shawmut Bank v. Joy, *supra* 315 Mass. at 476-477, 53 N.E.2d 113, we held that a settlor's reservation of the power to control investments did not impair the validity of a trust and noted that "[i]n Greeley v. Flynn, 310 Mass. 23, 36 N.E.2d 394 [1941], the settlor was herself the trustee and had every power of control, including the right to withdraw principal for her own use. Yet the gift over at her death was held valid and not testamentary." We did, however, leave open the question whether such a trust would be testamentary "had the trustees been reduced to passive impotence, or something near it." *Id.* 315 Mass. at 476, 53 N.E.2d 113. We have held an inter vivos trust valid where a settlor, having broad powers to revoke the trust and to demand trust principal, was a cotrustee with a friend (Ascher v. Cohen, *supra* 333 Mass. at 400, 131 N.E.2d 198) or with a bank whose tenure as trustee was at the whim of the settlor (Leahy v. Old Colony Trust Co., *supra* 326 Mass. at 51, 93 N.E.2d 238). In Theodore v. Theodore, 356 Mass. 297, 249 N.E.2d 3 (1969), the settlor was the sole trustee of two trusts and had the power to revoke the trusts and to withdraw principal. The court assumed that the trusts were not testamentary simply because of this arrangement. The *Theodore* case involved trust assets transferred to the trust only by third persons. For the purposes of determining whether a trust is testamentary, however, the origin of the assets, totally at the disposal of the settlor once received, should make no difference. See Gordon v. Feldman, 359 Mass. 25, 267 N.E.2d 895 (1971), in which the court and the parties implicitly accepted as valid an inter vivos trust in which A conveyed to himself as sole trustee with the power in A to withdraw income and principal. We believe that the law of the Commonwealth is correctly represented by the statement in Restatement (Second) of Trusts §57, comment h (1959), that a trust is "not testamentary and invalid for failure to comply with the requirements of the Statute of Wills merely because the settlor-trustee reserves a beneficial life interest and power to revoke and modify the trust. The fact that as trustee he controls the administration of the trust does not invalidate it."

We come then to the question whether, even if the trust was not testamentary on general principles, the widow has special interests which should be recognized. Courts in this country have differed considerably in their reasoning and in their conclusions in passing on this question. See 1 A. Scott, Trusts §57.5 at 509-511 (3d ed. 1967 & 1983 Supp.); Restatement (Second) of Property — Donative Transfers, Supplement to Tent. Draft No. 5, reporter's note to §13.7 (1982); Annot., 39 A.L.R.3d 14 (1971), Validity of Inter Vivos Trust Established by One Spouse Which Impairs the Other Spouse's Distributive Share or Other Statutory Rights in Property. In considering this issue at the May, 1982, annual meeting of the American Law Institute the members divided almost evenly on whether a settlor's surviving spouse should have rights, apart from specific statutory rights, with respect to the assets of an inter vivos trust over which the settlor retained a general power of appointment. See Proceedings of the American Law Institute, May, 1982, pp. 59-117; Restatement (Second) of Property — Donative Transfers, Supplement to Tent. Draft No. 5 at 28 (1982).[34b]

The rule of Kerwin v. Donaghy, *supra* 317 Mass. at 571, 59 N.E.2d 299, is that

> [t]he right of a wife to waive her husband's will, and take, with certain limitations, "the same portion of the property of the deceased, real and personal, that . . . she would have taken if the deceased had died intestate" (G.L. [Ter.Ed.] c.191, §15), does not extend to personal property that has been conveyed by the husband in his lifetime and does not form part of his estate at his death. Fiske v. Fiske, 173 Mass. 413, 419, 53 N.E. 916 [1899]. Shelton v. Sears, 187 Mass. 455, 73 N.E. 666 [1905]. In this Commonwealth a husband has an absolute right to dispose of any or all of his personal property in his lifetime, without the knowledge or consent of his wife, with the result that it will not form part of his estate for her to share under the statute of distributions (G.L. [Ter. Ed.] c.190, §§1,2), under his will, or by virtue of a waiver of his will. That is true even though his sole purpose was to disinherit her.

In the *Kerwin* case, we applied the rule to deny a surviving spouse the right to reach assets the deceased spouse had placed in an inter vivos trust of which the settlor's daughter by a previous marriage was trustee and over whose assets he had a general power of appointment. The rule of Kerwin v. Donaghy has been adhered to in this Commonwealth for almost forty years and was adumbrated even earlier. The bar has been entitled reasonably to rely on that rule in advising clients. In the area of property law, the

---

34b. In 1984 the members of the institute approved the following statement in §13.7 of the Restatement (Second) of Property — Donative Transfers at 116 (Tent. Draft No. 7, 1984):

§13.7 *Spousal Rights in Appointive Assets on Death of Donee*
Appointive assets are treated as owned assets of a deceased donee in determining the rights of a surviving spouse in the owned assets of the donee if, and only if, the deceased spouse is both the donor and donee of a general power that is exercisable by the donee alone, unless the controlling statute provides otherwise.

—Eds.

retroactive invalidation of an established principle is to be undertaken with great caution....

... We conclude that, whether or not Ernest G. Sullivan established the inter vivos trust in order to defeat his wife's right to take her statutory share in the assets placed in the trust and even though he had a general power of appointment over the trust assets, Mary A. Sullivan obtained no right to share in the assets of that trust when she made her election under G.L. c.191, §15.

We announce for the future that, as to any inter vivos trust created or amended after the date of this opinion, we shall no longer follow the rule announced in Kerwin v. Donaghy. There have been significant changes since 1945 in public policy considerations bearing on the right of one spouse to treat his or her property as he or she wishes during marriage. The interests of one spouse in the property of the other have been substantially increased upon the dissolution of a marriage by divorce.[34c] We believe that, when a marriage is terminated by the death of one spouse, the rights of the surviving spouse should not be so restricted as they are by the rule in Kerwin v. Donaghy. It is neither equitable nor logical to extend to a divorced spouse greater rights in the assets of an inter vivos trust created and controlled by the other spouse than are extended to a spouse who remains married until the death of his or her spouse.

The rule we now favor would treat as part of "the estate of the deceased" for the purposes of G.L. c.191, §15, assets of an inter vivos trust created during the marriage by the deceased spouse over which he or she alone had a general power of appointment, exercisable by deed or by will. This objec-

---

34c. At the time of a divorce or at any subsequent time, "the court may assign to either husband or wife all or any part of the estate of the other," on consideration of various factors, such as the length of the marriage, the conduct of the parties during the marriage, their ages, their employability, their liabilities and needs, and opportunity for future acquisition of capital assets and income. G.L. c.208, §34, as amended by St. 1982, c.642, §1. The power to dispose completely of the property of the divorced litigants comes from a 1974 amendment to G.L. c.208, §34. See St. 1974, c.565. It made a significant change in the respective rights of the husband and wife and in the power of Probate Court judges. See Bianco v. Bianco, 371 Mass. 420, 422-423, 358 N.E.2d 243 (1976). We have held that the "estate" subject to disposition on divorce includes not only property acquired during the marriage from the efforts of the husband and wife, but also all property of a spouse "whenever and however acquired." Rice v. Rice, 372 Mass. 398, 400, 361 N.E.2d 1305 (1977). Without suggesting the outer limits of the meaning of the word "estate" under G.L. c.208, §34, as applied to trust assets over which a spouse has a general power of appointment at the time of a divorce, after this decision there should be no doubt that the "estate" of such a spouse would include trust assets held in a trust created by the other spouse and having provisions such as the trust in the case before us.

tive test would involve no consideration of the motive or intention of the spouse in creating the trust. We would not need to engage in a determination of "whether the [spouse] has in good faith divested himself [or herself] of ownership of his [or her] property or has made an illusory transfer" (Newman v. Dore, 275 N.Y. 371, 379, 9 N.E.2d 966 [1937]) or with the factual question whether the spouse "intended to surrender complete dominion over the property" (Staples v. King, 433 A.2d 407, 411 [Me.1981]). Nor would we have to participate in the rather unsatisfactory process of determining whether the inter vivos trust was, on some standard, "colorable," "fraudulent," or "illusory."

What we have announced as a rule for the future hardly resolves all the problems that may arise. There may be a different rule if some or all of the trust assets were conveyed to such a trust by a third person. Cf. Theodore v. Theodore, 356 Mass. 297, 249 N.E.2d 3 (1969). We have not, of course, dealt with a case in which the power of appointment is held jointly with another person. If the surviving spouse assented to the creation of the inter vivos trust, perhaps the rule we announce would not apply. We have not discussed which assets should be used to satisfy a surviving spouse's claim. We have not discussed the question whether a surviving spouse's interest in the intestate estate of a deceased spouse should reflect the value of assets held in an inter vivos trust created by the intestate spouse over which he or she had a general power of appointment. That situation and the one before us, however, do not seem readily distinguishable. See Schnakenberg v. Schnakenberg, 262 A.D. 234, 236-237, 28 N.Y.S.2d 841 (N.Y.1941). A general power of appointment over assets in a trust created by a third person is said to present a different situation. Restatement (Second) of Property — Donative Transfers, Supplement to Tent. Draft No. 5, reporter's note to §13.7 at 29 (1982). Nor have we dealt with other assets not passing by will, such as a trust created before the marriage or insurance policies over which a deceased spouse had control. *Id.* at 30, 38.

The question of the rights of a surviving spouse in the estate of a deceased spouse, using the word "estate" in its broad sense, is one that can best be handled by legislation. See Uniform Probate Code, §§2-201, 2-202, 8 U.L.A. 74-75 (1983). See also Uniform Marital Property Act, §18 (Nat'l Conference of Comm'rs on Uniform State Laws, July, 1983), which adopts the concept of community property as to "marital property." But, until it is, the answers to these problems will "be determined in the usual way through the decisional process." Tucker v. Badoian, 376 Mass. 907, 918-919, 384 N.E.2d 1195 (1978) (Kaplan, J., concurring).

We affirm the judgment of the Probate Court dismissing the plaintiff's complaint.

So ordered.

E. RULES FURTHERING MARKETABILITY

Page 471. Delete Note 3 and insert the following case:

BROWN v. INDEPENDENT BAPTIST CHURCH OF WOBURN
Supreme Judicial Court of Massachusetts, 1950
325 Mass. 645, 91 N.E.2d 922

QUA, C.J. The object of this suit in equity, originally brought in this court, is to determine the ownership of a parcel of land in Woburn and the persons entitled to share in the proceeds of its sale by a receiver.

Sarah Converse died seised of the land on July 19, 1849, leaving a will in which she specifically devised it

> to the Independent Baptist Church of Woburn, to be holden and enjoyed by them so long as they shall maintain and promulgate their present religious belief and faith and shall continue a Church; and if the said Church shall be dissolved, or its religious sentiments shall be changed or abandoned, then my will is that this real estate shall go to my legatees hereinafter named, to be divided in equal portions between them. And my will further is, that if my beloved husband, Jesse Converse, shall survive me, that then this devise to the aforesaid Independent Church of Woburn, shall not take effect till from and after his decease; and that so long as he shall live he may enjoy and use the said real estate, and take the rents and profits thereof to his own use.

Then followed ten money legacies in varying amounts to different named persons, after which there was a residuary clause in these words,

> The rest and residue of my estate I give and bequeath to my legatees above named, saving and except therefrom the Independent Baptist Church; this devise to take effect from and after the decease of my husband; I do hereby direct and will that he shall have the use and this rest and residue during his life.

The husband of the testatrix died in 1864. The church named by the testatrix ceased to "continue a church" on October 19, 1939.

The parties apparently are in agreement, and the single justice ruled, that the estate of the church in the land was a determinable fee. We concur. First Universalist Society of North Adams v. Boland, 155 Mass. 171, 174. Institution for Savings v. Roxbury Home for Aged Women, 244 Mass. 583, 585-586. Dyer v. Siano, 298 Mass. 537, 540. The estate was a fee, since it might last forever, but it was not an absolute fee, since it might (and did) "automatically expire upon the occurrence of a stated event." Restatement: Property, §44. It is also conceded, and was ruled, that the specific executory devise over to the persons "hereinafter named" as legatees was void for remoteness. This conclusion seems to be required by Proprietors of the Church in

Future Interests Page 471

Brattle Square v. Grant, 3 Gray, 142, 152, 155-156. First Universalist Society of North Adams v. Boland, 155 Mass. 171, 173, and Institution for Savings v. Roxbury Home for Aged Women, 244 Mass. 583, 587. See Restatement: Property, §44, illustration 20. The reason is stated to be that the determinable fee might not come to an end until long after any life or lives in being and twenty-one years, and in theory at least might never come to an end, and for an indefinite period no clear title to the entire estate could be given.

Since the limitation over failed, it next becomes our duty to consider what became of the possibility of reverter which under our decisions remained after the failure of the limitation. First Universalist Society of North Adams v. Boland, 155 Mass. 171, 175. Institution for Savings v. Roxbury Home for Aged Women, 244 Mass. 583, 587. . . . A possibility of reverter seems, by the better authority, to be assignable inter vivos (Restatement: Property, §159; Simes, Future Interests, §715; see Tiffany, Real Property [3d ed.] §314, note 31) and must be at least as readily devisable as the other similar reversionary interest known as a right of entry for condition broken, which is devisable, though not assignable. . . . It follows that the possibility of reverter passed under the residuary clause of the will to the same persons designated in the invalid executory devise. It is of no consequence that the persons designated in the two provisions were the same. The same result must be reached as if they were different.

The single justice ruled that the residuary clause was void for remoteness, apparently for the same reason that rendered the executory devise void. With this we cannot agree, since we consider it settled that the rule against perpetuities does not apply to reversionary interests of this general type, including possibilities of reverter. Proprietors of the Church in Brattle Square v. Grant, 3 Gray, 142, 148. . . . For a full understanding of the situation here presented it is necessary to keep in mind the fundamental difference in character between the attempted executory devise to the legatees later named in the will and the residuary gift to the same persons. The executory devise was in form and substance an attempt to limit or create a new future interest which might not arise or vest in anyone until long after the permissible period. It was obviously not intended to pass such a residuum of the testatrix's existing estate as a possibility of reverter, and indeed if the executory devise had been valid according to its terms the whole estate would have passed from the testatrix and no possibility of reverter could have been left to her or her devisees. The residuary devise, on the other hand, was in terms and purpose exactly adapted to carry any interest which might otherwise remain in the testatrix, whether or not she had it in mind or knew it would exist. Thayer v. Wellington, 9 Allen, 283, 295. Wellman v. Carter, 286 Mass. 237, 249-250.

We cannot accept the contention made in behalf of Mrs. Converse's heirs that the words of the residuary clause "saving and except therefrom the

Independent Baptist Church" were meant to exclude from the operation of that clause any possible rights in the *land* previously given to the church. We construe these words as intended merely to render the will consistent by excluding the church which also had been "above named" from the list of "*legatees*" who were to take the residue.

The interlocutory decree entered December 16, 1947, is reversed, and a new decree is to be entered providing that the land in question or the proceeds of any sale thereof by the receiver shall go to the persons named as legatees in the will, other than the Independent Baptist Church of Woburn, or the successors in interest. Further proceedings are to be in accord with the new decree. Costs and expenses are to be at the discretion of the single justice.

So ordered.

NOTES AND QUESTIONS

1. Brown v. Independent Baptist Church of Woburn has been criticized on the ground that it assumes the testator died twice. 3 L. Simes & A. Smith, The Law of Future Interests §1241 (2d ed. 1956). Do you understand this criticism? Orthodox doctrine would hold that there is a possibility of reverter in Sarah's heirs, not in the residuary devisees. So held in In re Pruner's Estate, 400 Pa. 629, 162 A.2d 626 (1960).

Page 472. Renumber Note 4, making it Note 2.

Chapter Five
Co-Ownership and Marital Interests

A. COMMON LAW CONCURRENT INTERESTS

Page 489.   At the end of Problem 2(b), add:

See also Harms v. Sprague, 119 Ill. App. 3d 503, 456 N.E.2d 976 (1983).

Page 489.   At the end of Problem 3(b), add:

See generally Annot., 9 A.L.R.4th 1189 (1981).

Page 497.   At the end of the parenthetical remarks following the indented quote from Riddle v. Harmon, add:

Riddle v. Harmon was cited with approval and followed in Minonk State Bank v. Grassman, 95 Ill. 2d 392, 447 N.E.2d 822 (1983), noted in 17 J. Mar. L. Rev. 765 (1984). The court, however, made the following observation:

> Defendant argues that the creation of a joint tenancy is "akin to a quasi contract or shared common venture" and that, because of the appellate court's holding, the parties to this "joint venture no longer are able to rely upon the relationship that led to them originally entering into the purchase of the property in question." We recognize that in certain situations, e.g., where consideration is given for the creation of a joint tenancy or one of the joint tenants takes some irrevocable action in reliance upon the creation or existence of a joint tenancy, problems may arise if one tenant may unilaterally dissolve the joint tenancy. (See Hendrickson v. Minneapolis Federal Savings & Loan Association (1968), 281 Minn. 462, 466, 161 N.W.2d 688, 692; cf. 2 W. Blackstone, Commentaries 195.) Such a situation is not presented here; the record does not show that either party gave consideration for the creation of the joint tenancy or relied, to her detriment, on its continued existence. [95 Ill. 2d at 396, 447 N.E.2d at 825.]

See generally Annot., 7 A.L.R.4th 1268 (1981).

Page 511. After Problem 3, add:

4. Two brothers and two sisters own a parcel of land as tenants in common. One of the sisters files an action for partition. The trial court divides the land into four parts of equal value (in the court's judgment), then draws lots to see which sibling is to be awarded which part. One of the former cotenants, arguing that he should have been awarded the part adjacent to his home, appeals. What result? See Gray v. Crotts, 58 N.C. App. 365, 293 S.E.2d 626 (1982), and Annot., 32 A.L.R.4th 909 (1984).

Page 517. At the end of Question 2, add:

What of partition *by* co-owners of future interests? See Henry v. Kennedy, 273 Ark. 383, 619 S.W.2d 632 (1981), noted in 4 U. Ark. Little Rock L.J. 543 (1981).

Page 530. At the end of Problem 7, add:

See also Olwell v. Clark, 658 P.2d 585 (Utah 1982). Suppose the cotenant in exclusive possession of co-owned property, or the cotenant out of possession, or both, were unaware that a cotenancy existed. Would this have any bearing on the issue of adverse possession. See Annot., 27 A.L.R.4th 421 (1984). See also the following case.

ALLEN v. BATCHELDER
Appeals Court of Massachusetts, 1984
17 Mass. App. 453, 459 N.E.2d 129

KASS, J. Sebastian, the tobacco-chewing sheep, would have been disconcerted by this appeal. His status as a Martha's Vineyard tourist attraction was a function of his visibility on the Allen farm, astride the South Road in Chilmark. Sebastian could not have achieved the modest notoriety he enjoyed without tenure of the Allen farm by his owners, Henry and Maude Allen. The appellant, Batchelder, has called in question the exclusivity of the Allens' title, which has come down to Clarissa Allen (Clarissa). Batchelder espouses a theory that his predecessors in title, nonpossessory cotenants, were not affirmatively ousted from possession of the locus and that, therefore, the Allen family could not, as the Land Court judge determined, have acquired exclusive title to the farm by adverse possession. In light of 150 years of well developed case law, we conclude that the appellant's position is so untenable as to be frivolous.

The case began with a petition in the Land Court under G.L. c.185, §1,

Co-Ownership and Marital Interests

for registration. Clarissa occupies the locus, consisting of 116.7 acres, which her forebears acquired between 1762 and 1857. Land Court examiners (there were two) reported a record defect in Clarissa's title which developed upon the death of Tristam Allen, II, in 1864. Tristam left undivided fractional interests in a portion of the Allen farm to his widow, Tamson. Neither she, nor persons to whom her interests passed by devise, who were outside the Allen family, ever occupied the farm or made claim to any rents and profits from it. Batchelder claims under that line of title. Clarissa's line, in contrast, lived on and worked the farm actively.

After a long trial, the Land Court judge found that, at least from 1892, "the Allen farm was possessed by various members of the Allen family to the exclusion of any co-tenant in common." Clarissa's grandfather, Henry Allen, was well known in Chilmark. He held office as selectman, assessor, overseer of the poor and town moderator, manifesting a bent for public life which a witness, Captain Poole, attributed to Henry's being "lazier than hell . . . he was a typical small-town politician. He'd pat you on the back wherever you met him and agree with you 100 percent." Manifestly, his occupancy of the Allen farm was widely known and far from concealed. Maude, his wife, was the sheep's patroness. Henry's son, Roger, industrious by any measure, ran the farm and used some of the farm's outbuildings for a contracting business. Roger died in 1967, and farming came to a halt. His widow, however, continued to pay taxes on the locus, aggressively posted no trespassing signs, and routinely checked the farm. Clarissa, in 1975, came to live on the farm to rejuvenate it.

That the Allen family possessed the locus actually, openly and notoriously for at least ninety years is not in controversy. As the judge observed in his detailed and careful decision, the evidence on this score was overwhelming. Sebastian, the sheep, was but a minor example of how closely the Allen family were identified with the farm by residents of Martha's Vineyard. The judge found an equally strong case had been made that the Allens' possession was adverse and nonpermissive and that, accordingly, they had acquired good title by adverse possession to the seven parcels tainted with a record defect. For the elements of adverse possession, see Ryan v. Stavros, 348 Mass. 251, 262, 203 N.E.2d 85 (1964).

Batchelder's attack is on whether the Allens' possession was adverse and nonpermissive. It is uncontroverted that Clarissa's line was never aware of the claim now pressed on behalf of the Batchelder line and that no one in the Batchelder line was ever cognizant of the potential for that claim until publication of the registration petition in 1980 was called to Batchelder's attention by a William J. Devine. The judge found expressly that during the ninety-year period upon which he concentrated, no claim of title by Batchelder's predecessors was ever made.

Batchelder supports his claim with the argument that the interest of a cotenant cannot be wiped out by prescription without an ouster and, more to the point, communication of that ouster to the absent cotenant. It is correct that sole possession by one tenant in common is not in itself adverse to the interest of a nonpossessory cotenant; it could be consistent with the right of the cotenant. Rickard v. Rickard, 13 Pick. 251, 253-254 (1832). As early as that 1832 case, however, it was regarded by Chief Justice Shaw as equally "well settled, that a long exclusive and uninterrupted possession by one, without any possession, or claim for profits by the other, is evidence from which a jury may and ought to infer an actual ouster." *Ibid.* There need be no "turning out by the shoulders" to manifest a decisive intent to occupy to the exclusion of the absent cotenant. Doe v. Prosser, 1 Cowp. 217, 218, 98 Eng. Rep. 1052 (1774). The principle has been many times restated or applied. Lefavour v. Homan, 3 Allen 354, 355 (1862). Ingalls v. Newhall, 139 Mass. 268, 273, 30 N.E. 96 (1885). Joyce v. Dyer, 189 Mass. 64, 67-68, 75 N.E. 81 (1905). Nickerson v. Nickerson, 235 Mass. 348, 352-353, 126 N.E. 834 (1920). Snow v. E.L. Dauphinais, Inc., 13 Mass. App. Ct. 330, 334, 432 N.E.2d 730 (1982). In those cases the periods of exclusive possession which worked an ouster varied from thirty to forty-seven years. Clarissa's line has possessed the Allen farm for not less than ninety years. "[M]en do not ordinarily sleep on their rights for so long a period, and a strong presumption arises that actual proof of the original ouster has become lost by lapse of time." Lefavour v. Homan, *supra* at 355-356.

It distorts the cases cited to find in them a requirement that the absent cotenant must have knowledge that he is dispossessed. Knowledge, when the absent cotenant appeared to have it, was a convenient factor in the equation in Ingalls v. Newhall, *supra* 139 Mass. at 273-274, 30 N.E. 96, and in Nickerson v. Nickerson, *supra* 235 Mass. at 353, 126 N.E. 834. The underlying inquiry, however, has always been what knowledge the absent party "must be deemed to have had." Ingalls v. Newhall, *supra* 139 Mass. at 274, 30 N.E. 96. Precisely how long a possession should be to raise a presumption of ouster depends on many circumstances, *ibid.*, but it is apparent from the cases that ninety years is far more than enough. Lefavour v. Homan, *supra* at 355 emphasizes that absence and failure to make a claim, "if unexplained or controlled by any evidence tending to show a reason for such neglect or omission to assert a right," furnishes evidence from which the trier of fact ought to infer an actual ouster and adverse possession. Requiring actual knowledge of disseisin "would deprive the principle of prescription of much of its value in quieting controversy and giving sanction to long continued usages." Foot v. Bauman, 333 Mass. 214, 217-218, 129 N.E.2d 916 (1955). Long dormant claims to title could rise from the dust bin of history and many titles would become unsettled. This is particularly so in a case such as the instant one, where the absent parties did not live near the locus. Ada Cleveland, who took from Tamson, and her chain of title down

Co-Ownership and Marital Interests

to Batchelder, all lived off island. See also Ottavia v. Savarese, 338 Mass. 330, 333-334, 155 N.E.2d 432 (1959), which disposes of the proposition that the Allens' possession needed to be consciously adverse to the Batchelder line, i.e., that the Allens needed to be aware of the Batchelder claim to defeat it.

We have dwelled at some length on the extensive and decisive case law which defeats this appeal because it bears on how we deal with a motion by the appellee, Clarissa Allen, for damages and costs under Mass. R.A.P. 25, and Mass. R.A.P. 26, both as amended, 378 Mass. 925 (1979). Rule 25 authorizes assessment of damages, as well as double costs of the appeal, in instances where the appeal is frivolous. Mills v. Carlow, 15 Mass. App. Ct. 1104 (1983). See Good Hope Refineries, Inc. v. Brashear, 588 F.2d 846, 848 (1st Cir.1978). See the cases collected in 9 Moore's Federal Practice §238.02 (2d ed. 1983), in which the cognate Federal rule (Fed. R.A.P. 38) has been applied. See also Katz v. Savitsky, 10 Mass. App. Ct. 792, 798 n.8, 413 N.E.2d 354 (1980). When the law is well settled, when there can be no reasonable expectation of a reversal, an appeal is frivolous. See Note, Penalties for Frivolous Appeals, 43 Harv. L. Rev. 113, 114-116 (1929).

An appeal should not, however, be tarred as frivolous because it presents an argument that is novel, unusual or ingenious, or urges adoption of a new principle of law or revision of an old one. Compare G.L. c.231, §6F. In the instant case the appeal covers no ground not gone over by the cases, and the appellant has urged no policy consideration which would warrant reappraisal of the settled rule. Indeed, leading authorities are consistent with the Massachusetts decisions. Restatement of Property §458, comment *i*, illus. 9 (1944). 2 & 3 American Law of Property §§8.56 & 15.3 (1952). 7 Powell, The Law of Real Property §1013[2] (Rohan rev. ed. 1982).

Here, the appellant's case had lost all vestige of merit after the Land Court judge made his decision. A Land Court judge's findings in registration proceedings carry weight even beyond that generally accorded by an appellate court to findings of a trial judge. Norton v. West, 8 Mass. App. Ct. 348, 350, 394 N.E.2d 1125 (1979). Coupled with the strong evidence built up in favor of Clarissa, there was no hope for the appellant on any issue of fact and, indeed, the appellant, Batchelder, attempted no argument aimed at the judge's findings.

The judge's decision also contained a discussion of the relevant authorities, all of which had been copiously cited and discussed in a posttrial memorandum filed on behalf of Clarissa. Before he launched his appeal, therefore, the appellant was fully aware of the powerful precedents built up over the years against the appellant's position. There was no reasonable expectation of a reversal; the appeal was frivolous.

Another aspect of the case warrants comment. Batchelder, a candid witness, testified he resided in Winthrop and knew nothing about the Allen farm on Martha's Vineyard or a potential claim to an interest in it until, as we noted above, William J. Devine brought the possibility to attention. Devine proposed that he would pay the costs of mounting a legal campaign to assert the Batchelder claim and that he (Devine) and Batchelder would share the net proceeds of anything they realized from the litigation. To that end, Batchelder conveyed his interest in the locus, whatever it might be, to a trust of which he and Devine were equal beneficiaries.

This is the third occasion within a year in which we have come across the same pattern of a title challenge induced and financed by Devine. See Devine v. Nantucket, 16 Mass. App. Ct. 548, 452 N.E.2d 1167 (1983), and Hilde v. Dixon, 16 Mass. App. Ct. 981, 453 N.E.2d 1232 (1983). He appears to be a bounty hunter in troubled titles. The appellee has not raised the issue of champerty, but it is a subject to which a court may turn its attention on its own initiative. See Sherwin-Williams Co. v. J. Mannos & Sons, 287 Mass. 304, 312, 191 N.E. 438 (1934); Baskin v. Pass, 302 Mass. 338, 342, 19 N.E.2d 30 (1939). Champerty is the maintenance, at the champertor's expense, of a legal action in consideration of profit out of the action, if any. Sherwin-Williams Co. v. J. Mannos & Sons, 287 Mass. at 312, 191 N.E. 438. Pupecki v. James Madison Corp., 376 Mass. 212, 219, 382 N.E.2d 1030 (1978). Devine is not a lawyer, but it is not necessary to be a member of the bar to make a champertous agreement. Graustein v. Boston & Maine R.R., 304 Mass. 23, 27, 22 N.E.2d 594 (1939). Gill v. Richmond Co-op Assn., 309 Mass. 73, 76, 34 N.E.2d 509 (1941).

Champerty does not presuppose that the case to be maintained is a frivolous one. It is the latter characteristic which provides the occasion for invocation of Mass. R.A.P. 25. This case's champertous antecedents, however, bear on our willingness to apply the sanctions available under the rule and, as well, color our view of the damages which are appropriate.

Accordingly, the appellee, Clarissa Allen, is to have $5,000 damages on account of her legal fees for the appeal as well as double costs of the appeal.

The judgment is affirmed. Damages and costs shall be assessed in the Land Court as above provided.

B. MARITAL INTERESTS

Page 556. Before "2. The Community Property System," insert:

In 1983 the National Conference of Commissioners on Uniform State Laws approved the Uniform Marital Property Act. This act adopts community property principles, but it uses the term *marital property* rather than community property. It is too early to tell how many states will adopt the

Uniform Marital Property Act. Wisconsin adopted the act in 1984. Wis. Stat. Ann. §§766.001-.97, enacted by Wis. Acts. of 1984, Act. 186.

The following excerpt by Professor Mary Moers Wenig summarizes the basic features of the act.

WENIG, THE MARITAL PROPERTY ACT
12 Prob. & Prop., Summer 1983, at 9-11

It is news when William F. Buckley, Jr. and Phyllis Schlafly, on one end of the continuum, and the National Organization for Women on the other, agree. But agree they do. And in agreement with them, also, are others somewhere in between. For instance, the League of Women Voters of Wisconsin, The Older Women's League, Agri-Women, the 1963 President's Commission on the Status of Women, the 1976 National Commission on the International Women's Year, and the 1980 White House Conference on Families.

The concept that elicits this agreement is *sharing* — the equal sharing by husband and wife of the benefits and liabilities of the marriage partnership. The law which embodies this concept is community property law.

In a television program taped on November 30, 1982, William F. Buckley, Jr. stated that he "would welcome a change in the law that would grant community property rights, as they exist in eight states already, everywhere in the United States." A February 28, 1983 Newsweek interview with Phyllis Schlafly reported that she is working for passage of state community property laws. From the Wisconsin chapter of her Eagle Forum comes proof: a proposed community property act drafted for Phyllis Schlafly.

Judge Charles Sumner Lobingier, in an article in the ABA Journal, wrote that

> the introduction of the community [concept] would be a long step toward that juster and more equal status which the present condition of society demands. Moreover, it would relieve the state of diversity of marital property laws which is fast becoming intolerable. Here would seem to lie a promising field for the Commissioners on Uniform Laws.

The date of this article was 1928. Half a century later, the work was begun.

In 1977, the National Conference of Commissioners on Uniform State Laws (NCCUSL) appointed a special committee to study the subject of concurrent ownership and to determine if a uniform law might be desirable.... [In 1983 the Uniform Marital Property Act was promulgated.]

SUMMARY OF THE ACT

Rather than the terms *community* and *separate* property, used by the eight community property states, the act uses the terms *marital property* and *individual property*. Use of this terminology is not intended to belittle the community property roots. But the term *marital property* evokes the property distribution provisions of the Uniform Marriage and Divorce Act and of comparable provisions for equitable distribution on marriage dissolution, now adopted by all but two of the common law states. In addition, the terms *marital property* and *individual property* are employed in recognition that the Marital Property Act attempts to meld concepts from both community property and common law.

The act provides that property acquired during marriage is marital property. Both husband and wife have a present undivided one-half interest in their marital property. Individual property includes property owned before marriage, or acquired at any time by gift or inheritance, and appreciation of individual property not resulting from substantial personal effort of the other spouse. Presumptions aid in the identification of marital property and simple rules, based on a time continuum, are provided for the sorting out of marital and individual property components of life insurance, pension and other deferred employee benefits which straddle the date of marriage.

The act applies prospectively only, affecting interests acquired after the act's effective date by married couples within the adopting state.

While title no longer governs the ownership of property acquired after the act's effective date, title bestows rights of management and control. Title can be in the name of one spouse or the other or both. If title is in the name of husband *and* wife, there is joint management and control; if in the name of husband *or* wife, either can manage and control. Third persons who rely on title are protected in their dealings with a spouse but gifts to third persons in excess of a certain annual amount or in excess of the standard of giving set by the spouses can be set aside by the nondonor spouse who acts promptly. If necessary, a spouse may obtain judicial aid to add his or her name to the title of marital property (except for partnership interests or assets of an unincorporated business of the other spouse). Other judicial remedies, if sought promptly, may protect the interest of either spouse in marital property.

Claims of third persons arising during an obligee's marriage can be satisfied from the obligee's individual property or from marital property; claims which antedate the marriage can be satisfied from the obligee's individual property and from his or her earnings during marriage. Broad scope is granted to husbands and wives to enter into marital property agreements which may vary the effect of the act. Marital property can be held in survivorship form or transferred to trust without losing its marital property characteristics if this is what the spouses want.

The act is a property act, not a divorce act. Therefore, to use Reporter Cantwell's metaphor, in the event of divorce the act takes the couple up to the steps of the courthouse, each with his or her undivided one-half interest in marital property in hand, and leaves them there. The divorce law, and whatever power of equitable distribution the state has given to the court, then takes over. Because the act is a property act, at death of either spouse, that spouse has power of testamentary disposition over his or her undivided one-half interest in the couple's marital property.

Because of the act's prospective application, couples who are married before the effective date of the act or married couples who move into an adopting state from a state which has not adopted the act may have considerable individual property, possibly all or substantially all owned by only one of the spouses. To protect the nonowning spouse on divorce, or to protect a surviving spouse, a deferred interest is given to that spouse in the other spouse's property which would have been marital property under the act's definition but for the fact that the property was acquired during the couple's marriage before the adoption of the act or before their move to the adopting state. . . .

The act may sound unfamiliar to lawyers accustomed to common law. But almost one-fourth of the population of the United States now lives in the eight community property states — Arizona, California, Idaho, Louisiana, New Mexico, Nevada, Texas and Washington. Married couples travel; their domiciles change as their jobs move or as their retirement plans direct. While the population of many of the community property states is growing, couples in these states also move. Should their rights in marital property turn on the accident of their choice of residence?

The variegated marital property regimes of the common law states have been moving in many ways in the past two decades toward community property. "Creeping community property" is reflected in piecemeal judicial decisions or legislation providing for equitable distribution on divorce; protection against disinheritance on death; increases in intestate shares of surviving spouses; presumptions classifying household effects and other family assets as joint and survivor property; recognition of husband-and-wife partnerships in family businesses and family farms; imposition of constructive trusts to aid one spouse's claim of interest in property held in the name of the other spouse; increasing validation of marital contracts; and the growing trend of the states, both before and after the federal adoption in 1981 of the unlimited marital deduction, toward tax-free interspousal transfers. In addition, federal law pertaining to public and private pensions has in recent years reinforced state law in giving increasing recognition to the necessity of permitting one spouse to share in the benefits earned by the other spouse.

Justified by the trend exemplified by the many illustrations of creeping community property, the Marital Property Act would bring order and symmetry to the law of marital property. By looking at the length of the marriage and assuming that husband and wife are economic partners and that they have been acting as such during the course of the marriage, unless they agree that they have not, the act gives equal weight to the contributions of both spouses. The act smooths the jagged edges of laws that in one state may give a larger share to the surviving spouse of a decedent who dies intestate than to the surviving spouse of a decedent who dies with a will and that, in a neighboring state, may do the reverse. The act deals with nonprobate assets that are such a large part of wealth today, in a manner that neither the intestate nor elective share laws can provide. The act differentiates between marriages of short duration and longer marriages, not only upon divorce but in the course of the marriage and upon death of one of the spouses.

In a recent National Institute on Divorce and Estate Planning in an Uncertain Marital Climate, held jointly by this Section and the Family Law Section, the panel moderator asked questions not of the panel but of the audience, ten dozen lawyers from twenty states. After listening to the chaotic range of answers to each question asked, the moderator summed up with a McLuhan paraphrase: The chaos *is* the message. Uniformity and consistency are the desiderata.

The "strange bedfellow" proponents of community property — Buckley, Schlafly and NOW — may indicate that the Marital Property Act is the correct culmination and embodiment of a demand that the law recognize that marital property is not "his" or "hers" but "ours." Another proponent may have been revealed by a wedding that occurred two years ago. The Church of England marriage ceremony contains the traditional vow, "with my worldly goods I thee endow." The old English separate property regime grant of the limited right of dower is thus embodied in the marriage ritual. But those who watched the televised wedding of Prince Charles and Princess Diana two summers ago heard Prince Charles speak not that traditional vow but instead the words: "All my goods, with thee I *share*."

That is what the Marital Property Act is about. Creeping community property and the sharing concept has crept up on Prince Charles as well as the rest of us. The ritual vow has changed, and the law can too. The concept of marriage as an economic partnership, in which the contributions of both partners are adjudged equal may, finally, with the aid or inspiration of the Marital Property Act, become the law of all of the states.

Part 3
Voluntary Transfer of Property: Herein Mostly Sales of Land

Chapter Six
Transfer by Sale and by Gift

A. THE LAND TRANSACTIONS INDUSTRY

Page 637. At the end of Note 3, add:

In Fidelity First Federal Savings & Loan Association v. de la Cuesta, 458 U.S. 141 (1982), the Supreme Court held that the 1976 regulations of the Federal Home Loan Bank Board preempted state law and prevented the application of state due-on-sale laws to federally chartered associations.

In 1982 Congress intervened in the controversy over enforcement of due-on-sale clauses by enacting the Garn-St. Germain Depository Institutions Act of 1982, 12 U.S.C. §1701j-3 (1982). This act, effective October 15, 1982, preempted state law and generally provided that due-on-sale clauses in all mortgages are enforceable. The act contains exceptions similar to those provided in the 1976 regulations of the Federal Home Loan Bank Board. With respect to mortgages existing on October 15, 1982, the situation is complex. Federally chartered savings and loan associations may enforce the due-on-sale clauses in mortgages executed after the issuance of the 1976 regulations of the Federal Home Loan Bank Board, but these regulations may not apply to mortgages executed before 1976. Other existing mortgages are subject to the act, with one important exemption: If a state gave restrictive enforcement to due-on-sale clauses prior to October 15, 1982, any mortgage given or assumed in the state between the date the state first restricted enforcement and October 15, 1982 (the "window period"), is unaffected by the act for three years — until October 15, 1985. Before this latter date, the state legislature may, if it wishes, enact legislation extending indefinitely the protection of mortgages given or made during this window period. If the state legislature fails to act before October 15, 1985, the federal act making due-on-sale clauses enforceable becomes applicable to these window-period mortgages. See Nelson & Whitman, Congressional Preemption of Mortgage Due-on-Sale Law: An Analysis of the Garn-St. Germain Act, 35 Hastings L.J. 243 (1983).

Transfer by Sale and by Gift

B. THE CONTRACT OF SALE

Page 680. After Note 8, insert:

REED v. KING
California Court of Appeal, 1983
145 Cal. App. 3d 261, 193 Cal. Rptr. 130

BLEASE, J. — In the sale of a house, must the seller disclose it was the site of a multiple murder? Dorris Reed purchased a house from Robert King. Neither King nor his real estate agents (the other named defendants) told Reed that a woman and her four children were murdered there 10 years earlier. However, it seems "truth will come to light; murder cannot be hid long." (Shakespeare, Merchant of Venice, act II, scene II.) Reed learned of the gruesome episode from a neighbor after the sale. She sues seeking rescission and damages. King and the real estate agent defendants successfully demurred to her first amended complaint for failure to state a cause of action. Reed appeals the ensuing judgment of dismissal. We will reverse the judgment.

FACTS

We take all issuable facts pled in Reed's complaints as true. (See 3 Witkin, Cal. Procedure (2d ed. 1971) Pleading, §800.) King and his real estate agent knew about the murders and knew the event materially affected the market value of the house when they listed it for sale. They represented to Reed the premises were in good condition and fit for an "elderly lady" living alone. They did not disclose the fact of the murders. At some point King asked a neighbor not to inform Reed of that event. Nonetheless, after Reed moved in neighbors informed her no one was interested in purchasing the house because of the stigma. Reed paid $76,000, but the house is only worth $65,000 because of its past.

The trial court sustained the demurrers to the complaint on the ground it did not state a cause of action. The court concluded a cause of action could only be stated "if the subject property, by reason of the prior circumstances, were *presently* the object of community notoriety. . . ." (Original italics.) Reed declined the offer of leave to amend.

DISCUSSION

Does Reed's pleading state a cause of action? Concealed within this question is the nettlesome problem of the duty of disclosure of blemishes on real property which are not physical defects or legal impairments to use.

Reed seeks to state a cause of action sounding in contract, i.e. rescission, or in tort, i.e., deceit. In either event her allegations must reveal a fraud. (See Civ. Code, §§1571-1573, 1689, 1709-1710.)

> The elements of actual fraud, whether as the basis of the remedy in contract or tort, may be stated as follows: There must be (1) a *false representation* or concealment of a material fact (or, in some cases, an opinion) susceptible of knowledge, (2) made with *knowledge* of its falsity or without sufficient knowledge on the subject to warrant a representation, (3) with the *intent* to induce the person to whom it is made to act upon it; and such person must (4) act in *reliance* upon the representation (5) to his *damage*.

(Original italics.) (1 Witkin, Summary of Cal. Law (8th ed. 1973) Contracts, §315.)

The trial court perceived the defect in Reed's complaint to be a failure to allege concealment of a material fact. "Concealment" and "material" are legal conclusions concerning the effect of the issuable facts pled. As appears, the analytic pathways to these conclusions are intertwined.

Concealment is a term of art which includes mere nondisclosure when a party has a duty to disclose. (See, e.g., Lingsch v. Savage (1963) 213 Cal. App. 2d 729, 738 [29 Cal. Rptr. 201, 8 A.L.R.3d 537]; Rest. 2d Contracts, §161; Rest. 2d Torts, §551; Rest., Restitution, §8, esp. com. b.) Reed's complaint reveals only nondisclosure despite the allegation King asked a neighbor to hold his peace. There is no allegation the attempt at suppression was a cause in fact of Reed's ignorance. (See Rest. 2d Contracts, §§160, 162-164; Rest. 2d Torts, §550; Rest., Restitution, §9.) Accordingly, the critical question is: does the seller have a duty to disclose here? Resolution of this question depends on the materiality of the fact of the murders.

In general, a seller of real property has a duty to disclose:

> where the seller knows of facts *materially* affecting the value or desirability of the property which are known or accessible only to him and also knows that such facts are not known to, or within the reach of the diligent attention and observation of the buyer, the seller is under a duty to disclose them to the buyer.[48a] [Italics added; citations omitted.]

(Lingsch v. Savage, *supra*, 213 Cal. App. 2d at p.735.) This broad statement of duty has led one commentator to conclude: "The ancient maxim *caveat emptor* ('let the buyer beware.') has little or no application to California real estate transactions." (1 Miller & Starr, Current Law of Cal. Real Estate (rev. ed. 1975) §1:80.)

Whether information "is of sufficient materiality to affect the value or desirability of the property . . . depends on the facts of the particular case." (Lingsch, *supra*, 213 Cal. App. 2d at p.737.) Materiality "is a question of law,

---

[48a]. The real estate agent or broker representing the seller is under the same duty of disclosure. (Lingsch v. Savage, *supra*, 213 Cal. App. 2d at p.736.)

and is part of the concept of right to rely or justifiable reliance." (3 Witkin, Cal. Procedure (2d ed. 1971) Pleading, §578, p.2217.) Accordingly, the term is essentially a label affixed to a normative conclusion. Three considerations bear on this legal conclusion: the gravity of the harm inflicted by nondisclosure; the fairness of imposing a duty of discovery on the buyer as an alternative to compelling disclosure, and its impact on the stability of contracts if rescission is permitted.

Numerous cases have found nondisclosure of physical defects and legal impediments to use of real property are material. (See 1 Miller & Starr, *supra*, §181.)[48b] However, to our knowledge, no prior real estate sale case has faced an issue of nondisclosure of the kind presented here. . . . Should this variety of ill-repute be required to be disclosed? Is this a circumstance where "non-disclosure of the fact amounts to a failure to act in good faith and in accordance with reasonable standards of fair dealing[?]" (Rest. 2d Contracts, §161, subd. (b).)

The paramount argument against an affirmative conclusion is it permits the camel's nose of unrestrained irrationality admission to the tent. If such an "irrational" consideration is permitted as a basis of rescission the stability of all conveyances will be seriously undermined. Any fact that might disquiet the enjoyment of some segment of the buying public may be seized upon by a disgruntled purchaser to void a bargain.[48c] In our view, keeping this genie in the bottle is not as difficult a task as these arguments assume. We do not view a decision allowing Reed to survive a demurrer in these unusual circumstances as indorsing the materiality of facts predicating peripheral, insubstantial, or fancied harms.

48b. For example, the following have been held of sufficient materiality to require disclosure: the home sold was constructed on filled land (Burkett v. J.A. Thompson & Son (1957) 150 Cal. App. 2d 523, 526 [310 P.2d 56]); improvements were added without a building permit and in violation of zoning regulations (Barder v. McClung (1949) 93 Cal. App. 2d 692, 697 [209 P.2d 808]) or in violation of building codes (Curran v. Heslop (1953) 115 Cal. App. 2d 476, 480-481 [252 P.2d 378]); the structure was condemned (Katz v. Department of Real Estate (1979) 96 Cal. App. 3d 895, 900 [158 Cal. Rptr. 766]); the structure was termite-infested (Godfrey v. Steinpress (1982) 128 Cal. App. 3d 154 [180 Cal.Rptr. 95]); there was water infiltration in the soil (Barnhouse v. City of Pinole (1982) 133 Cal. App. 3d 171, 187-188 [183 Cal. Rptr. 881]); the correct amount of net income a piece of property would yield (Ford v. Cournale (1973) 36 Cal. App. 3d 172, 179-180 [111 Cal. Rptr. 334, 81 A.L.R.3d 704]).

48c. Concern for the effects of an overly indulgent rescission policy on the stability of bargains is not new. Our Supreme Court early on quoted with approval the sentiment: "'The power to cancel a contract is a most extraordinary power. It is one which should be exercised with great caution, — nay, I may say, with great reluctance, — unless in a clear case. A too free use of this power would render all business uncertain, and, as has been said, make the length of a chancellor's foot the measure of individual rights. The greatest liberty of making contracts is essential to the business interests of the country. In general, the parties must look out for themselves.'" (Colton v. Stanford (1980) 82 Cal. 351, 398 [23 P. 16].)

The murder of innocents is highly unusual in its potential for so disturbing buyers they may be unable to reside in a home where it has occurred. This fact may foreseeably deprive a buyer of the intended use of the purchase. Murder is not such a common occurrence that *buyers* should be charged with anticipating and discovering this disquieting possibility. Accordingly, the fact is not one for which a duty of inquiry and discovery can sensibly be imposed upon the buyer.

Reed alleges the fact of the murders has a quantifiable effect on the market value of the premises. We cannot say this allegation is inherently wrong and, in the pleading posture of the case, we assume it to be true. If information known or accessible only to the seller has a significant and measurable effect on market value and, as is alleged here, the seller is aware of this effect, we see no principled basis for making the duty to disclose turn upon the character of the information. Physical usefulness is not and never has been the sole criterion of valuation. Stamp collections and gold speculation would be insane activities if utilitarian considerations were the sole measure of value. (See also Civ. Code, §3355 [deprivation of property of peculiar value to owner]; Annot. (1950) 12 A.L.R.2d 902 [Measure of Damages for Conversion or Loss of, or Damage to, Personal Property Having No Market Value].)

Reputation and history can have a significant effect on the value of realty. "George Washington slept here" is worth something, however physically inconsequential that consideration may be. Ill-repute or "bad will" conversely may depress the value of property. Failure to disclose such a negative fact where it will have a foreseeably depressing effect on income expected to be generated by a business is tortious. (See Rest. 2d Torts, §551, illus. 11.) Some cases have held that *unreasonable* fears of the potential buying public that a gas or oil pipeline may rupture may depress the market value of land and entitle the owner to incremental compensation in eminent domain. (See Annot., Eminent Domain: Elements and Measure of Compensation for Oil or Gas Pipeline Through Private Property (1954) 38 A.L.R.2d 788, 801-804.)

Whether Reed will be able to prove her allegation the decade-old multiple murder has a significant effect on market value we cannot determine. If she is able to do so by competent evidence she is entitled to a favorable ruling on the issues of materiality and duty to disclose.[48d] Her demonstra-

---

[48d]. The ruling of the trial court requiring the additional element of notoriety, i.e. widespread public knowledge, is unpersuasive. Lack of notoriety may facilitate resale to yet another unsuspecting buyer at the "market price" of a house with no ill-repute. However, it appears the buyer will learn of the possibly unsettling history of the house soon after moving in. Those who suffer no discomfort from the specter of residing in such quarters per se, will nonetheless be discomforted by the prospect they have bought a house that may be difficult to sell to less hardy souls. Nondisclosure must be evaluated as fair or unfair regardless of the ease with which a buyer may escape this discomfort by foisting it upon another.

tion of objective tangible harm would still the concern that permitting her to go forward will open the floodgates to rescission on subjective and idiosyncratic grounds.

A more troublesome question would arise if a buyer in similar circumstances were unable to plead or establish a significant and quantifiable effect on market value. However, this question is not presented in the posture of this case. Reed has not alleged the fact of the murders has rendered the premises useless to her as a residence. As currently pled, the gravamen of her case is pecuniary harm. We decline to speculate on the abstract alternative.

The judgment is reversed.

Chapter Seven
Methods of Title Assurance

B. TITLE INSURANCE

Page 780. Insert the following before Southern Title Guaranty Co., Inc. v. Prendergast:

L. SMIRLOCK REALTY CORP. v. TITLE GUARANTY CO.
New York Supreme Court, Appellate Division, 1983
97 App. Div. 2d 208, 469 N.Y.S.2d 415

[In 1969 plaintiff purchased a warehouse for $600,000 at a proceeding foreclosing a mortgage. Plaintiff paid $65,000 down and borrowed $535,000 to pay the balance, giving the lender a mortgage on the property. Plaintiff purchased a title insurance policy from defendant, insuring plaintiff's interest for $600,000. At the time of sale, access to the property was over three public streets: Carvel Place to the north and St. George Place and Jeanette Avenue to the east. The loading docks for large trucks were located at the east end of the building with direct access to St. George Place and Jeanette Avenue. In addition, an alley connected Carvel Place with this loading dock area, but because it was narrow, large trucks could not use this route.

Unknown to plaintiff, some two years before the purchase the town of Hempstead had condemned, paid for, and taken title to the roadbeds of St. George Place and Jeanette Avenue for urban renewal purposes. No exception was listed in the title insurance policy for the condemnations. Apparently, defendant's title searcher had neglected to make the appropriate inquiry in the county clerk's office, which would have revealed the condemnations.

Some two years after the purchase the Town of Hempstead began to rip up Jeanette Avenue and St. George Place, pursuant to its urban renewal plan. That plan required the closing of the warehouse access routes via these streets. The only access to the warehouse now was by way of Carvel

Place, and the alley connecting Carvel Place to the loading area would admit only small trucks. Plaintiff sued the title insurance company on the policy, seeking to recover the sum of $600,000 in damages. In Smirlock Realty Corp. v. Title Guarantee Co., 52 N.Y.2d 179, 437 N.Y.S.2d 57, 418 N.E.2d 650 (1981), the New York Court of Appeals held that the company was liable on the policy for damages resulting from loss of access and remanded the case for determination of damages.

On remand, plaintiff advanced its theory of damages: Its loss should be measured by "the difference in market value between the property with the encumbrance and without the encumbrance." The trial court agreed. The trial court found that the market value of the property on the date of sale, with access via St. George Place and Jeanette Avenue, was $800,000 (the 1969 purchase price of $600,000 was not considered important, because the sale was made in a foreclosure proceeding). The court further found that the market value of the property on the date of sale without access to St. George Place and Jeanette Avenue was $206,150 for a net difference of $593,850.

The warehouse was subject to a purchase money mortgage of $535,000 given by plaintiff and held by a bank. In 1975 the bank foreclosed its mortgage and sold the property for $300,000. The bank also made a claim against defendant under a separate mortgagee's policy of title insurance issued by defendant. The bank settled its claim against defendant for $32,500. The record does not reveal whether the bank sued plaintiff for a deficiency judgment.

On the theory that defendant was subrogated to the bank, the trial court, after deducting the value of the property without access ($200,000) from the $535,000 mortgage subrogation claim, found that defendant was entitled to a setoff of $335,000. This left net damages at $258,850, which the trial court awarded as damages.

Defendant appealed, alleging that plaintiff's damages should be measured by the plaintiff's equity in the property. Plaintiff appealed, alleging that defendant was entitled only to a setoff of $32,500, the amount actually paid in settling the mortgagee's claim. (The facts have been changed slightly by the editors to eliminate peripheral issues.)]

GIBBONS, J. . . . It follows from the nature of title insurance that an insured is entitled to be reimbursed for his actual loss, up to the limit of the policy (Empire Dev. Co. v. Title Guar. & Trust Co., 225 N.Y. 53, 121 N.E. 468; see 9 [rev.] Appleman, Insurance Law & Prac, §5216; 15A Couch, Insurance [2d ed.], §57:179). This is, at once, a restrictive and expansive statement of damages. It is restrictive in that conjectural lost profits are not included (see 15A Couch, Insurance [2d ed.], §57:179). It is expansive in that the insured is protected against more than just nominal damages or out-of-pocket expenses (Montemarano v. Home Title Ins. Co., 258 N.Y. 478, 180 N.E. 241).

Methods of Title Assurance

Generally speaking, what the words "loss or damage" mean is to be determined by the definitions and standards accepted by the parties (Empire Dev. Co. v. Title Guar. & Trust Co., *supra*, 225 N.Y. pp. 59-60, 121 N.E. 468), subject to any applicable government regulation. In this case, the policy does explictly and in detail set forth the types of, and occasions for, losses covered by the policy. However, it is practically silent on the question of how to measure the value of loss or damage. There is no provision which expressly addresses this very important issue. We thus must resort to general rules of contract interpretation, in particular, taking into account the purpose and object of the contract.

. . . As already mentioned, plaintiff contends that it is entitled to the difference in market value between the property with the defect in title and without such defect. Reliance is placed on, among other sources, the case of Glyn v. Title Guar. & Trust Co. 132 App. Div. 859, 117 N.Y.S. 424. Defendant, on the other hand, argues that actual loss is to be measured by the insured's equity in the property, citing our decision in Grimsey v. Lawyers Tit. Ins. Corp. 38 A.D.2d 572, 328 N.Y.S.2d 474, *mod. on other grounds* 31 N.Y.2d 953, 341 N.Y.S.2d 100, 293 N.E.2d 249. A similar view is expressed in the brief of the New York State Land Title Association as amicus curiae. According to that organization, a title policy is a species of valued policy, the value being set by the purchase price. The loss to be recompensed is measured by the purchase price less the amount due on any mortgage agreement.

In Glyn v. Title Guar. & Trust Co. (*supra*) the plaintiff purchased property which was encroached upon by neighboring structures which had been in existence for over 20 years. Noting that the encumbrances were such that "the owner could not at will remove [them]", the court held that the measure of the plaintiff's damages was "the difference between the value of the property when purchased, as it was with the encroachment, and its value as it would have been if there had been no such encroachment" (Glyn v. Title Guar. & Trust Co., *supra*, 132 A.D. p.863, 117 N.Y.S. 424). In *Glyn*, the insured suffered a partial loss in the value of the property.

Defendant argues that the applicable case is not *Glyn*, but rather Grimsey v. Lawyers Tit. Ins. Corp. (*supra*), wherein this court said "[b]ecause indemnity is the nature of the title insurance contract at bar, plaintiffs are entitled only to the recovery of their actual loss and *may not recover the value of the fee*" (38 A.D.2d 572, 573, 328 N.Y.S.2d 474, *supra*, emphasis supplied). *Grimsey* was a total loss case wherein the plaintiff bought land that did not belong to the grantor. The purchase price was $65,000, with the plaintiff paying $25,000 cash and giving a purchase-money mortgage for the balance. Almost one year after the purchase, the plaintiff learned that the county held the fee. The trial court, among other things, held that the plaintiff was entitled on his policy to $65,000 for the loss of the fee. This court disagreed, allowing the plaintiff only $25,000, the amount of his initial investment. The case was appealed to the Court of Appeals, but only by the defendant title company, with respect to an award of the plaintiff's counsel fees (Grimsey v. Lawyers Tit. Ins. Corp., 31 N.Y.2d 953, *supra*, 341 N.Y.S.2d 100, 293 N.E.2d 249). Thus, we have no final determination by the Court of Appeals in *Grimsey* regarding the correctness of the valuation of the loss in that case.

Because *Grimsey* was a total loss case, whereas the case at bar involves a partial loss, as did *Glyn*, it is tempting to simply say that *Glyn* and not *Grimsey* sets forth the controlling rule as to damages. However, such would result in a very dissatisfying situation, wherein a fee holder facing a total loss may be entitled to far less compensation, other things being equal, than a fee holder facing a partial loss, because of the radically different formulae utilized. The application of one formula, predicated on the influence a defect has on the value of the property, and another formula, utilized when the defect is total, wherein the value of the property is irrelevant and the loss is measured by the consideration or equity, does not provide a particularly coherent theory of loss. Rather, we should search for an underlying principle of damages which would lead to harmonious results, whether the loss is partial or total.

The roots of the difficulty appear to go back to the early development of the concept of title insurance, when it made its appearance in this country during the last half of the nineteenth century (see Johnstone, Title Insurance, 66 Yale L.J. 492). The writers considering this new form of insurance gave short shrift to the question of damages by simply analogizing them to those found in an action brought by a grantee against his grantor for breach of the various covenants of title (see, e.g. 3 Sutherland, Damages [4th ed.], §840a). Thus, where there was a total absence or loss of title, it was stated that an insured under a title policy should receive as damages what he would receive for a breach of the covenant of seizin or warranty of title, that is, the consideration paid (see Murphy v. United States Tit. Guar. Co., 104 Misc. 607, 172 N.Y.S. 243; see, also, Hunt v. Hay, 214 N.Y. 578, 108 N.E. 851). On the other hand, where the breach of the title policy pertained only to an encumbrance, damages were analogized to those existing where there had been a breach of the covenant against encumbrances (Murphy v. United States Tit. Guar. Co., *supra*). The measure of damages in the latter context is that set forth in *Glyn* 132 App. Div. 859, 117 N.Y.S. 424, *supra*: either the cost of removal, or, alternatively, the difference in value between the land with the servitude and without it (City of New York v. The New York & South Brooklyn Ferry and Steam Transp. Co., 231 N.Y. 18, 24, 131 N.E. 554).

By indiscriminately extending the law of covenants of title to the measure of damages for breach of a title insurance policy, the early authorities ignored the unique history of covenants of title. The covenant of seizin and

Methods of Title Assurance

the warranty of title do not generally follow the rules of contract law and are not covenants of indemnity. They are derived from the rules of feudal tenure and the relationships of lord and vassal (see Ann., Measure of Damages for Breach of Covenants of Title in Conveyances or Mortgages of Real Property, 61 A.L.R. 10). In the system of feudal tenure, land did not have a market price; the value of land "depended not upon a pecuniary rental but upon the personal services which its holding entailed" (3 Sedgwick, Damages [9th ed.], §951). A lord had the obligation of ensuring his vassal's enjoyment of his feud. The latter's remedy, if the land were, for whatever reason, taken, was to be put in possession of lands as good as those lost, a kind of specific performance.

> The idea of the loss of a good pecuniary bargain was foreign to the existing legal and social order. As the value of land was not measured in money, so there was no fluctuation in the market, and purchasers did not acquire title with the intention of subsequently conveying to a new purchaser at a profit. Even when the next step was taken and the ordinary purchase and sale of lands began to become common, the idea of fluctuation in value was not thought of, and the consideration named in the deed began to be regarded as a pecuniary equivalent for the old agreement to enfeoff of lands of equal value. Instead of getting land of equal value the plaintiff was to get what both parties had by consent substituted for it — the consideration

(3 Sedgwick, Damages [9th ed.], §951, pp. 1966-1967).

A covenant or warranty against encumbrances differs from a covenant of seizin or a warranty of title in that many elements or principles of contract law appear applicable. Thus, a covenant against encumbrances looks past the time of sale, in the sense that the warrantor must make good on his warranty, putting the warrantee in as good a state as if the covenant or warranty had been kept (Thayer v. Clemence, 22 Pick 490 [Mass]). A covenant against encumbrances is distinguishable from a covenant of seizin in that it "is to be regarded as a covenant of indemnity" (Ann., Measure of Damages for Breach of Covenants of Title in Conveyances or Mortgages of Real Property, 61 A.L.R. 10, 61; see McGuckin v. Milbank, 152 N.Y. 297, 302, 46 N.E. 490). Not surprisingly, courts have been quick to seize on this difference and the rule that the appropriate measure of damages, where there is a breach of a covenant against encumbrances, is the diminution of value rather than the consideration paid, in order to grant justice to an injured grantee (see, e.g., Hymes v. Esty, 133 N.Y. 342, 348, 31 N.E. 105).

The measure of damages for a breach of the covenant of seizin or warranty of title based on the consideration paid was criticized by the Court of Appeals as long ago as 1892, in the case of Hymes v. Esty (*supra*). The rule's ancient origins were emphasized, and the fact that when applied to a market economy, the rule leads to unjust results in favor of the covenantor (133

N.Y. 342, 347, 31 N.E. 105, *supra*). The rule simply violates the general measure of damages where there has been a breach of contract, which is the recovery of foreseeable damages and the value of what has been lost (Ann., Measure of Damages for Breach of Covenants of Title in Conveyances or Mortgages of Real Property, 61 A.L.R. 10, 20-38; 3 Sedgwick, Damages [9th ed.], §951, p.1967). Nonetheless, using the consideration as the measure of damages where there has been a breach of the covenant of seizin, perhaps because of its venerable tradition, apparently remains the law in many, if not most, of the states, including New York (see Hunt v. Hay, 214 N.Y. 578, 108 N.E. 851, *supra*).

The wholesale grafting of the law of covenants of title onto the law of damages with respect to title insurance was questioned, at least implicitly, by former Chief Judge (then Justice) Lehman in the case of Murphy v. United States Tit. Guar. Co. 104 Misc. 607, 172 N.Y.S. 243, *supra*. Examining both the covenant of seizin and the covenant against encumbrances, Chief Judge Lehman stated that the latter "is essentially more nearly like the agreement of a title insurance company" (104 Misc. 607, 611, 172 N.Y.S., 243, *supra*). Chief Judge Lehman pointed out that a title policy goes further than the covenant of seizin in that it concerns unmarketability of title, and, also, like the warranty against encumbrances, is a covenant of indemnity. . . .

A bare two months after Murphy v. United States Tit. Guar. Co. 104 Misc. 607, 172 N.Y.S. 243, *supra* was decided by the Appellate Term, First Department, in October, 1918, the Court of Appeals handed down Empire Dev. Co. v. Title Guar. & Trust Co. 225 N.Y. 53, 121 N.E. 468, *supra*. There the court noted that a title insurance policy is akin to a covenant against encumbrances (Empire Dev. Co. v. Title Guar. & Trust Co., *supra*, p.61, 121 N.E. 468). The court also remarked that it was a contract of indemnity and, then, in determining the meaning of the word "loss", stated that "[f]ailure to keep what a man has or *thinks he has is a loss*" (Empire Dev. Co. v. Title Guar. & Trust Co., *supra*, p. 59, 121 N.E. 468, emphasis supplied). What an owner of real property "thinks he has" will generally be more than the consideration paid. Clearly, the Court in the *Empire Dev. Co.* case would have agreed with the view, quoted with approval by the Court of Appeals in Smirlock Realty Corp. v. Title Guar. Co. 52 N.Y.2d 179, 187, 437 N.Y.S.2d 57, 418 N.E.2d 650, that "[a] policy of title insurance means the opinion of the company which issues it, as to the validity of the title, *backed by an agreement to make that opinion good*, in case it should prove to be mistaken" (First Nat. Bank & Trust Co. of Port Chester v. New York Tit. Ins. Co., 171 Misc. 854, 859, 12 N.Y.S.2d 703, emphasis supplied).

The statements expressed in the preceding paragraph concerning the nature of title insurance seem almost obvious, yet they mark a significant, if unrecognized, departure from the traditional view that compared title insurance, at least in the total loss case, to a covenant of seizin. It follows from

Methods of Title Assurance

Empire Dev. Co. (supra) and like cases that an insured may recover under the policy for the *loss of what he supposed he had* rather than the consideration he paid (see Foehrenbach v. German-American Tit. & Trust Co., 217 Pa. 331, 66 A. 561). Thus, for example, it may be that the insured will be compensated for the loss of profit on a resale of the property, where the loss is readily ascertainable (Montemarano v. Home Tit. Ins. Co., 258 N.Y. 478, 180 N.E. 241, *supra*). An insured is not limited solely to a theory of recovery based on the fact that he received nothing for what he paid out and, therefore, should only be reimbursed to the extent of his consideration. He can also seek to be placed in the equivalent position which he reasonably thought he occupied in the first place. That is the fundamental or underlying principle of loss in a title insurance case. . . .

Applying the fundamental principle of recovery above discussed where there has been a total loss of title, the measure of loss will generally be the market value of the property within the limit of the policy (Ann., Measure, Extent, or Amount of Recovery on Policy of Title Insurance, 60 A.L.R.2d 972, 977; 15A Couch, Insurance [2d ed.], §57:182). While the purchase price certainly may be a factor in determining value, it should not be considered necessarily dispositive (see Hartman v. Shambaugh, 96 N.M. 359, 630 P.2d 758). The value may be considerably greater than the purchase price. On the other hand, where the actual value is less than the purchase price, the insured is entitled to the latter amount as compensation for a total breach of the warranty of title, that being his out-of-pocket injury (Dallas Tit. & Guar. Co. v. Valdes, 445 S.W.2d 26 [Tex.]; 15A Couch, Insurance [2d ed.], §57:182).

Where there is a partial loss of title and where the partial loss cannot readily be rectified, such as where an encumbrance cannot be removed, the standard ordinarily will be, as set forth in *Glyn* 132 App. Div. 859, 117 N.Y.S. 424, *supra*, the value of the property without the defect in title less its value with the defect (15A Couch, Insurance [2d ed.], §57:184; 9 [rev.] Appleman, Insurance Law & Prac., §5216, p. 102). In essence, the formula in the total loss case is but an application of this formula, wherein it is assumed that the value of the property with the defect is zero, the defect being total.

We would be remiss if we did not again examine the *Grimsey* case 38 A.D.2d 572, 573, 328 N.Y.S.2d 474, *supra*, relied on by defendant, wherein we stated that the plaintiff insured could not recover the value of the fee. This language does hearken back to the days when title insurance was likened to a covenant of seizin (cf. Matter of Boylan, 119 Misc. 545, 547, 197 N.Y.S. 710 [holding that the measure of damages for the breach of a covenant of seizin is the purchase price, less the amount owed on a purchase money mortgage]). To that extent *Grimsey* should not be considered as a valid statement of the law. However, we note that *Grimsey*, nonetheless, reached the correct result. The record in that case reveals that the actual value of the property at issue was apparently less than the plaintiff's $25,000 down payment. Therefore, the plaintiff was entitled to his consideration, representing his out-of-pocket loss (Dallas Tit. & Guar. Co. v. Valdes, 445 S.W.2d 26 [Tex.], *supra*).

Returning to the case at bar, we conclude that the trial court utilized the correct standard for determining plaintiff's loss, that is, the diminution in the value of the property caused by the denial of access via St. George Place and Jeanette Avenue. . . .

The primary contention on plaintiff's appeal is that defendant should not be entitled to subrogation except, possibly, to the extent of the $32,500 it paid to the bank. Section 8 of the conditions of both plaintiff's and the bank's respective title policies, entitled "SUBROGATION", states in relevant part that:

> This company shall to the extent of any payment by it of loss under this policy, be subrogated to all rights of the insured with respect thereto. The insured shall execute such instruments as may be requested to transfer such rights to this company. The rights so transferred shall be subordinate to any remaining interest of the insured.

Relying on this section, the trial court held that defendant was entitled to subrogation. It determined the amount to be setoff at $335,000, being the difference between the amount of the mortgage title policy and the value of the land without access by large trucks. . . .

It is well settled that where a mortgagee has a separate insurance policy protecting it, the insurer, on making compensation, may be subrogated as against the owner mortgagor. . . . Plaintiff's point is well taken, however, that defendant's right of subrogation should be limited to the amount it expended in settling the bank's claim. The subrogation clause itself contains such a limitation. That provision in the contract conforms with the general rule that a subrogee is only entitled to the amount actually paid by him (Broad Exchange Assoc. v. Hirsch & Co., 51 A.D.2d 896, 380 N.Y.S.2d 682; 57 N.Y. Jur., Subrogation, §27).

The trial court, as well as the defendant, was apparently of the view that to limit the offset to the actual payment made to the mortgagee would give the plaintiff a huge windfall which could not possibly be the intent of its title policy. We are sympathetic to the court's concern. However, the subrogation clause as it is written is satisfactorily designed to prevent just such a windfall. With its presence, the title company is not vulnerable to a cumulative or double recovery, equivalent to the total amounts of both title policies (see Scinta v. Kazmierczak, 59 A.D.2d 313, 316, 399 N.Y.S.2d 545). It is as though, in the case where only one policy might be issued, there is a provision in the policy allowing for a *pro tanto* reduction in what is owed the homeowner resulting from a payment made to the homeowner's mortgagee (see Grady v. Utica Mut. Ins. Co., 69 A.D.2d 668, 673-674, 419 N.Y.S.2d 565).

The record does not contain any instruments which purportedly assign the bank's mortgage to defendant, but, presumably, if such exist, they constitute, at most, a partial assignment, reflective of the $32,500 payment. This is evidenced by the small size of the settlement between the bank and the title company. It is also evidenced by the formula for determining the loss under a mortgage title policy, which is the difference in the market value of the mortgage on the property without the title defect and its value with the defect (5A Warren's Weed, N.Y. Real Prop., Title Ins., §2.06). The amount of loss derived from this formula is clearly less than the amount owed on the mortgage itself.

As section 8 of the conditions of the policy states, rights transferred pursuant to subrogation shall be subordinate to "any remaining interest of the insured [mortgagee]". Resulting in only a partial assignment, the payment of compensation by the insurer to the mortgagee did not eradicate the latter's rights, if any, to seek a deficiency judgment after the foreclosure sale (see Dollar Fed. Sav. & Loan Assn. v. Herbert Kallen, Inc., 66 A.D.2d 793, 410 N.Y.S.2d 1004). If it appears that plaintiff is getting more than it should, because the offset should only be $32,500, this has nothing to do with the title company. Rather, it is a result of the record's silence as to whether the bank obtained a deficiency judgment against the plaintiff. Assuming the bank never obtained a deficiency judgment, defendant cannot use that fact to somehow increase that to which it is subrogated as though it were the one entitled to recover the deficiency. If the bank did obtain a deficiency judgment pursuant to section 1371 of the Real Property Actions and Proceedings Law and has not, up until now, collected on it, presumably, on satisfaction of the judgment to be issued herein, it could have execution.

Defendant's right of subrogation impinges on another issue in this case, already discussed, which is whether or not the measure of loss is plaintiff's equity in the property. Assume that there was a complete loss of title. According to defendant, plaintiff would be entitled, at most, to $65,000, under its title policy. Defendant would, very likely, be subject to a claim from the mortgagee for the full $535,000 of the mortgage title policy. With subrogation, plaintiff would owe defendant the $535,000, the bottom line being that defendant would only be out $65,000 on both policies together, the same as though it had only issued a fee policy. In effect, defendant would be receiving the benefit of two subrogations, one on the mortgage policy, the other a hidden subrogation right in the fee title policy allowing for a *pro tanto* reduction in the fee holder's benefit corresponding to what is owed the mortgagee. With such a scheme, the title company would be the one receiving a double or cumulative benefit, with the fee holder getting less than nothing. Such could hardly be the intent of parties entering into a contract of title insurance!

[The court affirmed the award of damages to plaintiff of $593,850, with a setoff of only $32,500, or a total damage award of $561,350. In addition, the court held that plaintiff was entitled to attorney's fees and to interest on the award for loss in value of the property from 1972, when the city began to dig up St. George Place and Jeanette Avenue and access was lost. The court held that plaintiff could recover the entire amount of attorney's fees and interest, even though these sums caused the total recovery to exceed the face amount of the policy.]

The judgment dated May 4, 1982 should be modified in accordance with this decision.

Part 4

More on Voluntary and Involuntary Transfer: Control of Land Use through "Private" and "Public" Means

Chapter Eight
Nuisances Private and Public

A. An Introduction to the Substantive Law

Page 927. At the end of the last full paragraph, add:

On recovery in trespass for damages caused by air pollutants, see Annot., 2 A.L.R.4th 1054 (1980). In Wilson v. Interlake Steel Co., 32 Cal. 3d 229, 649 P.2d 922, 185 Cal. Rptr. 280 (1982), plaintiff property owners bothered by noise from a steel factory brought an action based on trespass. The court held that noise alone will not support a trespass action, absent some kind of physical invasion or physical damage to property. Intangible intrusions, according to the court, must be dealt with on a nuisance theory.

Page 928. After Problem 3, insert:

NOTE: SOLAR ENERGY AND THE LAW OF NUISANCE

Suppose a homeowner installs a solar collector to help heat her house. Has she a legal right to stop neighboring property owners from obstructing the sun's rays? The law of servitudes may provide one set of answers, and some states have legislation on solar access. See Notes 2 and 3, pages 1003-1004 of the main text. Nuisance law provides another approach to the question. Consider the following case.

PRAH v. MARETTI
Supreme Court of Wisconsin, 1982
108 Wis. 2d 223, 321 N.W.2d 182

ABRAHAMSON, J. This appeal from a judgment of the circuit court for Waukesha county, Max Raskin, circuit judge, was certified to this court by the court of appeals, sec. (Rule) 809.61, Stats.1979-80, as presenting an issue of first impression, namely, whether an owner of a solar-heated residence states a claim upon which relief can be granted when he asserts that his neighbor's proposed construction of a residence (which conforms to existing deed restrictions and local ordinances) interferes with his access to an unobstructed path for sunlight across the neighbor's property. This case thus involves a conflict between one landowner (Glenn Prah, the plaintiff) interested in unobstructed access to sunlight across adjoining property as a natural source of energy and an adjoining landowner (Richard D. Maretti, the defendant) interested in the development of his land.

The circuit court concluded that the plaintiff presented no claim upon which relief could be granted and granted summary judgment for the defendant. We reverse the judgment of the circuit court and remand the cause to the circuit court for further proceedings.

According to the complaint, the plaintiff is the owner of a residence which was constructed during the years 1978-1979. The complaint alleges that the residence has a solar system which includes collectors on the roof to supply energy for heat and hot water and that after the plaintiff built his solar-heated house, the defendant purchased the lot adjacent to and immediately to the south of the plaintiff's lot and commenced planning construction of a home. The complaint further states that when the plaintiff learned of defendant's plans to build the house he advised the defendant that if the house were built at the proposed location, defendant's house would substantially and adversely affect the integrity of plaintiff's solar system and could cause plaintiff other damage. Nevertheless, the defendant began construction. The complaint further alleges that the plaintiff is entitled to "unrestricted use of the sun and its solar power" and demands judgment for injunctive relief and damages.

After filing his complaint, the plaintiff moved for a temporary injunction to restrain and enjoin construction by the defendant. In ruling on that motion the circuit court heard testimony, received affidavits and viewed the site.

The record made on the motion reveals the following additional facts: Plaintiff's home was the first residence built in the subdivision, and although plaintiff did not build his house in the center of the lot it was built in accordance with applicable restrictions. Plaintiff advised defendant that if the defendant's home were built at the proposed site it would cause a shadowing effect on the solar collectors which would reduce the efficiency of the system and possibly damage the system. To avoid these adverse effects, plaintiff requested defendant to locate his home an additional several feet away from the plaintiff's lot line, the exact number being disputed. Plaintiff and defendant failed to reach an agreement on the location of defendant's home before defendant started construction. The Architectural Control Committee of the subdivision and the Planning Commission of the City of Muskego approved the defendant's plans for his home, including its location on the lot. After such approval, the defendant apparently changed the grade of the property without prior notice to the Architectural Control Committee. The problem with defendant's proposed construction, as far as the plaintiff's interests are concerned, arises from a combination of the grade and the distance of defendant's home from the defendant's lot line.

The circuit court denied plaintiff's motion for injunctive relief, declared it would entertain a motion for summary judgment and thereafter entered judgment in favor of the defendant. . . .

The plaintiff presents three legal theories to support his claim that the defendant's continued construction of a home justifies granting him relief: (1) the construction constitutes a common law private nuisance; (2) the construction is prohibited by sec. 844.01, Stats.1979-80;[3a] and (3) the construction interferes with the solar easement plaintiff acquired under the doctrine of prior appropriation.[3b]

As to the claim of private nuisance the circuit court concluded that the law of private nuisance requires the court to make "a comparative evaluation of the conflicting interests and to weigh the gravity of the harm to the plaintiff against the utility of the defendant's conduct." The circuit court concluded: "A comparative evaluation of the conflicting interests, keeping in mind the omissions and commissions of both Prah and Maretti, indicates that defendant's conduct does not cause the gravity of the harm which the plaintiff himself may well have avoided by proper planning." The circuit court also concluded that sec. 844.01 does not apply to a home constructed in accordance with deed and municipal ordinance requirements. Further,

3a. Sec. 844.01, Stats.1979-80, provides:

"(1) Any person owning or claiming an interest in real property may bring an action claiming physical injury to, or interference with, the property or his interest therein; the action may be to redress past injury, to restrain further injury, to abate the source of injury, or for other appropriate relief.

(2) Physical injury includes unprivileged intrusions and encroachments; the injury may be surface, subsurface or suprasurface; the injury may arise from activities on the plaintiff's property, or from activities outside the plaintiff's property which affect plaintiff's property.

(3) Interference with an interest is any activity other than physical injury which lessens the possibility of use or enjoyment of the interest.

(4) The lessening of a security interest without physical injury is not actionable unless such lessening constitutes waste."

We can find no reported cases in which sec. 844.01 has been interpreted and applied, and the parties do not cite any.

3b. Under the doctrine of prior appropriation the first user to appropriate the resource has the right of continued use to the exlusion of others.

The doctrine of prior appropriation has been used by several western states to allocate water, Paug Vik v. Wards Cove, 633 P.2d 1015 (Alaska 1981), and by the New Mexico legislature to allocate solar access, secs. 47-3-1 to 47-3-5, N.M. Stats.1978. See also Note, The Allocation of Sunlight: Solar Rights and the Prior Appropriation Doctrine, 47 Colo. L. Rev. 421 (1976).

the circuit court rejected the prior appropriation doctrine as "an intrusion of judicial egoism over legislative passivity."

We consider first whether the complaint states a claim for relief based on common law private nuisance. This state has long recognized that an owner of land does not have an absolute or unlimited right to use the land in a way which injures the rights of others. The rights of neighboring landowners are relative; the uses by one must not unreasonably impair the uses or enjoyment of the other. VI-A American Law of Property sec. 28.22, pp. 64-65 (1954). When one landowner's use of his or her property unreasonably interferes with another's enjoyment of his or her property, that use is said to be a private nuisance. Hoene v. Milwaukee, 17 Wis. 2d 209, 214, 116 N.W.2d 112 (1962); Metzger v. Hochrein, 107 Wis. 267, 269, 83 N.W. 308 (1900). See also Prosser, Law of Torts sec. 89, p.591 (2d ed. 1971).

The private nuisance doctrine has traditionally been employed in this state to balance the conflicting rights of landowners, and this court has recently adopted the analysis of private nuisance set forth in the Restatement (Second) of Torts. CEW Mgmt. Corp. v. First Federal Savings & Loan Association, 88 Wis. 2d 631, 633, 277 N.W.2d 766 (1979). The Restatement defines private nuisance as "a nontrespassory invasion of another's interest in the private use and enjoyment of land." Restatement (Second) of Torts sec. 821D (1977). The phrase "interest in the private use and enjoyment of land" as used in sec. 821D is broadly defined to include any disturbance of the enjoyment of property. The comment in the Restatement describes the landowner's interest protected by private nuisance law as follows:

> The phrase "interest in the use and enjoyment of land" is used in this Restatement in a broad sense. It comprehends not only the interests that a person may have in the actual present use of land for residential, agricultural, commercial, industrial and other purposes, but also his interests in having the present use value of the land unimpaired by changes in its physical condition. Thus the destruction of trees on vacant land is as much an invasion of the owner's interest in its use and enjoyment as is the destruction of crops or flowers that he is growing on the land for his present use. "Interest in use and enjoyment" also comprehends the pleasure, comfort and enjoyment that a person normally derives from the occupancy of land. Freedom from discomfort and annoyance while using land is often as important to a person as freedom from physical interruption with his use or freedom from detrimental change in the physical condition of the land itself.

Restatement (Second) of Torts, Sec. 821D, Comment *b*, p.101 (1977)

Although the defendant's obstruction of the plaintiff's access to sunlight appears to fall within the Restatement's broad concept of a private nuisance as a nontrespassory invasion of another's interest in the private use and enjoyment of land, the defendant asserts that he has a right to develop his property in compliance with statutes, ordinances and private covenants without regard to the effect of such development upon the plaintiff's access to sunlight. In essence, the defendant is asking this court to hold that the private nuisance doctrine is not applicable in the instant case and that his right to develop his land is a right which is per se superior to his neighbor's interest in access to sunlight. This position is expressed in the maxim "cujus est solum, ejus est usque ad coelum et ad infernos," that is, the owner of land owns up to the sky and down to the center of the earth. The rights of the surface owner are, however, not unlimited. U.S. v. Causby, 328 U.S. 256, 260-1, 66 S. Ct. 1062, 1065, 90 L. Ed. 1206 (1946). See also 114.03, Stats. 1979-80.

The defendant is not completely correct in asserting that the common law did not protect a landowner's access to sunlight across adjoining property. At English common law a landowner could acquire a right to receive sunlight across adjoining land by both express agreement and under the judge-made doctrine of "ancient lights." Under the doctrine of ancient lights if the landowner had received sunlight across adjoining property for a specified period of time, the landowner was entitled to continue to receive unobstructed access to sunlight across the adjoining property. Under the doctrine the landowner acquired a negative prescriptive easement and could prevent the adjoining landowner from obstructing access to light.[3c]

Although American courts have not been as receptive to protecting a landowner's access to sunlight as the English courts, American courts have afforded some protection to a landowner's interest in access to sunlight. American courts honor express easements to sunlight. American courts initially enforced the English common law doctrine of ancient lights, but later every state which considered the doctrine repudiated it as inconsistent with the needs of a developing country. Indeed, for just that reason this court concluded that an easement to light and air over adjacent property could not be created or acquired by prescription and has been unwilling to recognize such an easement by implication. Depner v. United States National Bank, 202 Wis. 405, 408, 232 N.W. 851 (1930); Miller v. Hoeschler, 126 Wis. 263, 268-69, 105 N.W. 790 (1905).

Many jurisdictions in this country have protected a landowner from malicious obstruction of access to light (the spite fence cases) under the common law private nuisance doctrine. If any activity is motivated by malice it lacks utility and the harm it causes others outweighs any social values. VI-A Law of Property sec. 28.28, p.79 (1954). This court was reluctant to protect

---

3c. Pfeiffer, Ancient Lights: Legal Protection of Access to Solar Energy, 68 ABAJ 288 (1982). No American common law state recognizes a landowner's right to acquire an easement of light by prescription. Comment, Solar Lights: Guaranteeing a Place in the Sun, 57 Ore. L. Rev. 94, 112 (1977).

a landowner's interest in sunlight even against a spite fence, only to be overruled by the legislature. Shortly after this court upheld a landowner's right to erect a useless and unsightly sixteen-foot spite fence four feet from his neighbor's windows, Metzger v. Hochrein, 107 Wis. 267, 83 N.W. 308 (1900), the legislature enacted a law specifically defining a spite fence as an actionable private nuisance. Thus a landowner's interest in sunlight has been protected in this country by common law private nuisance law at least in the narrow context of the modern American rule invalidating spite fences. See, e.g., Sundowner, Inc. v. King, 95 Idaho 367, 509 P.2d 785 (1973); Restatement (Second) of Torts, sec. 829 (1977).

This court's reluctance in the nineteenth and early part of the twentieth century to provide broader protection for a landowner's access to sunlight was premised on three policy considerations. First, the right of landowners to use their property as they wished, as long as they did not cause physical damage to a neighbor, was jealously guarded. Metzger v. Hochrein, 107 Wis. 267, 272, 83 N.W. 308 (1900).

Second, sunlight was valued only for aesthetic enjoyment or as illumination. Since artificial light could be used for illumination, loss of sunlight was at most a personal annoyance which was given little, if any weight by society.

Third, society had a significant interest in not restricting or impeding land development. Dillman v. Hoffman, 38 Wis. 559, 574 (1875). This court repeatedly emphasized that in the growth period of the nineteenth and early twentieth centuries change is to be expected and is essential to property and that recognition of a right to sunlight would hinder property development. The court expressed this concept as follows:

> As the city grows, large grounds appurtenant to residences must be cut up to supply more residences. . . . The cistern, the outhouse, the cesspool, and the private drain must disappear in deference to the public waterworks and sewer; the terrace and the garden, to the need for more complete occupancy. . . . Strict limitation [on the recognition of easements of light and air over adjacent premises is] in accord with the popular conception upon which real estate has been and is daily being conveyed in Wisconsin and to be essential to easy and rapid development at least of our municipalities.

Miller v. Hoeschler, *supra*, 126 Wis. at 268, 270, 105 N.W. 790; quoted with approval in Depner, *supra*, 202 Wis. at 409, 232 N.W. 851.

Considering these three policies, this court concluded that in the absence of an express agreement granting access to sunlight, a landowner's obstruction of another's access to sunlight was not actionable. Miller v. Hoeschler, *supra*, 126 Wis. at 271, 105 N.W. 790; Depner v. United States National Bank, *supra*, 202 Wis. at 410, 232 N.W. 851. These three policies are no longer fully accepted or applicable. They reflect factual circumstances and social priorities that are now obsolete.

First, society has increasingly regulated the use of land by the landowner for the general welfare. Euclid v. Ambler Realty Co., 272 U.S. 365, 47 S. Ct. 114, 71 L.Ed. 303 (1926); Just v. Marinette, 56 Wis. 2d 7, 201 N.W.2d 761 (1972).

Second, access to sunlight has taken on a new significance in recent years. In this case the plaintiff seeks to protect access to sunlight, not for aesthetic reasons or as a source of illumination but as a source of energy. Access to sunlight as an energy source is of significance both to the landowner who invests in solar collectors and to a society which has an interest in developing alternative sources of energy.

Third, the policy of favoring unhindered private development in an expanding economy is no longer in harmony with the realities of our society. State v. Deetz, 66 Wis. 2d 1, 224 N.W.2d 407 (1974). The need for easy and rapid development is not as great today as it once was, while our perception of the value of sunlight as a source of energy has increased significantly.

Courts should not implement obsolete policies that have lost their vigor over the course of the years. The law of private nuisance is better suited to resolve landowners' disputes about property development in the 1980's than is a rigid rule which does not recognize a landowner's interest in access to sunlight. As we said in Ballstadt v. Pagel, 202 Wis. 484, 489, 232 N.W. 862 (1930), "What is regarded in law as constituting a nuisance in modern times would no doubt have been tolerated without question in former times." We read State v. Deetz, 66 Wis. 2d 1, 224 N.W.2d 407 (1974), as an endorsement of the application of common law nuisance to situations involving the conflicting interests of landowners and as rejecting per se exclusions to the nuisance law reasonable use doctrine.

In *Deetz* the court abandoned the rigid common law common enemy rule with respect to surface water and adopted the private nuisance reasonable use rule, namely that the landowner is subject to liability if his or her interference with the flow of surface waters unreasonably invades a neighbor's interest in the use and enjoyment of land. Restatement (Second) of Torts, secs. 822, 826, 829 (1977). This court concluded that the common enemy rule which served society "well in the days of burgeoning national expansion of the mid-nineteenth and early-twentieth centuries" should be abandoned because it was no longer "in harmony with the realities of our society." *Deetz, supra,* 66 Wis. 2d at 14-15, 224 N.W.2d 407. We recognized in *Deetz* that common law rules adapt to changing social values and conditions.

Yet the defendant would have us ignore the flexible private nuisance law as a means of resolving the dispute between the landowners in this case and would have us adopt an approach, already abandoned in *Deetz,* of favoring the unrestricted development of land and of applying a rigid and inflexible rule protecting his right to build on his land and disregarding any interest of the plaintiff in the use and enjoyment of his land. This we refuse to do.[3d]

Private nuisance law, the law traditionally used to adjudicate conflicts between private landowners, has the flexibility to protect both a landowner's right of access to sunlight and another landowner's right to develop land. Private nuisance law is better suited to regulate access to sunlight in modern society and is more in harmony with legislative policy and the prior decisions of this court than is an inflexible doctrine of non-recognition of any interest in access to sunlight across adjoining land.

We therefore hold that private nuisance law, that is, the reasonable use doctrine as set forth in the Restatement, is applicable to the instant case. Recognition of a nuisance claim for unreasonable obstruction of access to sunlight will not prevent land development or unduly hinder the use of adjoining land. It will promote the reasonable use and enjoyment of land in a manner suitable to the 1980's. That obstruction of access to light might be found to constitute a nuisance in certain circumstances does not mean that it will be or must be found to constitute a nuisance under all circumstances. The result in each case depends on whether the conduct complained of is unreasonable.

Accordingly we hold that the plaintiff in this case has stated a claim under which relief can be granted. Nonetheless we do not determine whether the plaintiff in this case is entitled to relief. In order to be entitled to relief the

---

[3d]. Defendant's position that a landowner's interest in access to sunlight across adjoining land is not "legally enforceable" and is therefore excluded per se from private nuisance law was adopted in Fontainebleau Hotel Corp. v. Forty-five Twenty-five, Inc., 114 So. 2d 357 (Fla. App. 1959), *cert. den.* 117 So. 2d 842 (Fla.1960). The Florida district court of appeals permitted construction of a building which cast a shadow on a neighboring hotel's swimming pool. The court asserted that nuisance law protects only those interests "which [are] recognized and protected by law," and that there is no legally recognized or protected right to access to sunlight. A property owner does not, said the Florida court, in the absence of a contract or statute, acquire a presumptive or implied right to the free flow of light and air across adjoining land. The Florida court then concluded that a lawful structure which causes injury to another by cutting off light and air — whether or not erected partly for spitspite — does not give rise to a cause of action for damages or for an injunction. See also People ex rel. Hoogasian v. Sears, Roebuck & Co., 52 Ill. 2d 301, 287 N.E.2d 677 (1972).

We do not find the reasoning of *Fountainebleau* persuasive. The court leaped from rejecting an easement by prescription (the doctrine of ancient lights) and an easement by implication to the conclusion that there is no right to protection from obstruction of access to sunlight. The court's statement that a landowner has no right to light should be the conclusion, not its initial premise. The court did not explain why an owner's interest in unobstructed light should not be protected or in what manner an owner's interest in unobstructed sunlight differs from an owner's interest in being free from obtrusive noises or smells or differs from an owner's interest in unobstructed use of water. The recognition of a per se exception to private nuisance law may invite unreasonable behavior. [The *Fontainebleau* case appears at page 998 of the main text. — Eds.]

plaintiff must prove the elements required to establish actionable nuisance, and the conduct of the defendant herein must be judged by the reasonable use doctrine.

The defendant asserts that even if we hold that the private nuisance doctrine applies to obstruction of access to sunlight across adjoining land, the circuit court's granting of summary judgment should be affirmed.

Although the memorandum decision of the circuit court in the instant case is unclear, it appears that the circuit court recognized that the common law private nuisance doctrine was applicable but concluded that defendant's conduct was not unreasonable. The circuit court apparently attempted to balance the utility of the defendant's conduct with the gravity of the harm. Sec. 826, Restatement (Second) of Torts (1977). The defendant urges us to accept the circuit court's balance as adequate. We decline to do so.

The circuit court concluded that because the defendant's proposed house was in conformity with zoning regulations, building codes and deed restrictions, the defendant's use of the land was reasonable. This court has concluded that a landowner's compliance with zoning laws does not automatically bar a nuisance claim. Compliance with the law "is not the controlling factor, though it is, of course, entitled to some weight." Bie v. Ingersoll, 27 Wis. 2d 490, 495, 135 N.W.2d 250 (1965). The circuit court also concluded that the plaintiff could have avoided any harm by locating his own house in a better place. Again, plaintiff's ability to avoid the harm is a relevant but not a conclusive factor. See secs. 826, 827, 828, Restatement (Second) of Torts (1977).

Furthermore, our examination of the record leads us to conclude that the record does not furnish an adequate basis for the circuit court to apply the proper legal principles on summary judgment. The application of the reasonable use standard in nuisance cases normally requires a full exposition of all underlying facts and circumstances. Too little is known in this case of such matters as the extent of the harm to the plaintiff, the suitability of solar heat in that neighborhood, the availability of remedies to the plaintiff, and the costs to the defendant of avoiding the harm. Summary judgment is not an appropriate procedural vehicle in this case when the circuit court must weigh evidence which has not been presented at trial. 6 (Pt. 2) Moore's *Federal Practice*, 56.15[7], pp. 56-638 (1982); 10 Wright and Miller, *Federal Practice and Procedure — Civil*, secs. 2729, 2731 (1973).

Because the plaintiff has stated a claim of common law private nuisance upon which relief can be granted, the judgment of the circuit court must be reversed. We need not, and do not, reach the question of whether the complaint states a claim under sec. 844.01, Stats.1979-80, or under the doctrine of prior appropriation. Attoe v. Madison Professional Policemen's Assoc., 79 Wis. 2d 199, 205, 255 N.W.2d 489 (1977).

For the reasons set forth, we reverse the judgment of the circuit court dismissing the complaint and remand the matter to circuit court for further proceedings not inconsistent with this opinion.

The judgment of the circuit court is reversed and the cause remanded for proceedings not inconsistent with this opinion.

CALLOW, J. (dissenting). The majority has adopted the Restatement's reasonable use doctrine to grant an owner of a solar heated home a cause of action against his neighbor who, in acting entirely within the applicable ordinances and statutes, seeks to design and build his home in such a location that it may, at various times during the day, shade the plaintiff's solar collector, thereby impeding the efficiency of his heating system during several months of the year. Because I believe the facts of this case clearly reveal that a cause of action for private nuisance will not lie, I dissent.

The majority arrives at its conclusion that the common law private nuisance doctrine is applicable by analogizing this situation with the spite fence cases which protect a landowner from *malicious* obstruction of access to light. . . .

The majority then concludes that this court's past reluctance to extend protection to a landowner's access to sunlight beyond the spite fence cases is based on obsolete policies which have lost their vigor over the course of the years. The three obsolete policies cited by the majority are: (1) Right of landowners to use their property as they desire as long as no physical damage is done to a neighbor; (2) In the past, sunlight was valued only for aesthetic value, not a source of energy; and (3) Society has a significant interest in not impeding land development. . . . The majority has failed to convince me that these policies are obsolete. . . . I firmly believe that a landowner's right to use his property within the limits of ordinances, statutes, and restrictions of record where such use is necessary to serve his legitimate needs is a fundamental precept of a free society which this court should strive to uphold. . . .

I know of no cases repudiating policies favoring the right of a landowner to use his property as he lawfully desires or which declare such policies are "no longer fully accepted or applicable" in this context.[3e] The right of a property owner to lawful enjoyment of his property should be vigorously protected, particularly in those cases where the adjacent property owner

---

[3e]. Perhaps one reason courts have been hesitant to recognize a cause of action for solar blockage is that such a suit would normally only occur between two abutting landowners, and it is hoped that neighbors will compromise and reach agreement between themselves. This has, undoubtedly, been done in a large percentage of cases. To now recognize a cause of action for solar blockage may thwart a policy of compromise between neighbors. See Williams, Solar Access and Property Rights: A Maverick Analysis, 11 Conn. L. Rev. 430, 441-42 (1979). See also S. Kraemer, Solar Law, 138 (1978) ("[a] deterring factor to the use of private nuisance to assure access to direct sunlight is the resultant litigation between neighbors").

could have insulated himself from the alleged problem by acquiring the land as a defense to the potential problem or by provident use of his own property.

The majority concludes that sunlight has not heretofore been accorded the status of a source of energy, and consequently it has taken on a new significance in recent years. Solar energy for home heating is at this time sparingly used and of questionable economic value because solar collectors are not mass produced, and consequently, they are very costly. Their limited efficiency may explain the lack of production.

Regarding the third policy the majority apparently believes is obsolete (that society has a significant interest in not restricting land development), it cites State v. Deetz, 66 Wis. 2d 1, 224 N.W.2d 407 (1974). I concede the law may be tending to recognize the value of aesthetics over increased volume development and that an individual may not use his land in such a way as to harm the *public*. The instant case, however, deals with a *private* benefit. I note that this court in *Deetz* stated: "The reasonable use rule retains . . . a policy of favoring land improvement and development." *Id.* at 20, 224 N.W.2d 407. See also *id.* at 15, 224 N.W.2d 407. Accord Moritz v. Buglewicz, 187 Neb. 819, 194 N.W.2d 215 (1972). I find it significant that community planners are dealing with this country's continued population growth and building revitalization where "[t]he number of households is expected to reach almost 100 million by the end of the decade; that would be 34 percent higher than the number in 1970." F. Strom, 1981 Zoning and Planning Law Handbook, sec. 22.02[3], 396 (1981). It is clear that community planners are acutely aware of the present housing shortages, particularly among those two groups with limited financial resources, the young and the elderly. *Id.* While the majority's policy arguments may be directed to a cause of action for public nuisance, we are presented with a private nuisance case which I believe is distinguishable in this regard.[3f]

I would submit that any policy decisions in this area are best left for the legislature. . . .

The legislature has recently acted in this area. Chapter 354, Laws of 1981

3f. I am amused at the majority's contention that what constitutes a nuisance today would have been accepted without question in earlier times. This calls to mind the fact that, in early days of travel by horses, the first automobiles were considered nuisances. Later, when automobile travel became developed, the horse became the nuisance. Ellickson, Alternatives to Zoning: Covenants, Nuisance Rules, and Fines as Land Use Controls, 40 U. Chi. L. Rev. 681, 731 (1973). This makes me wonder if we are examining the proper nuisance in the case before us. In other words, could it be said that the solar energy user is creating the nuisance when others must conform their homes to accommodate his use? I note that solar panel glare may temporarily blind automobile drivers, reflect into adjacent buildings causing excessive heat, and otherwise irritate neighbors. Certainly in these instances the solar heating system constitutes the nuisance.

(effective May 7, 1982), was enacted to provide the underlying legislation enabling local governments to enact ordinances establishing procedures for guaranteeing access to sunlight. This court's intrusion into an area where legislative action is being taken is unwarranted, and it may undermine a legislative scheme for orderly development not yet fully operational. . . .

. . . This legislative scheme would deal with the type of problem presented in the present case and precludes the need for judicial activism in this area.

I examine with interest the definition of nuisance as set out in the Restatement (Second) of Torts and adopted in the majority opinion: "A private nuisance is a nontrespassory *invasion* of another's interest in the private use and enjoyment of land." Restatement (Second) of Torts sec. 821D (1977) (emphasis added). The majority believes that the defendant's obstruction of the plaintiff's access to sunlight falls within the broad definition of "use and enjoyment of land." I do not believe the defendant's "obstruction" of the plaintiff's access to sunlight falls within the definition of "invasion," as it applies to the private use and enjoyment of land. Invasion is typically synonymous with "entry," "attack," "penetration," "hostile entrance," "the incoming or spread of something unusually hurtful." Webster's Third International Dictionary, 1188 (1966). Most of the nuisance cases arising under this definition involve noxious odors, smoke, blasting, flooding, or *excessive light* invading the plaintiff's right to the use or enjoyment of his property. See Prosser, Law of Torts, sec. 89, 591-92 (4th ed. 1971). See Williams, Solar Access and Property Rights: A Maverick Analysis, 11 Conn. L. Rev. at 441 (there are significant practical differences between dust and noise, on the one hand, and solar access blockage on the other). Clearly, an owner who merely builds his home in complaince with all building code and municipal regulations is not "invading" another's right to the use and enjoyment of his property. To say so is to acknowledge that all construction may be an "invasion" because all construction has some restrictive impact on adjacent land. A "view," for example, is modified by any construction simply because it is there.

In order for a nuisance to be actionable in the instant case, the defendant's conduct must be "intentional and unreasonable." It is impossible for me to accept the majority's conclusion that Mr. Maretti, in lawfully seeking to construct his home, may be intentionally and unreasonably interfering with the plaintiff's access to sunlight. In addressing the "unreasonableness" component of the actor's conduct, it is important to note that "[t]here is liability for a nuisance only to those to whom it causes significant harm, of a kind that would be suffered by a normal person in the community or by property in normal condition and used for a normal purpose." Restatement (Second) of Torts sec. 821F (1979). The comments to the Restatement further reveal that "[if] normal persons in that locality would not be substantially annoyed or disturbed by the situation, then the invasion is not a significant one, even though the idiosyncracies of the particular plaintiff may make it unendurable to him." *Id.* Comment d. . . .

I conclude that plaintiff's solar heating system is an unusually sensitive use. In other words, the defendant's proposed construction of his home, under ordinary circumstances, would not interfere with the use and enjoyment of the usual person's property. *See* W. Prosser, *supra*, sec. 87 at 578-79. "The plaintiff cannot, by devoting his own land to an unusually sensitive use, such as a drive-in motion picture theater easily affected by light, make a nuisance out of conduct of the adjoining defendant which would otherwise be harmless." *Id.* at 579 (footnote omitted).[3g] . . .

I believe the facts of the instant controversy present the classic case of the owner of a solar collector who fails to take any action to protect his investment. There is nothing in the record to indicate that Mr. Prah disclosed his situation to Mr. Maretti prior to Maretti's purchase of the lot or attempted to secure protection for his solar collector prior to Maretti's submission of his building plans to the architectural committee. Such inaction should be considered a significant factor in determining whether a cause of action exists.

The majority's failure to recognize the need for notice may perpetuate a vicious cycle. Maretti may feel compelled to sell his lot because of Prah's solar collector's interference with his plans to build his family home. If so, Maretti will not be obliged to inform prospective purchasers of the problem. Certainly, such information will reduce the value of his land. If the presence of collectors is sufficient notice, it cannot be said that the seller of the lot has a duty to disclose information peculiarly within his knowledge. I do not believe that an adjacent lot owner should be obliged to experience the substantial economic loss resulting from the lot being rendered unbuildable by the contour of the land as it relates to the location and design of the adjoining home using solar collectors.[3h]

3g. Amicus curiae United States of America in its brief to this court advances the proposition that even a sensitive use is entitled to protection from unreasonable interference. Amicus analogizes to several "mink cases" which involve negligence actions. See Bell v. Gray-Robinson Construction Company, 265 Wis. 652, 62 N.W.2d 390 (1954); Maitland v. Twin City Aviation Corp., 254 Wis. 541, 37 N.W.2d 74 (1949). A thorough reading of these decisions reveals that they are clearly distinguishable from the case at bar. No cases have been cited in this jurisdiction which limit this.

I note that the federal government supports the plaintiff's position in the instant case. If solar energy is in the national interest, federal legislation should be enacted.

3h. Mr. Prah could have avoided this litigation by building his own home in the center of his lot instead of only ten feet from the Maretti lot line and/or by purchasing the adjoining lot for his own protection. Mr. Maretti has already moved the proposed location of his home over an additional ten feet to accommodate Mr. Prah's solar collector, and he testified that moving the home any further would interfere with his view of the lake on which the property faces.

I am troubled by the majority's apparent retrospective application of its decision. I note that the court in *Deetz* saw the wisdom and fairness in rendering a prospective decision. 66 Wis. 2d at 24, 224 N.W.2d 407. Surely, a decision such as this should be accorded prospective status. Creating the cause of action after the fact results in such unfair surprise and hardship to property owners such as Maretti.

Because I do not believe that the facts of the present case give rise to a cause of action for private nuisance, I dissent.

NOTE

Like the sun itself, Prah v. Maretti has generated much heat and light. The case is noted — sometimes favorably, sometimes not — in 1984 Det. C.L. Rev. 1449 (1983); 11 Ecology L.Q. 47 (1983); 48 Mo. L. Rev. 769 (1983); 78 Nw. U.L. Rev. 861 (1984); 29 Wayne L. Rev. 1449 (1983); 1983 Wis. L. Rev. 1263.

Page 929. At the end of the last full paragraph on the page, add:

But see Friendswood Development Co. v. Smith-Southwest Industries, reprinted below.

Page 930. After line 2, insert:

FRIENDSWOOD DEVELOPMENT CO. v. SMITH-SOUTHWEST INDUSTRIES

Supreme Court of Texas, 1978
576 S.W.2d 21

DANIEL, J. The question in this case is whether landowners who withdrew percolating ground waters from wells located on their own land are liable for subsidence which resulted on lands of others in the same general area.

Smith-Southwest Industries and other landowners located in the Seabrook and Clear Lake area of Harris County brought this class action in 1973 against Friendswood Development Company and its corporate parent, Exxon Corporation, alleging that severe subsidence of their lands was caused by the defendants' past and continuing withdrawals of vast quantities of underground water from wells on defendants' nearby lands. Friendswood, alleged to be the operator of the wells, joined as third party defendants numerous parties alleged to be withdrawing ground water in the same general area. Friendswood and Exxon moved for a summary judgment against the plaintiffs, and it was granted by the trial court along with denial of relief in the third party actions.

The trial court followed a long-established common law rule that, in the absence of willful waste or malicious injury, a landowner has the right to withdraw ground waters from wells located on his own land without liability for resulting damage to his neighbor's land. The Court of Civil Appeals reversed and remanded, holding that plaintiffs' petition stated a cause of action in nuisance and negligence and that the summary judgment record raises genuine issues of material fact with regard thereto. 546 S.W.2d 890. We reverse the judgment of the Court of Civil Appeals and affirm the judgment of the trial court.

Our decision results from what we conceive to be our duty to apply a rule of property law as it existed during the time of the actions complained of in this suit, even though we disagree with certain aspects of the existing rule. As to future subsidence caused by wells hereinafter drilled or produced, this Court, in the manner hereinafter set forth, will recognize and apply the law of negligence along with willful waste and malicious injury as limitations on the present rule applicable to subsidence resulting from withdrawal of underground waters.

ALLEGATIONS AND SUMMARY JUDGMENT PROOF

The petition of Smith-Southwest, the name by which all of the plaintiffs will be identified, recites that plaintiffs are landowners in the area of Seabrook and Clear Lake, and as a class include all owners of fee simple and leasehold estates along the west bank of Galveston Bay from the north dike of the Houston Yacht Club, following the shore line south to the mouth of Clear Creek and inclusive of the entire shore line of Clear Lake, Armand's Bayou, and Taylor Bayou from the shore line to a contour line with elevation 15 feet above the shore line, except the land owned by the defendants.

The trial court had before it depositions, interrogatories, affidavits and exhibits which showed rather clearly that Friendswood had pumped large amounts of subsurface waters from its own property for sale primarily to industrial users in the Bayport industrial area developed by Friendswood and Exxon. These wells were drilled from 1964 through 1971, even though previous engineering reports to defendants showed that production therefrom would result in a certain amount of land subsidence in the area. Plaintiffs alleged that the wells were negligently spaced too close together, too near the common boundary of lands owned by plaintiffs and defendants, and that excessive quantities were produced with knowledge that this would cause subsidence and flooding of plaintiffs' lands. Plaintiffs alleged that this extensive withdrawal of ground water proximately caused the sinking and loss of elevation above mean sea level of their property and the property of others similarly situated along the shores of Galveston Bay and Clear Lake, resulting in the erosion and flooding of their lands and damage to their residences, businesses and improvements. Plaintiffs further allege that the manner in which Friendswood Development Company continues to use its property for the withdrawal and sale of large amounts of fresh water to commercial users on other lands constitutes a continuing nuisance and permanent loss and damage to their property.

The defendants, Friendswood Development Company and its parent company, Exxon, are sought to be held jointly liable for the damages alleged in this case on the theory that they jointly planned and pursued the operations complained of. Among other defenses, Friendswood and Exxon contend that subsidence was a problem in the area before their operations began and that owners of other water wells throughout Harris and Galveston Counties caused or contributed to the subsidence. Friendswood's third party action for contribution and indemnity was filed against twenty-two companies and municipalities in Harris and Galveston Counties, alleging that they contributed to any existing subsidence by pumping large quantities of ground water from the common aquifers underlying the lands in question. Plaintiffs concede that subsidence in the area complained of was known to be a "potential problem" before defendants' operations began, but they allege that Friendswood and Exxon knew that the problem "would be severely aggravated" by the withdrawals which the companies contemplated. There was summary judgment proof of such knowledge and aggravation.

Reports in the record and publications of official agencies reflect that land subsidence in Harris County is not peculiar to or confined within the Galveston Bay and Clear Creek areas described in plaintiffs' petition. Rather it is a problem which has existed for many years in Harris and Galveston Counties. Harris County alone had 2,635 ground water wells in the inventory compiled by the U.S. Geological Survey in cooperation with the Texas Water Development Board in 1972. The Chicot and Evangeline aquifers underlie the Houston-Galveston region, which includes all of Harris and Galveston Counties and parts of adjacent counties. These two aquifers furnish all of the ground water pumped in the Houston-Galveston region, according to the U.S. Geological Report prepared by R.K. Gabrysch and C. W. Bonnet in 1974. This report states that water level declines of as much as 200 feet have resulted in wells completed in the Chicot aquifer and as much as 325 feet in the Evangeline aquifer during 1943-73, and "the declines in artesian pressures have resulted in a pronounced regional subsidence of the land surface." It states that the area in which there has been subsidence of one foot or more has increased from 350 square miles in 1954 to about 2,500 square miles in 1973. The contour lines of this area encompass practically all of Harris and Galveston Counties and include all of the principal areas of ground water withdrawals. Maps in the report indicate that the land and wells involved in this suit are in or near the "Johnson

Space Center Area," where the land surface subsided about 2.12 feet between 1964 and 1973.

The general and widespread problem of subsidence in Harris and Galveston Counties has been considered in numerous other writings, and more notably by action of the Legislature, which created the Harris-Galveston Coastal Subsidence District in 1975. This is a comprehensive measure "to provide for the regulation of the withdrawal of ground water within the boundaries of the district for the purpose of ending subsidence which contributes to or precipitates flooding, inundation, or overflow of any area within the district. . . ." It includes all of Harris and Galveston Counties and provides for a board of fifteen members with the power to grant or decline permits for new wells, regulate spacing and production, require metering devices, and adopt any rules necessary to prevent further subsidence.

The magnitude of the problem has been reviewed in depth because it is relevant to our determination of whether existing rules of law are applicable and appropriate, or whether new rules should be adopted by this Court or recommended for consideration by the Legislature.

NATURE OF PLAINTIFF'S ACTION

Plaintiffs have alleged an action in tort based upon the general rule that a landowner has a duty not to use his property so as to injure others — *sic utere tuo ut alienum non laedas.* Storey v. Central Hide & Rendering Co., 148 Tex. 509, 226 S.W.2d 615 (1950); Turner v. Big Lake Oil Co., 128 Tex. 155, 96 S.W.2d 221 (1936); Gulf, C. & S.F. Ry. Co. v. Oakes, 94 Tex. 155, 58 S.W. 999 (1900). The Court of Civil Appeals cited the above cases and this general rule of tort law in holding that plaintiffs were entitled to a trial on the allegations of nuisance and negligence. The problem is that those cases, none of which related to ground water withdrawals, involved liability for the *unreasonable use* of correlative property rights or the balancing of legal and equitable rights between property owners. This is a concept which was deliberately rejected with respect to withdrawals of underground water when this Court adopted the common law rule that such rights are not correlative, but are absolute, and thus are not subject to the conflicting *"reasonable use"* rule. Houston & T. C. Ry. Co. v. East, 98 Tex. 146, 81 S.W. 279 (1904).

Plaintiffs insist that this is not a case involving conflicting claims to the ownership or nontortuous use of water and that, therefore, the "archaic and awkward" common law rule adopted in *East* as to "absolute" ownership should not insulate the defendants from damages due to nuisance in fact or negligence in the manner by which they made use of their property. This is, in effect, a contention that the "reasonable use" doctrine should apply to ground water the same as it does to other real property.

The plaintiff in *East* argued for the "reasonable use" rule in that case, and it was adopted by the Court of Civil Appeals. East v. Houston & T. C. Ry. Co., 77 S.W. 646 (Tex. Civ. App. 1903, error granted). In that case the railroad company, with full knowledge of the long existence of Mr. East's small shallow well on his homestead, dug a well twenty feet in diameter and 66 feet deep on its own adjacent property, from which it pumped 25,000 gallons of water per day. This resulted in lowering the water level on plaintiff's land and drying up his well. The trial court found that the railroad's well was not a reasonable use of its property, and that plaintiff *and his land* had sustained damage in the sum of $206.00. Nevertheless, the trial court granted judgment for the railroad. The Court of Civil Appeals reversed and rendered judgment in favor of East. It followed what has since become known as the "reasonable use" or "American rule" as set forth in Bassett v. Salisbury Mfg. Co., 43 N.H. 569, 82 Am. Dec. 179 (1862), which held that the right of a landowner to draw underground water from his land was not absolute, but limited to the amount necessary for the reasonable use of his land, and that the rights of adjoining landowners are correlative and limited to reasonable use. The court also noted the contrary English doctrine laid down in Acton v. Blundell, 12 M. & W. 324, 152 E.R. 1223 (Ex. 1843), that, "if a man digs a well on his own field and thereby drains his neighbor's, he may do so unless he does it maliciously." The court said that "to apply that rule under the facts shown here would shock our sense of justice."

ADOPTION OF THE COMMON LAW RULE OF ABSOLUTE OWNERSHIP

Thus, on the appeal of the *East* case to this Court, the conflicting aspects of the "reasonable use" rule and the common law rule, later referred to as the "English rule" or "absolute ownership rule," were clearly presented. This Court discussed both rules and made a deliberate choice of the common law rule as announced in Acton v. Blundell, *supra*, reciting that it had been followed since 1843 in the courts of England "and probably by all the courts of last resort in this country before which the [subject] has come, except the Supreme Court of New Hampshire." Houston & T. C. Ry. Co. v. East, 98 Tex. 146, 81 S.W. 279, 280 (1904). In reversing the Court of Civil Appeals and rejecting the "reasonable use" rule, this Court adopted the absolute ownership doctrine of underground percolating waters. It cited approvingly the language of the Supreme Court of Ohio in Frazier v. Brown, 12 Ohio St. 294 (1861): "In the absence of express contract and a positive authorized legislation, as between proprietors of adjoining land, the law recognizes no correlative rights in respect to underground water percolating, oozing, or filtrating through the earth; and this mainly from considerations of public policy. . . ."[3i]

[3i]. The public policy considerations were said to be (1) "because the existence, origin, movement and course of such waters, . . . are so secret, occult and concealed that an attempt to administer any set of legal rules in respect to them would be involved in hopeless uncertainty, and would, therefore, be practically impossible"; and (2) "because any such recognition of correlative rights would interfere, to the material detriment of the commonwealth, with drainage and agriculture, mining, . . ." etc. 81 S.W. 279 at p.281. . . .

In holding that the owner may withdraw water from beneath his land without liability for lowering the water table and thus damaging his neighbor's well and land, the Court mentioned only waste and malice as possible limitations to the rule. Absent these, the Court clearly embraced the doctrine stated in Acton v. Blundell, *supra*, that this type of damage "falls within the description damnum absque injuria, which cannot become the ground of action." This legal maxim denotes a loss without injury in the legal sense, that is, without the invasion of a legal right or the violation of a legal duty. Langbrook Properties, Ltd. v. Surrey County Council, 3 All E.R. 1424 (Ch. 1969). In *Langbrook*, which was an action for subsidence caused by withdrawal of ground water, the court held that the law of negligence and nuisance did not apply under the English rule because pumping of the water was lawful and there was no duty to protect against the injury. We have been cited no case from a jurisdiction which adheres to the English rule in which actions in tort for subsidence have been recognized.

The English rule of so-called "absolute ownership" was applied by this Court in Texas Co. v. Burkett, 117 Tex. 16, 296 S.W. 273 (1927), which held that a landowner has the absolute right to sell percolating ground water for industrial purposes off the land. At a time when the trend in other jurisdictions was away from the English rule and toward the "reasonable use" rule, the English rule was reaffirmed by this Court in City of Corpus Christi v. City of Pleasanton, 154 Tex. 289, 276 S.W.2d 798 (1955). The Court said:

> With both rules before it, this Court in 1904 adopted, unequivocally, the "English" or "Common Law" rule. Houston & T. C. R. Co. v. East, 98 Tex. 146, 81 S.W. 279, 280, 66 L.R.A. 738, 107 Am. St. Rep. 620. The opinion in the case shows quite clearly that the court weighed the merits of the two rules — "The practical reasons upon which the courts base their conclusions [applying the 'English' rule] fully meet the more theoretical view of the New Hampshire Court [applying the 'American' rule] and satisfy us of the necessity of the doctrine" — and, whether wisely or unwisely, made a deliberate choice....
>
> Having adopted the "English" rule it may be assumed that the court adopted it with only such limitations as existed in the common law. What were these limitations? About the only limitations applied by those jurisdictions retaining the "English" rule are that the owner may not maliciously take water for the sole purpose of injuring his neighbor, 55 A.L.R. 1395-1398; 67 C.J., sec. 257, p.840; or wantonly and willfully waste it. 56 Am. Jur., sec. 119, p.602; Stillwater Water Co. v. Farmer, 89 Minn. 58, 93 N.W. 907, 60 L.R.A. 875....

For similar recognition that percolating ground waters belong to the landowner and may be produced by him at his will, absent waste or malice, see Pecos County Water Control & Imp. Dist. No. 1 v. Williams, 271 S.W.2d 503 (Tex. Civ. App. 1954, *writ ref'd n. r. e.*), which was pending in this Court simultaneously with the *Corpus Christi* case, *supra*; City of Altus v. Carr, 255

F. Supp. 828 (W.D. Tex.1966), *aff'd mem.* Carr v. City of Altus, 385 U.S. 35, 87 S. Ct. 240, 17 L. Ed. 2d 34 (1966); and U.S. v. Shurbet, 347 F.2d 103 (5th Cir. 1965). See also Brown v. Humble Oil & Ref. Co., 126 Tex. 296, 83 S.W.2d 935 (1935), one of the basic cases recognizing private ownership of oil and gas in place, which cites *East* as the earliest case establishing the "law of capture" in Texas. Other writers have traced both the Texas ownership and capture theories to the English rule relating to underground percolating waters, and it is interesting to note in this connection that the courts did not attempt to afford protection against the rule of capture of oil and gas until the Legislature enacted policy guidelines for the prevention of waste and protection of correlative rights. By the same token, it has been suggested that regulation of ground water production is primarily a legislative, not a judicial problem.

As heretofore mentioned in 1975 the Legislature undertook to retard further subsidence in Harris and Galveston Counties by creating a subsidence district with power to prevent future well spacing and excessive pumping of the nature alleged to have occurred in this case. Previously, in 1949 the Legislature provided for the creation of districts for the purpose of "conservation, preservation, protection, recharging, and prevention of waste of underground water. . . ." In 1973, the Legislature added to such purposes the authority "to control subsidence caused by withdrawal of water. . . ."

It is of some importance to note that in the laws authorizing these regulatory Underground Water Districts and the Harris-Galveston Coastal Subsidence District, the Legislature specifically confirmed private ownership of underground water. It provided: "The ownership and rights of the owner of land and his lessees and assigns in underground water are hereby recognized, and nothing in this Act shall be construed as depriving or divesting the owner or his lessees and assigns of the ownership or rights . . . ," subject only to the regulatory rules to be promulgated by the districts. See Vernon's Tex. Water Code Ann. §52.002 and Sec. 29, Ch. 284, Acts 64 Leg. 1975.

SUBSIDENCE CASES UNDER THE COMMON LAW RULE

Although the *East, Corpus Christi,* and *Williams* cases involved damages to wells and lands of the plaintiffs because the water tables beneath their lands were lowered by ground water withdrawals of the defendants, none of these nor any other Texas case has dealt specifically with land subsidence resulting from such pumping of underground waters. In other jurisdictions adhering to the English ground water rule, liability for neighboring land subsidence has been denied. Langbrook Properties, Ltd. v. Surrey County Council, [1969] 3 All E.R. 1424 (Ch. 1969); New York Continental Jewell Filtration Co. v. Jones, 37 App. D.C. 511 (D.C. Cir. 1911); English v. Metropolitan Water Board, 1 K.B. 588 (1907); Elster v. City of Springfield, 30 N.E. 274 (Ohio 1892); Popplewell v. Hodgkinson, [1861-73] All E.R. 996 (Ex. 1869). See also Finley v. Teeter Stone, Inc., 251 M.D. 428, 248 A.2d 106 (1968), in which the same holding was made in a jurisdiction which follows the reasonable use rule.

On the basis of the earlier decisions cited above, the Restatement of Torts §818 (1939), adopted the following rule:

> §818. *Withdrawing Subterranean Water*
> To the extent that a person is not liable for withdrawing subterranean waters from the land of another, he is not liable for a subsidence of the other's land which is caused by the withdrawal.

The foregoing statement in §818 fairly represents the law on the subject as pronounced in common law jurisdictions. In 1840, Texas adopted the common law of England, with exceptions not relevant here. Our present Article 1, Texas Revised Civil Statutes, reads: "The common law of England, so far as it is not inconsistent with the Constitution and laws of this State, shall together with such Constitution and laws, be the rule of decision, and shall continue in force until altered or replaced by the Legislature."

We have found nothing in our Constitution, laws, or decisions inconsistent with the common law rule. On the contrary, our decisions in *East, City of Pleasanton*, and *Williams*, denying liability for damages to neighboring property because of lowering the water tables beneath neighboring lands, are consistent with the rule as stated above. It has been suggested, but not by respondents, that another rule applicable to destruction of subjacent land support caused by withdrawal of minerals should be applied in this case. We disagree, because the common law has recognized a clear distinction between subsidence caused by withdrawal of water and that caused by withdrawal of minerals, especially when solid minerals were involved. Restatement of Torts §820 (1939), relating to withdrawal of subjacent support, reflects this distinction by a specific exception of water withdrawals referred to in §818, *supra*, as follows:

> §820. *Withdrawing Naturally Necessary Subjacent Support*
> (1) Except as stated in §818, a person who withdraws the naturally necessary subjacent support of land in another's possession or the support which has been substituted for the naturally necessary support is liable for a subsidence of such land of the other as was naturally dependent upon the support withdrawn, in the absence of a superseding cause or other reason for relieving him.

Although a tentative revision of §818 was adopted by the American Law Institute in 1969, which would completely reverse this rule, it is important to our decision in this case that the Restatement of Torts rule as quoted above was in effect, without any tentative change, from 1939 to 1969[3j]. The defendants began drilling and production from their wells in 1964 and the majority of their wells were completed by 1969.

The facts and legal issues in *Langbrook, supra,* were most similar to those in the instant case. In *Langbrook,* the plaintiffs alleged nuisance and negligence in an action for damages to their property due to subsidence alleged to have been caused by defendants in the manner by which they withdrew underground water from their own nearby property. The only question before the court was whether plaintiffs' suit, cast in nuisance and negligence, stated a cause of action. The court, after an exhaustive review of the English cases, held that the law of nuisance and negligence was not applicable in the case by reason of the acts complained of because there was no duty to take care against the resulting damage and no unlawful act of interference with lawful rights of the plaintiffs. The court said:

> The authorities cited on behalf of the defendants in my judgment establish that a man may abstract the water under his land which percolates in undefined channels to whatever extent he pleases, notwithstanding that this may result in the abstraction of water percolating under the land of his neighbour and, thereby, cause him injury. In such circumstances the principle of *sic utere tuo ut alienum non laedas* [use your property so as not to injure the property of another] does not operate and the damage is *damnum sine injuria* [damages suffered without the invasion of a legal right or the violation of a legal duty].
>
> Is there then any room for the law of nuisance or negligence to operate? In my judgment there is not . . . if there were, it seems to me highly probable that the courts would already have said so, and yet I have not been referred to any case in which that was done.

[1969] 3 All E.R. Rep. at 1439-40.

The above holding is in accord with Texas rules of tort law that (1) in order to create liability for the maintenance of a nuisance, the act com-

---

3j. The tentative change of §818 from non-liability to strict liability, with the addition of other substances, reads as follows:

§818. Withdrawing Subterranean Substances
One who is privileged to withdraw subterranean water, oil, minerals or other substances from under the land of another is not for that reason privileged to cause a subsidence of the other's land by such withdrawal.

The proceedings of the American Law Institute reflect that this change was proposed by the Reporter, Dean Prosser, in what he termed "a rather bob-tailed session," with the explanation that instead of fixing liability, this revision of §818 would simply "knock out the absolute privilege to withdraw water without liability for the consequences." 1969 Proceedings of the American Law Institute 268, 273. The Reporter's Note to Institute appended to the tentative draft states that "[t]he Advisors and the Council, meeting the problem for the first time, are in some doubt, but express themselves as willing to follow the majority of the cases." [Most of which related to substances other than water.] See tentative draft proposal #15, Restatement (Second) of Torts §818, Ch. 39.

plained of must in some way constitute an unlawful invasion of the right of another, Gotcher v. City of Farmersville, 137 Tex. 12, 151 S.W.2d 565 (1941); and (2) for redress in negligence actions there must be a violation of a legal right and the breach of a legal duty, State v. Brewer, 141 Tex. 1, 169 S.W.2d 468 (1943).

STARE DECISIS

We agree that some aspects of the English or common law rule as to underground waters are harsh and outmoded, and the rule has been severely criticized since its reaffirmation by this Court in 1955. Most of the critics, however, recognize that it has become an established rule of property law in this State, under which many citizens own land and water rights. The rule has been relied upon by thousands of farmers, industries, and municipalities in purchasing and developing vast tracts of land overlying aquifers of underground water. Approximately 50,000 wells are used to irrigate 2,800,000 acres in the thirteen county High Plains area of West Texas. As shown in the official reports earlier in this opinion, over 2,600 water wells have been drilled in Harris County alone while this rule of immunity from liability was in effect. The very wells which brought about this action were drilled after the English rule had been reaffirmed by this Court in 1955.

On this subject, we are not writing on a clean slate. Even though good reasons may exist for lifting the immunity from tort actions in cases of this nature, it would be unjust to do so retroactively. The doctrine of stare decisis has been and should be strictly followed by this Court in cases involving established rules of property rights. Southland Royalty Co. v. Humble Oil and Refining Co., 151 Tex. 324, 249 S.W.2d 914 (1952); Tanton v. State National Bank of El Paso, 125 Tex. 16, 79 S.W.2d 833 (1935). It is for this reason that, as to past actions complained of in this case, we follow the English rule and Restatement of Torts §818 (1939) in holding that defendants are not liable on plaintiff's allegations of nuisance and negligence. The same reasoning applies to plaintiff's other allegations in tort (wrongful diversion of surface waters onto and across plaintiffs' lands and wrongful taking and conversion of plaintiffs' property), which the Court of Civil Appeals did not reach. We have considered all of plaintiffs' points of error in the Court of Civil Appeals complaining of the trial court's judgment and find them to be without merit.

AS TO FUTURE WELLS AND SUBSIDENCE

As heretofore mentioned, the Legislature has entered the field of regulation of ground water withdrawals and subsidence. This occurred after geologists, hydrologists, and engineers had developed more accurate knowledge concerning the location, source, and measurement of percolating underground waters, and after legislators became aware of the potential conflicts inherent in the unregulated use of ground water under the English rule of ownership. With a rule that recognizes ownership of underground water by each individual under his own land, but with no limitation on the manner and amount which another individual landowner might produce (absent willful waste and malicious malice), legislative action was essential in order to provide for conservation and protection of public interests.

The legislative policy contained in Chapter 52 of the Texas Water Code is designed to limit the exercise of that portion of the English rule which has been interpreted as giving each landowner the right to take all the water he pleases without regard to the effect on other lands in the same area. For instance, §52.117 of the Water Code, applicable to Underground Water Conservation Districts, provides:

> *§52.117. Regulation of Spacing and Production*
> In order to minimize as far as practicable the drawdown of the water table or the reduction of artesian pressure, to control subsidence, or to prevent waste, the district may provide for the spacing of water wells and may regulate the production of wells.

Ten of these Underground Water Conservation Districts are active in an area embracing much of West Texas. 33rd Report, Texas Water Rights Commission for Fiscal Year 1977. The need for additional legislation for creation of districts to cover unregulated ground water reservoirs and to solve other conflicts which may arise in this area of water law and subsidence seems to be inevitable. Providing policy and regulatory procedures in this field is a legislative function. It is well that the Legislature has assumed its proper role, because our courts are not equipped to regulate ground water uses and subsidence on a suit-by-suit basis.

This case, however, gives the Court its first opportunity to recognize, and to encourage compliance with, the policy set forth by the Legislature and its regulatory agencies in an effort to curb excessive underground water withdrawals and resulting land subsidence. It also affords us the opportunity to discard an objectionable aspect of the court-made English rule as it relates to subsidence by stating a rule for the future which is more in harmony with expressed legislative policy. We refer to the past immunity from negligence which heretofore has been afforded ground water producers solely because of their "absolute" ownership of the water.

As far as we can determine, there is no other use of private real property which enjoys such an immunity from liability under the law of negligence. This ownership of underground water comes with ownership of the surface; it is part of the soil. Yet, the use of one's ground-level surface and other elements of the soil is without such insulation from tort liability. Our consideration of this case convinces us that there is no valid reason to continue this special immunity insofar as it relates to future subsidence proximately caused by negligence in the manner which wells are drilled or produced in the future. It appears that the ownership and rights of all landowners will be better protected against subsidence if each has the duty to produce water from his land in a manner that will not negligently damage or destroy the lands of others.

Therefore, if the landowner's manner of withdrawing ground water from his land is negligent, willfully wasteful, or for the purpose of malicious injury, and such conduct is a proximate cause of the subsidence of the land of others, he will be liable for the consequences of his conduct. The addition of negligence as a ground of recovery shall apply only to future subsidence proximately caused by future withdrawals of ground water from wells which are either produced or drilled in a negligent manner after the date this opinion becomes final.

While this addition of negligence as a ground of recovery in subsidence cases applies to future negligence in producing water from existing wells and those drilled or produced in a negligent manner in the future, it has been suggested that this new ground of recovery should be applied in the present cause of action. This is often done when a court writes or adds a new rule applicable to personal injury cases, but seldom when rules of property law are involved. Klocke v. Klocke, 276 Mo. 572, 208 S.W. 825 (1919); 10 A.L.R.3d 1371, 1388; Currier, Time and Change in Judge-Made Law: Prospective Overruling, 51 Va. L. Rev. 201, 242-43 (1965). This is because precedent is necessarily a highly important factor when problems regarding land or contracts are concerned. In deeds, property transactions, and land developments, the parties should be able to rely on the law which existed at the time of their actions. For the power of the courts in this regard, see Great Northern Ry. Co. v. Sunburst Oil and Refining Co., 287 U.S. 358, 53 S. Ct. 145, 77 L. Ed. 360 (1932).

JUDGMENT

Accordingly, the judgment of the Court of Civil Appeals is reversed and the judgment of the trial court is affirmed.

Dissenting Opinion by POPE, J., in which SAM D. JOHNSON, J., joins.

CHADICK, J., not sitting.

POPE, J., dissenting.

I respectfully dissent. The court has decided this cause upon the mistaken belief that the case is governed by the ownership of ground water. Plaintiffs assert no ownerships to the percolating waters pumped and extracted from the ground by defendants. They make no complaint that their own wells have been or will be pumped dry. They seek no damages for the defendants' sale of the water. Plaintiffs' action calls for no change in nor even a review of the English rule of "absolute ownership" of ground water, the American rule of "reasonable use" of ground water, nor the Texas rule of "nonwasteful" use of ground water. They claim no correlative rights in the

Nuisances Private and Public

water. The Texas law of percolating waters is not put in issue by this suit, and there is no occasion to overrule that law either now or prospectively. There is a question whether this court can or ought to do so after the Texas legislature has so often and so recently stated its intent that the law of ground waters should be respected. Tex. Water Code Ann. §§21.004, 52.002; 1975 Tex. Gen. Laws, ch. 284, §40, at 682 (creating Harris-Galveston Coastal Subsidence District).

Plaintiffs' complaint is that defendants are causing subsidence of their land. They assert an absolute right to keep the surface of their land at its natural horizon. The landowners' right to the subjacent support for their land is the only right in suit, and this is a case of original impression. Other areas of the law should not be disturbed, but the majority opinion needlessly does so. It is no more logical to say that this is a case concerning the right to ground water than it would be correct in a case in which an adjoining landowner removed lateral support by a caterpillar to say that the case would be governed by the law of caterpillars. In making this decision about one's right to subjacent support, I would use as analogies other kinds of cases concerning support, such as the right to lateral support.

A landowner's right to lateral support for his land is an absolute right. The instrument employed in causing land to slough off, cave in or wash away is not the real subject of inquiry. The inquiry is whether the adjoining owner actually causes the loss of support. Whether the support is destroyed by excavation, ditching, the flowing of water, the pumping of water, unnatural pressure, unnatural suction, or explosives, the right to support is the same, and it is an absolute right....

Respectable American authority supports the rule that a landowner has the right to the support afforded by subterranean waters. New York Central R. Co. v. Marinucci Bros. & Co., 337 Mass. 469, 149 N.E.2d 680 (1958); Gamer v. Milton, 346 Mass. 617, 195 N.E.2d 65 (1963), [rejecting the decision in Popplewell v. Hodkinson, L.R. 4 Ex. 248 (1869)]; Cabot v. Kingman, 166 Mass. 403, 44 N.E. 344 (1896); Bjorvatn v. Pacific Mechanical Construction, Inc., 77 Wash. 2d 563, 464 P.2d 432 (1970); Muskatell v. City of Seattle, 10 Wash. 2d 221, 116 P.2d 363 (1941); Farnandis v. Great Northern Ry. Co., 41 Wash. 486, 84 P. 18 (1906); 1 Am. Jur. 2d Adjoining Landowners §80 (1962); 2 C.J.S. Adjoining Landowners §38 (1972); Annot., 4 A.L.R. 1104.

A second analogous rule which protects one's subsurface from damage by an operator on other lands is found in Gregg v. Delhi-Taylor Oil Corp., 162 Tex. 26, 33, 344 S.W.2d 411, 416 (1961). Mr. Gregg, in the development of his mineral lease, was preparing to use a sand fracturing technique to open cracks and veins extending some distance from his lease and to alter the substructure of neighboring land. By use of hydraulic pressure the ruptures of the subsurface formations would free greater quantities of gas. The rupture beneath the Delhi-Taylor's lands would create only small veins about one-tenth of an inch in diameter. This court regarded the creation of fissures on another's land as an invasion of property rights. "The invasion alleged is direct and the action taken is intentional. . . . While the drilling bit of Gregg's well is not alleged to have extended into Delhi-Taylor's land, the same result is reached if in fact the cracks or veins extend into its land and gas is produced therefrom by Gregg." This court denied one landowner the right to interfere with the subsurface of lands beyond his own lease boundaries. The same principle was applied in Gregg v. Delhi-Taylor Oil Corp., 162 Tex. 38, 344 S.W.2d 419 (1961), and in Delhi-Taylor Oil Corp. v. Holmes, 162 Tex. 39, 344 S.W.2d 420 (1961).

In my judgment, the examples are indistinguishable from the present case. The geologic changes that the defendants are creating beneath the surface of the plaintiffs' land in the instant case are more severe than in the *Gregg* and *Holmes* cases. The plaintiffs made summary judgment showing that the defendants squeeze the water from the clay beneath plaintiffs' lands, and the clay is then compressed and compacted so that the layers become thinner. The subterranean strata beneath plaintiffs' land is wholly altered by the process. The process is permanent and irreversible. If one may not use pressure that alters the geologic status of one's subsurface estate, how can we approve a process which reduces the pressure and which more grievously alters the subsurface estate? With respect I suggest, had we used the same argument in the *Gregg* and *Holmes* cases that is today employed, we would have approached the problem by looking at *Gregg's* and *Holmes's* right to capture the oil through its wellbore on its own lease. Once we determine that they had the right to capture and own the oil, we would have ruled that the case was solved. In *Gregg* and *Holmes*, we correctly looked at the damage to the neighbors' subsurface estate that was threatened by one who had a complete legal right to capture from a wellbore on his own land the oil from beneath another's land. The right of capture did not carry with it the right to destroy or interfere with the geology beneath another's land.

Elliff v. Texon Drilling Co., 146 Tex. 575, 210 S.W.2d 558, 4 A.L.R.2d 191 (1948), was another example in which this court looked at the damage done a neighbor's subsurface estate by an oil driller who had the right to capture oil through the wellbore on his own lease. This court expressly rejected holdings by the Louisiana Supreme Court which held that an adjoining owner has no action against one who negligently destroys a reservoir. This court also rejected the defense that one's right to capture the oil rendered him immune from damages for his negligence in wasting it.

We thus reach the end result. Under our prior holdings compared with today's, one who mines for oil may not destroy his neighbor's subjacent geology; but the right to pump water, we inconsistently say, is the right to destroy the subsurface geology, the subjacent support and even the surface of the land. Defendants may pump the plaintiffs' land to the bottom of Galveston Bay. . . .

The error of the majority is its narrow focus upon the right of the defendants to pump ground water. We should enlarge our vision so we can see what this lawsuit is about. I do not believe it is sound law that the right to pump water is the power to destroy the surface of surrounding landowners. If defendants argue that they have an absolute right to pump groundwater, plaintiffs reply that they too have an absolute right to the support of their natural surface. According to some of the summary judgment proofs, the defendants with knowledge have destroyed and are destroying the natural surface estate of the plaintiffs. The summary judgment proofs include showings that the plaintiffs own lands that were originally seven feet above sea level; today their land is flooded or subject to periodic flooding and the situation is getting worse. The natural shoreline banks which once protected lands from Galveston Bay and Clear Lake have now fallen below sea level. Lands are innundated. More lands will be innundated in the future. Lands that were once above sea level are now under salt water.

There is yet another legal principle that we should observe. Many things, though lawful, when done to excess, become remediable. Church bells may toll the knell of parting day or announce the time for solemn services, but when bells continuously clang without interruption for many days, the rights of others spring into being. What we do cannot be understood except in relation to those we touch. We have in this case the pleadings and showing that the defendants have abused their right to pump water to the point that property and the rights of others are ignored and destroyed.

Plaintiffs asserted their action upon theories of negligence, intentional tort, nuisance, and a taking of their property. In my opinion, subject to proof, they have an action on the first three theories.

I therefore dissent from this court's treatment of this case as one which concerns ownership of ground water. I dissent from this court's endorsement of English water cases that have been rejected in this country. I dissent from this court's adherence to the Restatement of Torts §818. As discussed above, Texas has its own developed and developing law in this area of the law that is fair and equitable. The members of the Restatement Committee are neither legislators nor members of the Congress, and we do not need their help in this instance.

I dissent from the court's holding that this case is governed by the stare decisis of ground water cases. There has not previously been a case like this in Texas and there is no stare decisis applicable. Damages for subsidence was not the issue when courts were writing City of Corpus Christi v. City of Pleasanton, 154 Tex. 289, 276 S.W.2d 798 (1955), and Texas Co. v. Burkett,

117 Tex. 16, 296 S.W. 273 (1927), and Houston & T. C. Ry. Co. v. East, 98 Tex. 146, 81 S.W. 279 (1904). The parties in these cases were fighting over water rights. Nor was that the issue in Acton v. Blundell, 12 Meeson & Welsby 324, 152 Eng. Rep. 1223 (Ex.1843). The law stated by those cases need not and should not be disturbed by today's opinion. Because there is no stare decisis, I also dissent from the court's holding that plaintiffs can have no remedy except by a retroactive application of the law. The defendants, according to some of the summary judgment proofs, had knowledge from expert opinions that their course of action would cause subsidence. When the defendants, after warning, elect to take their risks in an area in which there are no precedents, I see no reason to apply our holding prospectively. No property law had attached in this instance. I dissent from the court's dicta that the legislature has in some fashion recognized or legislated about the defendants' immunity. Where is that legislation found?

Finally, and importantly, I dissent from the majority's holding that landowners in the future may prosecute a suit for damages for the destruction of their property if, and only if the action is one for negligence, wilful waste, or malicious injury. I rather assume that pumpers of ground water will carefully do so, will not waste their water, and will bear no ill will toward those whose property they are destroying. In fact, pumpers more probably, will feel benignly toward those who regrettably must suffer the loss of their lands under the law of Friendswood Development Company v. Smith-Southwest Industries, Inc.

I would hold that an owner of land may assert an action against one who destroys the lateral or subjacent support to his land in its natural state when: (1) he engages in conduct knowing that it will cause damages to another's land by loss or destruction of the subjacent support, Paris Purity Coal Co. v. Pendergrass, 193 Ark. 1031, 104 S.W.2d 455 (1937); or (2) the plaintiff proves negligence, or (3) the plaintiff proves a nuisance, and here a balancing will be a factor.

I also dissent from the court's denial of rights to the plaintiffs, while acknowledging that future landowners may have an action at least in negligence. This court, in recent years, has recognized a number of new actions, and each time, the successful party was allowed the victory. Among the recent examples are Whittlesey v. Miller, 572 S.W.2d 665 (Tex.1978) [consortium]; Parker v. Highland Park, Inc., 565 S.W.2d 512 (Tex.1978) [abolition of no-duty doctrine in premises cases]; Bounds v. Caudle, 560 S.W.2d 925 (Tex.1977) [interspousal tort immunity abolished in case of wilful and intentional torts]; Farley v. M M Cattle Company, 529 S.W.2d 751 (Tex.1975) [abolition of voluntary assumption of risk]; Felsenthal v. McMillan, 493 S.W.2d 729 (Tex.1973) [criminal conversation]; Getty Oil Company v. Jones, 470 S.W.2d 618 (Tex.1971) [dominant estate limited by rule of reasonable necessity]. In my opinion, it is basically unfair to treat the plaintiffs in this case unequally by recognizing that they possess an action, but by denying them the remedy.

I would affirm the judgment of the court of civil appeals.

NOTES AND QUESTIONS

1. See generally Annot., 5 A.L.R.4th 614 (1981).

2. It is one thing to observe, as the majority opinion in the *Friendswood* case does, that Texas adopted the common law of England in 1840. It is another to say that it also adopted at that time decisions by English courts *subsequently* to be rendered. Yet the English cases relied on by the court — Acton v. Blundell and *Langbrook* — were decided in 1843 and 1969, respectively. *Acton,* moreover, did not involve subsidence. And if the Texas courts were obliged to follow the English common law before, why may they change it now? Is there anything at all to be said for the English rule of absolute ownership that was (only) prospectively overruled in *Friendswood*? If there is not, is there anything to be said for overruling it only prospectively? Judging from the opinion, the defendants in the case *will* be liable in the future for negligent withdrawal from the very wells involved in the litigation. Is that fair to the defendants? They must, one gathers from the opinion, have relied on the English rule when they purchased their land and sunk their wells. Presumably the advantages of the English rule were reflected in the price they paid for the land and in the amounts they were willing to invest in wells. Now those advantages — which the majority regards as property rights — are reduced. If this is fair, then why would it be unfair to apply retroactively against the defendants the new rule announced in *Friendswood*?

3. Under the new rule announced by the court, those withdrawing groundwater will be liable for subsidence caused by negligent operations. The dissent argues that pumpers of ground water will in the future pump just as much — but "carefully." (Page 126.) Does the dissent understand the law of negligence?

4. A colleague, William Ian Miller, who has lent us several insights into *Friendswood,* regards the case (and the English rule it only prospectively changes) as utterly indefensible. He believes the court does so as well, and that the product is a very tortured opinion — as illustrated by some of the questions asked above, or by the court's suggesting that the problem of subsidence is one to be resolved by the legislature and then going on to resolve the problem itself, but only prospectively. Miller says: "A Freudian might find an unconscious admission of the court's uncertainty about the justice of its opinion in the misuse of 'nontortuous' for 'nontortious.'" (See page 114.)

B. REMEDIES (AND MORE ON THE SUBSTANTIVE LAW)

Page 935. At the end of the first full paragraph, add:

On the subject of effective bargaining between the parties after injunctive relief has been granted, see Hoffman & Spitzer, The Coase Theorem: Some Experimental Tests, 25 J. Law & Econ. 73, 97 (1982), concluding — on the basis of a set of experiments — that in two-party (plaintiff-defendant) situations, the parties will bargain to efficient outcomes. (For further discussion of Hoffman and Spitzer's conclusions, see below.) Refer back to the case of Prah v. Maretti, reprinted at page 98 of this supplement. Do the findings of Hoffman and Spitzer suggest that the court could just as well have ignored the problem presented to it, instead relying on the market to resolve the issue? Why didn't Prah and Maretti bargain over the right to solar access? If effective bargaining is unlikely to occur, should a case like Prah v. Maretti conclude with a damage award rather than injunctive relief? See Comment, Wisconsin Recognizes the Power of the Sun: *Prah v. Maretti* and the Solar Access Act, 1983 Wis. L. Rev. 1263, 1281-1289.

Page 945. In the last line, after the reference to the Note on "Externalities," add:

Hoffman & Spitzer, The Coase Theorem: Some Experimental Tests, 25 J. Law & Econ. 73, 97 (1982), found that in "many-party" situations (e.g., multiple plaintiffs, as in *Boomer*), post-litigation bargaining difficulties might well arise. The study notes, however, the difficulty of making accurate generalizations on the issue. Bargaining may go forth more smoothly, for example, if the plaintiff homeowners are denied all relief than if the defendant factory is enjoined. A subsequent study, Hoffman & Spitzer, Experimental Tests of the Coase Theorem with Large Bargaining Groups (forthcoming in the Journal of Legal Studies), does venture a generalization — a rather startling one — based on further experiments: Even in situations involving up to twenty parties (whether one defendant and nineteen plaintiffs, vice versa, or any mix), post-litigation bargaining will lead to efficient solutions with no problems of free-riding or holding out whatsoever!

Page 953. At the end of the first full paragraph, add:

On attempts to control obscenity through public nuisance statutes, see Vance v. Universal Amusement Co., 445 U.S. 308 (1980) (regulation of a communicative activity such as the exhibition of motion pictures must adhere to more narrowly drawn procedures than is necessary for the abatement of ordinary nuisances), noted in 26 N.Y.L.S.L. Rev. 1122 (1981). See Gorman, The Demise of Civil Nuisance Actions in Obscenity Control, 14

Loy. U. Chi. L.J. 31 (1982); Note, Pornography, Padlocks and Prior Restraints: The Constitutional Limits of the Nuisance Power, 58 N.Y.U.L. Rev. 1478 (1983).

Page 955. At the end of the carryover paragraph, add:

4. *Spur II.* Pending at the time of the *Spur* litigation reported in the main text was a suit by residents of Sun City seeking damages from Spur for maintaining a nuisance. After the *Spur* decision, Spur filed a third-party complaint against Webb to obtain indemnity from Webb for damages for which Spur might be held liable in the residents' suit. The trial court dismissed Spur's complaint, apparently on the ground that the *Spur* decision was res judicata and resolved against Spur the issues Spur hoped to raise again in its third-party complaint. The Supreme Court of Arizona reversed, holding that the *Spur* decision was not res judicata because it concerned only Spur and Webb, and only the questions whether (1) Spur should be enjoined, and (2) who was to pay for the costs of the injunction. The suit in which Spur filed its third-party complaint, on the other hand, involved different parties, and different questions: (1) whether the residents had been damaged as a result of Spur's operations, and (2) whether Webb's conduct as to each of the residents was such that Webb should be required to indemnify Spur for any damages the residents might be awarded. Spur Feeding Co. v. Superior Court, 109 Ariz. 105, 505 P.2d 1377 (1973).

The dissenting opinion argued that Spur had clearly operated a nuisance, then added:

> Today the Court apparently holds that Webb must indemnify the wrongdoer for any damages caused to property owners by the operation of the nuisance.
>
> If these Spur cases are adhered to by this Court in the future, every operator of a nuisance which sends smoke, fumes, dust, stench, etc. onto his neighbors may be guaranteed economic protection should anyone be annoyed or harassed enough to try and stop the wrongful activity by court action. Such a result should not be allowed under the law of this state. [109 Ariz. at 108, 505 P. 2d at 1380.]

Chapter Nine
Private Land-Use Arrangements: A Comparative Study of Servitudes

A. AN OVERVIEW OF SERVITUDES

Page 968. After Note 4, add:

5. For an excellent discussion of the issues raised in this chapter, see the Symposium Issue, 55 S. Cal. L. Rev. 1177-1447 (1982), and particularly French, Toward a Modern Law of Servitudes: Reweaving the Ancient Strands, *id.* at 1261, and Reichman, Toward a Unified Concept of Servitudes, *id.* at 1177.

B. CREATION OF SERVITUDES

Page 990. At the end of Problem 2, add:

On ways of necessity where access exists but is inconvenient, or makes only part of the land accessible, see respectively Annots., 10 A.L.R.4th 447, 500 (1981).

Page 1003. In Note 2, line 5, after the reference to Chapter 8, add:

See also pages 98-111 of this supplement.

Page 1004. At the end of the first paragraph of Note 3, add:

See generally Pedowitz, Solar Energy Easements, 15 Real Prop., Prob. & Tr. J. 797 (1980).

E. TERMINATION OF SERVITUDES

Page 1083. At the end of the carryover paragraph, add:

See generally Comment, Termination of Servitudes: Expanding the Remedies for "Changed Conditions," 31 U.C.L.A.L. Rev. 226 (1983) (endorsing damage remedies for breach of restrictive covenants).

Page 1084. After Note 6, insert:

CRANE NECK ASSOCIATION, INC. v. NEW YORK CITY/LONG ISLAND COUNTY

Court of Appeals of New York, 1984
61 N.Y.2d 154, 460 N.E.2d 1336

KAYE, J. Beginning in 1945, as the Long Island estate of Eversley Childs was divided into residential parcels, each deed within the tract (called Crane Neck Farm) included an identical covenant restricting buildings to "single family dwellings." Respondent agencies, implementing a long-standing State policy to deinstitutionalize retarded persons and place them in community settings, in 1980 leased property within Crane Neck to house and care for eight severely retarded adults. Appellants, Crane Neck property owners, contending that this use violates the restrictive covenant, seek a judgment enforcing the covenant and enjoining continuation of the lease.

Special Term granted appellants partial summary judgment, concluding that the State facility was not a single-family dwelling and therefore violated the covenant, yet finding that there were fact issues as to whether the restrictions of the covenant had been waived by past violations and whether the character of the neighborhood had so changed as to render the covenant unenforceable in equity. The Appellate Division, 92 A.D.2d 119, 460 N.Y.S.2d 69, reversed and dismissed the complaint, determining that the facility could be considered a single-family dwelling consistent with the restrictive covenant, and that in any event the covenant could not be enforced to prevent the residence as a matter of public policy. On the latter ground, we affirm the order of the Appellate Division.

I

Pursuant to a lease effective September 1, 1980 between the owners of the subject property (respondents Jonathan Pool and Bernard Grofman) and respondent New York City/Long Island County Services Group (an agency of respondent New York State Department of Mental Retardation and Developmental Disabilities), eight profoundly retarded adults formerly

Private Land-Use Arrangements

in institutions came to reside in a six-bedroom home situated on two wooded acres at 3 Johns Hollow Road in the Hamlet of Crane Neck, Village of Old Field. These adults were in need of uninterrupted supervision.

According to the State's program, a nonresident professional staff of approximately 16 persons cares for the residents, trains them, and provides therapy where needed. While resident "houseparents" are in theory part of the program, it is not clear from the record that there have in fact been houseparents at 3 Johns Hollow Road. At least three supervisory persons are to be within the home around the clock.

In a family-type environment and under constant supervision, the disabled persons residing in Crane Neck are taught socialization as well as basic physical skills. Structured "day programming" lasting six or more hours a day is conducted in feeding, toilet training, personal grooming and health habits, dressing, housekeeping, and caring for property. After the initial period of intensive training, once sufficient independence is developed, the residents are enrolled in sheltered workshops in the area, such as the United Cerebral Palsy Center in Commack, the Industrial Home for the Blind in Melville, and the Suffolk Child Development Center in Smithtown, returning to 3 Johns Hollow Road each day. As they are able, also, they begin interacting with merchants and others in the neighborhood. The stays at 3 Johns Hollow are of indefinite duration, but it appears that residents upon reaching a certain degree of development are expected to leave and be replaced by others in need of care and training.

II

The question presented on this appeal is whether use of the leased premises at 3 Johns Hollow Road should be enjoined by equitable enforcement of the restrictive covenant in the lessors' deed. Any analysis of this issue of course must begin with language of the covenant.

Starting in 1945, and continuing for about 10 years, uniform deed restrictions were imposed on all parcels comprising the tract of Crane Neck. Each of these deeds, including the deed from which respondent lessors derived title, included the following:

> Subject to the following covenants and restrictions, which shall be construed as real covenants running with the land and shall be binding upon and enure to the benefit of the parties hereto, and their respective heirs, devisees, legal representatives, successors and assigns:
>
> (a) There shall not be constructed nor maintained upon the said premises any buildings other than single family dwellings and outbuildings. That no house or dwelling costing less than $3500 on the basis of 1944 material and labor costs shall be erected on the said premises, and that no building other than Cape Cod or Colonial design and architecture (and additional buildings shall conform in

architecture to the main dwelling) shall be erected on said premises unless plans and specifications therefor have first been submitted to and approved in writing by the parties of the first part, or their duly authorized agent.

From a reading of the covenant and the undisputed evidence regarding the intent of the grantor, we conclude that the deed restriction was imposed to preserve Crane Neck as a neighborhood of single-family dwellings, not only architecturally but also functionally. We are therefore in agreement with both courts below that, to give the effect intended by its creator, the covenant must be read to apply not only to the physical construction of single-family dwellings within Crane Neck but also to their actual use. (Baumert v. Malkin, 235 N.Y. 115, 139 N.E. 210.)

We cannot agree, however, with the conclusion of the Appellate Division that the community residence at 3 Johns Hollow Road functions as a single-family dwelling. It fits neither a traditional concept of a single-family unit known in 1945 (see What Constitutes a "Family" Within Meaning of Zoning Regulation or Restrictive Covenant, Ann., 172 A.L.R. 1172), by which its use must be measured (Clark v. Devoe, 124 N.Y. 120, 123, 26 N.E. 275), nor even the expanded definitions of "family" of more recent origin (see City of White Plains v. Ferraioli, 34 N.Y.S.2d 300, 306, 357 N.Y.2d 449, 313 N.E.2d 756).

In support of their argument that the use is consonant with the covenant, respondent agencies point to the fact that the residence in theory functions as one housekeeping unit providing a homelike atmosphere for individuals who cannot remain in their natural families, meanwhile teaching them basic skills which will enable them to live independently. But these indicia of family life do not create a family.

We found in City of White Plains v. Ferraioli, 34 N.Y.2d 300, 357 N.Y.S.2d 449, 313 N.E.2d 756, *supra* that a group home consisting of a married couple, their two children and 10 foster children qualified as a family for purposes of a zoning ordinance, and in Group House of Port Washington v. Board of Zoning & Appeals, 45 N.Y.2d 266, 271, 408 N.Y.S.2d 377, 380 N.E.2d 207, we concluded that a group home of seven children with two surrogate parents could not be distinguished from a natural family for that same purpose. Those decisions, which have in effect been codified in subdivision (f) of section 41.34 of the Mental Hygiene Law, are not controlling here. This case concerns the application of a private covenant, not a zoning ordinance. Furthermore, a much different factual situation is presented.

In this context, a home inhabited by eight unrelated adults each receiving uninterrupted professional supervision and care is not a single-family unit. The residents are twice outnumbered by a changing, nonresident staff of nurses, physical and recreational therapists, dieticians and others finding no equivalent in a biologically unitary family, or indeed in any expanded concept of the word "family." While neither the size of the resident group nor the nature of its daily activities would necessarily determine the issue (see Incorporated Vil. of Freeport v. Association for Help of Retarded Children, 94 Misc. 2d 1048, 1049, 406 N.Y.S.2d 221, *affd.* 60 A.D.2d 644, 400 N.Y.S.2d 724), the absence of regular houseparents and, most significantly, the presence of a large complement of nonresident professional attendants distinguish the residence at 3 Johns Hollow Road from a single-family unit.

The residence being operated by respondent agencies within Crane Neck, then, cannot be considered a single-family dwelling as contemplated by the deed restriction.

III

But even if use of the property violates the restrictive covenant, that covenant cannot be equitably enforced because to do so would contravene a long-standing public policy favoring the establishment of such residences for the mentally disabled.

Over the past three decades this State has developed a policy favoring the deinstitutionalization of mentally and developmentally disabled persons, and their placement in supervised residences housing small groups, called "community residences" (Mental Hygiene Law, §1.03, subd. 28). The Mental Hygiene Law authorizes the Commissioner of Mental Retardation and Developmental Disabilities to operate these residences (Mental Hygiene Law, §41.33), and provides for grants and reimbursements to others who offer such services (Mental Hygiene Law, §§41.36, 41.37, 41.38). . . .

While the community residence program was at first directed to placement of mildly retarded persons, in 1975 Governor Carey pledged this State to a major program of deinstitutionalization of more severely disabled persons, such as those involved in this action, in the consent decree issued in New York State Assn. for Retarded Children v. Carey, 393 F. Supp. 715. In 1978, the Department of Mental Hygiene issued a five-year plan for community placement and support of the chronically mentally ill, stating that "[t]he needs of the chronically mentally ill are now better understood and appropriate community support alternatives to institution have been identified; every effort should be made to provide what has been found to be needed." (New York State Dept of Mental Hygiene, Division of Mental Health, "Appropriate Community Placement and Support: Phase One, Five Year Mental Health Plan," p.ii [Jan., 1978].)

The State policy was further reaffirmed by the passage in 1978 of what has come to be known as the "Padavan Law" (L.1978, ch. 468, codified in Mental Hygiene Law, §41.34), which established site selection procedures for community residences. As the Legislature declared: "It is the intention of this legislation to meet the needs of the mentally disabled in New York state by providing, wherever possible, that such persons remain in normal community settings, receiving such treatment, care, rehabilitation and education as may be appropriate to each individual." (L.1978, ch. 468, §1.) . . .

As late as last month, Governor Cuomo stressed in his message to the Legislature that the State remains dedicated to a program of deinstitutionalization and placement of mentally disabled persons in community residences, and that "additional efforts are required to ensure the availability of structured residential settings for all individuals unable to function independently in the community." (Message to Legislature, p. 49-50[Jan. 4, 1984].)

Thus, the consistent, unequivocal legislative and executive pronouncements over the past 30 years leave no doubt that it is an important State policy to deinstitutionalize mentally and developmentally retarded individuals, and to house and teach them in "community residences" such as the one now maintained at 3 Johns Hollow Road, in Crane Neck.

Even more directly pertinent to the present issues is the enactment of subdivision (f) of section 41.34 of the Mental Hygiene Law. Section 41.34 was added to the Mental Hygiene Law in 1978 to provide for a fair distribution of community residences and to bring municipalities into the process of site selection, thereby minimizing resistance and avoiding legal battles that had impeded the community residence program. The latter concern was a very real one as attempts to develop community residences and similar group homes in some areas had met with resistance in the form of injunctive actions based upon local ordinances limiting the use of property to single-family residences. In an effort to keep such legal challenges from frustrating the program, the Legislature provided as follows in the concluding subdivision of section 41.34 of the Mental Hygiene Law: "(f) A community residence established pursuant to this section and family care homes shall be deemed a family unit, for purposes of local laws and ordinances."

While the statute is limited to local laws and ordinances, this provision cannot be read without reference to the purpose that engendered it. A major purpose of section 41.34, and the very purpose for which subdivision (f) was enacted, was to eliminate the legal challenges that were impeding implementation of the State policy. . . . Private covenants restricting the use of property to single-family dwellings pose the same deterrent to the effective implementation of the State policy as the local laws and ordinances that had actually been the subject of the legal challenges. Given the avowed purpose of this law, we conclude that the Legislature did not enact subdivision (f) to erase the impediment resulting from single-family requirements found in laws and ordinances while leaving it intact in private covenants, and that the subdivision applies to such deed restrictions as well. . . .

Since the State's policy regarding placement of the mentally disabled as set forth in subdivision (f) would be frustrated by enforcement of the restrictive covenant, it cannot as a matter of public policy be enforced against the community residence at 3 Johns Hollow Road.

IV

Appellants urge that this court may not refuse to enjoin violation of the restrictive covenant on public policy grounds because it is a private contract which cannot be impaired by the State absent emergency circumstances not present here. (U.S. Const., art. I, §10; Home Bldg. & Loan Assn. v. Blaisdell, 290 U.S. 398, 54 S. Ct. 231, 78 L. Ed. 413.) Appellants' argument, however, misconstrues the law.

Although the language of the contract clause is facially absolute, this court has long recognized that the State's interest in protecting the general good of the public through social welfare legislation is paramount to the interests of parties under private contracts, and the State may impair such contracts by subsequent legislation or regulation so long as it is reasonably necessary to further an important public purpose and the measures taken that impair the contract are reasonable and appropriate to effectuate that purpose. . . .

Here the State's interest in protecting the welfare of mentally and developmentally disabled individuals is clearly an important public purpose, and the means used to select the sites for community residences are reasonable and appropriate to effectuate the State's program of providing the most effective care in the least restrictive environment. In such circumstances, appellants' private contract rights may not override State policy.

V

Since public policy prohibits enforcement of the restrictive covenant against the "community residence" at 3 Johns Hollow Road, appellants' action seeking to enjoin such use was properly dismissed. Accordingly, the order of the Appellate Division should be affirmed, with costs.

QUESTIONS

1. If, as the court acknowledges, certain "nonfamilies" qualify as "families" for purposes of zoning ordinances that restrict defined areas to single-family dwellings, why should not the same follow in the case of restrictive covenants?

Page 1084 — Private Land-Use Arrangements

2. Has not the state policy given effect in *Crane Neck* essentially destroyed the benefit of the otherwise perfectly legitimate restrictive covenant at issue in the case? If so, should not the beneficiaries of the covenant be entitled to compensation, on the ground that the government has "taken" their property interest? See the main text at pages 1085-1092, and Chapter 10, section D3.

Chapter Ten

Eminent Domain and the Implicit Taking Problem

B. THE PUBLIC-USE PUZZLE

Page 1097. Replace the *Courtesy Sandwich Shop* case with the following (retain the Notes and Questions after *Courtesy Sandwich Shop*):

HAWAII HOUSING AUTHORITY v. MIDKIFF
Supreme Court of the United States, 1984
104 S. Ct. 2321

Justice O'CONNOR delivered the opinion of the Court.

The Fifth Amendment of the United States Constitution provides, in pertinent part, that "private property [shall not] be taken for public use, without just compensation." These cases present the question whether the Public Use Clause of that Amendment, made applicable to the States through the Fourteenth Amendment, prohibits the State of Hawaii from taking, with just compensation, title in real property from lessors and transferring it to lessees in order to reduce the concentration of ownership of fees simple in the State. We conclude that it does not.

The Hawaiian Islands were originally settled by Polynesian immigrants from the eastern Pacific. These settlers developed an economy around a feudal land tenure system in which one island high chief, the ali'i nui, controlled the land and assigned it for development to certain subchiefs. The subchiefs would then reassign the land to other lower ranking chiefs, who would administer the land and govern the farmers and other tenants working it. All land was held at the will of the ali'i nui and eventually had to be returned to his trust. There was no private ownership of land. . . .

Beginning in the early 1800's, Hawaiian leaders and American settlers repeatedly attempted to divide the lands of the kingdom among the crown, the chiefs, and the common people. These efforts proved largely unsuccessful, however, and the land remained in the hands of a few. In the mid-1960's, after extensive hearings, the Hawaii Legislature discovered that, while the State and Federal Governments owned almost 49% of the State's land, another 47% was in the hands of only 72 private landowners.... The legislature further found that 18 landholders, with tracts of 21,000 acres or more, owned more than 40% of this land and that, on Oahu, the most urbanized of the islands, 22 landowners owned 72.5% of the fee simple titles.... The legislature concluded that concentrated land ownership was responsible for skewing the State's residential fee simple market, inflating land prices, and injuring the public tranquility and welfare.

To redress these problems, the legislature decided to compel the large landowners to break up their estates. The legislature considered requiring large landowners to sell lands which they were leasing to homeowners. However, the landowners strongly resisted this scheme, pointing out the significant federal tax liabilities they would incur. Indeed, the landowners claimed that the federal tax laws were the primary reason they previously had chosen to lease, and not sell, their lands. Therefore, to accommodate the needs of both lessors and lessees, the Hawaii Legislature enacted the Land Reform Act of 1967 (Act), Haw. Rev. Stat., ch. 516, which created a mechanism for condemning residential tracts and for transferring ownership of the condemned fees simple to existing lessees. By condemning the land in question, the Hawaii Legislature intended to make the land sales involuntary, thereby making the federal tax consequences less severe while still facilitating the redistribution of fees simple....

Under the Act's condemnation scheme, tenants living on single-family residential lots within developmental tracts at least five acres in size are entitled to ask the Hawaii Housing Authority (HHA) to condemn the property on which they live. Haw. Rev. Stat. §§516-1(2), (11), 516-22 (1977). When 25 eligible tenants,[5a] or tenants on half the lots in the tract, whichever is less, file appropriate applications, the Act authorizes HHA to hold a public hearing to determine whether acquisition by the State of all or part of the tract will "effectuate the public purposes" of the Act. §516-22. If HHA finds that these public purposes will be served, it is authorized to designate some or all of the lots in the tract for acquisition. It then acquires, at prices set either by condemnation trial or by negotiation between lessors and lessees,[5b] the former fee owners' full "right, title, and interest" in the land. §516-25.

5a. An eligible tenant is one who, among other things, owns a house on the lot, has a bona fide intent to live on the lot or be a resident of the State, shows proof of ability to pay for a fee interest in it, and does not own residential land elsewhere nearby. Haw. Rev. Stat. §516-33(3), (4), (7) (1979).

5b. See §516-56 (Supp. 1983). In either case, compensation must equal the fair market value of the owner's leased fee interest. §516-1(14). The adequacy of compensation is not before us.

After compensation has been set, HHA may sell the land titles to tenants who have applied for fee simple ownership. HHA is authorized to lend these tenants up to 90% of the purchase price, and it may condition final transfer on a right of first refusal for the first 10 years following sale. §§516-30, 516-34, 516-35. If HHA does not sell the lot to the tenant residing there, it may lease the lot or sell it to someone else, provided that public notice has been given. §516-28. However, HHA may not sell to any one purchaser, or lease to any one tenant, more than one lot, and it may not operate for profit. §§516-28, 516-32. In practice, funds to satisfy the condemnation awards have been supplied entirely by lessees. See App. 164. While the Act authorizes HHA to issue bonds and appropriate funds for acquisition, no bonds have issued and HHA has not supplied any funds for condemned lots. . . .

In April 1977, HHA held a public hearing concerning the proposed acquisition of some of appellees' lands. HHA made the statutorily required finding that acquisition of appellees' lands would effectuate the public purposes of the Act. Then, in October 1978, it directed appellees to negotiate with certain lessees concerning the sale of the designated properties. Those negotiations failed, and HHA subsequently ordered appellees to submit to compulsory arbitration.

Rather than comply with the compulsory arbitration order, appellees filed suit, in February 1979, in United States District Court, asking that the Act be declared unconstitutional and that its enforcement be enjoined. The District Court temporarily restrained the State from proceeding against appellees' estates. Three months later, while declaring the compulsory arbitration and compensation formulae provisions of the Act unconstitutional,[5c] the District Court refused preliminarily to enjoin appellants from conducting the statutory designation and condemnation proceedings. Finally, in December 1979, it granted partial summary judgment to appellants, holding the remaining portion of the Act constitutional under the Public Use Clause. See 483 F. Supp. 62 (Haw. 1979). The District Court found that the Act's goals were within the bounds of the State's police powers and that the means the legislature had chosen to serve those goals were not arbitrary, capricious, or selected in bad faith.

The Court of Appeals for the Ninth Circuit reversed. 702 F.2d 788 (CA9 1983). . . . [It] determined that the Hawaii Land Reform Act could not pass the requisite judicial scrutiny of the Public Use Clause. It found that the transfers contemplated by the Act were unlike those of takings previously

---

5c. As originally enacted, lessor and lessee had to commence compulsory arbitration if they could not agree on a price for the fee simple title. Statutory formulae were provided for the determination of compensation. The District Court declared both the compulsory arbitration provision and the compensation formulae unconstitutional. No appeal was taken from these rulings, and the Hawaii legislature subsequently amended the statute to provide only for mandatory negotiation and for advisory compensation formulae. These issues are not before us.

held to constitute "public uses" by this Court. The court further determined that the public purposes offered by the Hawaii Legislature were not deserving of judicial deference. The court concluded that the Act was simply "a naked attempt on the part of the state of Hawaii to take the private property of *A* and transfer it to *B* solely for *B*'s private use and benefit." *Id.,* at 798. One judge dissented.

On applications of HHA and certain private appellants who had intervened below, this Court noted probable jurisdiction.... We now reverse....

The starting point for our analysis of the Act's constitutionality is the Court's decision in Berman v. Parker, 348 U.S. 26, 75 S. Ct. 98, 99 L. Ed. 27 (1954). In *Berman,* the Court held constitutional the District of Columbia Redevelopment Act of 1945. That Act provided both for the comprehensive use of the eminent domain power to redevelop slum areas and for the possible sale or lease of the condemned lands to private interests. In discussing whether the takings authorized by that Act were for a "public use," *id.,* at 31, 75 S. Ct., at 101, the Court stated

> We deal, in other words, with what traditionally has been known as the police power. An attempt to define its reach or trace its outer limits is fruitless, for each case must turn on its own facts. The definition is essentially the product of legislative determinations addressed to the purposes of government, purposes neither abstractly nor historically capable of complete definition. Subject to specific constitutional limitations, when the legislature has spoken, the public interest has been declared in terms well-nigh conclusive. In such cases the legislature, not the judiciary, is the main guardian of the public needs to be served by social legislation, whether it be Congress legislating concerning the District of Columbia . . . or the States legislating concerning local affairs. . . . This principle admits of no exception merely because the power of eminent domain is involved. . . .

Id., at 32, 75 S. Ct., at 102 (citations omitted). The Court explicitly recognized the breadth of the principle it was announcing, noting:

> Once the object is within the authority of Congress, the right to realize it through the exercise of eminent domain is clear. For the power of eminent domain is merely the means to the end. . . . Once the object is within the authority of Congress, the means by which it will be attained is also for Congress to determine. Here one of the means chosen is the use of private enterprise for redevelopment of the area. Appellants argue that this makes the project a taking from one businessman for the benefit of another businessman. But the means of executing the project are for Congress and Congress alone to determine, once the public purpose has been established.

Id., at 33, 75 S. Ct., at 102. The "public use" requirement is thus coterminous with the scope of a sovereign's police powers.

There is, of course, a role for courts to play in reviewing a legislature's judgment of what constitutes a public use, even when the eminent domain power is equated with the police power. But the Court in *Berman* made clear that it is "an extremely narrow" one. *Id.,* at 32, 75 S. Ct., at 102. The Court in *Berman* cited with approval the Court's decision in Old Dominion Co. v. United States, 269 U.S. 55, 66, 46 S. Ct. 39, 40, 70 L. Ed. 162 (1925), which held that deference to the legislature's "public use" determination is required "until it is shown to involve an impossibility." The *Berman* Court also cited to United States ex rel. TVA v. Welch, 327 U.S. 546, 552, 66 S. Ct. 715, 718, 90 L. Ed. 843 (1946), which emphasized that "[a]ny departure from this judicial restraint would result in courts deciding on what is and is not a governmental function and in their invalidating legislation on the basis of their view on that question at the moment of decision, a practice which has proved impracticable in other fields." In short, the Court has made clear that it will not substitute its judgment for a legislature's judgment as to what constitutes a public use "unless the use be palpably without reasonable foundation." United States v. Gettysburg Electric R. Co., 160 U.S 668, 680, 16 S. Ct. 427, 429, 40 L. Ed. 576 (1896).

To be sure, the Court's cases have repeatedly stated that "one person's property may not be taken for the benefit of another private person without a justifying public purpose, even though compensation be paid." Thompson v. Consolidated Gas Corp., 300 U.S. 55, 80, 57 S. Ct. 364, 376, 81 L. Ed. 510 (1937).... Thus, in Missouri Pacific R. Co. v. Nebraska, where the "order in question was not, *and was not claimed to be,* ... a taking of private property for a public use under the right of eminent domain," the Court invalidated a compensated taking of property for lack of a justifying public purpose. 164 U.S. 403, 416, 17 S. Ct. 130, 135, 41 L. Ed. 2d 489 (1896) (emphasis added). But where the exercise of the eminent domain power is rationally related to a conceivable public purpose, the Court has never held a compensated taking to be proscribed by the Public Use Clause. See Berman v. Parker, *supra*; Rindge v. Los Angeles, 262 U.S. 700, 43 S. Ct. 689, 67 L. Ed. 1186 (1923); Block v. Hirsh, 256 U.S. 135, 41 S. Ct. 458, 65 L. Ed. 865 (1921); cf. Thompson v. Consolidated Gas Corp., *supra* (invalidating an *uncompensated* taking).

On this basis, we have no trouble concluding that the Hawaii Act is constitutional. The people of Hawaii have attempted, much as the settlers of the original 13 Colonies did,[5d] to reduce the perceived social and economic evils of a land oligopoly traceable to their monarchs. The land oligopoly

---

5d. After the American Revolution, the colonists in several states took steps to eradicate the feudal incidents with which large proprietors had encumbered land in the colonies. See, e.g., Act of May 1779, 10 Henning's Statutes At Large 64, ch. 13, §6 (1822) (Virginia statute); Divesting Act of 1779, 1775-1781 Pa. Acts 258, ch. 139 (1782) (Pennsylvania statute). Courts have never doubted that such statutes served a public purpose. See, e.g., Wilson v. Iseminger, 185 U.S. 55, 60-61, 22 S. Ct. 573, 574-575, 46 L. Ed. 804 (1902); Stewart v. Gorter, 70 Md. 242, 243, 16 A. 644, 645 (Md. 1889).

has, according to the Hawaii Legislature, created artificial deterrents to the normal functioning of the State's residential land market and forced thousands of individual homeowners to lease, rather than buy, the land underneath their homes. Regulating oligopoly and the evils associated with it is a classic exercise of a State's police powers.... We cannot disapprove of Hawaii's exercise of this power.

Nor can we condemn as irrational the Act's approach to correcting the land oligopoly problem. The Act presumes that when a sufficiently large number of persons declare that they are willing but unable to buy lots at fair prices the land market is malfunctioning. When such a malfunction is signalled, the Act authorizes HHA to condemn lots in the relevant tract. The Act limits the number of lots any one tenant can purchase and authorizes HHA to use public funds to ensure that the market dilution goals will be achieved. This is a comprehensive and rational approach to identifying and correcting market failure.

Of course, this Act, like any other, may not be successful in achieving its intended goals. But "whether *in fact* the provision will accomplish its objectives is not the question: the [constitutional requirement] is satisfied if . . . the . . . [state] Legislature *rationally could have believed* that the [Act] would promote its objective." Western & Southern Life Ins. Co. v. State Bd. of Equalization, 451 U.S. 648, 671-672, 101 S. Ct. 2070, 2084-2085, 68 L. Ed. 2d 514 (1981).... When the legislature's purpose is legitimate and its means are not irrational, our cases make clear that empirical debates over the wisdom of takings — no less than debates over the wisdom of other kinds of socioeconomic legislation — are not to be carried out in the federal courts. Redistribution of fees simple to correct deficiencies in the market determined by the state legislature to be attributable to land oligopoly is a rational exercise of the eminent domain power. Therefore, the Hawaii statute must pass the scrutiny of the Public Use Clause.

The Court of Appeals read our cases to stand for a much narrower proposition. First, it read our "public use" cases, especially *Berman*, as requiring that government possess and use property at some point during a taking. Since Hawaiian lessees retain possession of the property for private use throughout the condemnation process, the court found that the Act exacted takings for private use. 702 F.2d, at 796-797. Second, it determined that these cases involved only "the review of . . . *congressional* determination[s] that there was a public use, *not* the review of . . . state legislative determination[s]." *Id.*, at 798 (emphasis in original). Because state legislative determinations are involved in the instant cases, the Court of Appeals decided that more rigorous judicial scrutiny of the public use determinations was appropriate. The court concluded that the Hawaii Legislature's professed purposes were mere "statutory rationalizations." *Ibid.* We disagree with the Court of Appeals' analysis.

The mere fact that property taken outright by eminent domain is transferred in the first instance to private beneficiaries does not condemn that taking as having only a private purpose. The Court long ago rejected any literal requirement that condemned property be put into use for the general public. "It is not essential that the entire community, nor even any considerable portion, . . . directly enjoy or participate in any improvement in order [for it] to constitute a public use." Rindge Co. v. Los Angeles, 262 U.S., at 707, 43 S. Ct., at 692. "[W]hat in its immediate aspect [is] only a private transaction may . . . be raised by its class or character to a public affair." Block v. Hirsh, 256 U.S., at 155, 41 S. Ct., at 459. As the unique way titles were held in Hawaii skewed the land market, exercise of the power of eminent domain was justified. The Act advances its purposes without the State taking actual possession of the land. In such cases, government does not itself have to use property to legitimate the taking; it is only the taking's purpose, and not its mechanics, that must pass scrutiny under the Public Use Clause.

Similarly, the fact that a state legislature, and not the Congress, made the public use determination does not mean that judicial deference is less appropriate. Judicial deference is required because, in our system of government, legislatures are better able to assess what public purposes should be advanced by an exercise of the taking power. State legislatures are as capable as Congress of making such determinations within their respective spheres of authority. See Berman v. Parker, 348 U.S., at 32, 75 S. Ct., at 102. Thus, if a legislature, state or federal, determines there are substantial reasons for an exercise of the taking power, courts must defer to its determination that the taking will serve a public use.

The State of Hawaii has never denied that the Constitution forbids even a compensated taking of property when executed for no reason other than to confer a private benefit on a particular private party. A purely private taking could not withstand the scrutiny of the public use requirement; it would serve no legitimate purpose of government and would thus be void. But no purely private taking is involved in this case. The Hawaii Legislature enacted its Land Reform Act not to benefit a particular class of identifiable individuals but to attack certain perceived evils of concentrated property ownership in Hawaii — a legitimate public purpose. Use of the condemnation power to achieve this purpose is not irrational. Since we assume for purposes of this appeal that the weighty demand of just compensation has been met, the requirements of the Fifth and Fourteenth Amendments have been satisfied. Accordingly, we reverse the judgment of the Court of Appeals, and remand these cases for further proceedings in conformity with this opinion.

NOTES AND QUESTIONS

1. What does the court mean when it says (at page 146) that the "'public use' requirement is . . . coterminous with the scope of a sovereign's police powers"? The public-use requirement should be read *more* broadly than the police power, should it not?

> The police power question is designed to ask whether the state may go forward without paying at all; the public use requirement asks whether it may go forward if it is prepared to pay. It is therefore wholly improper to allow the very broad tests of public use to play any role in answering the more stringent police power question.

Epstein, Not Deference, but Doctrine: The Eminent Domain Clause, 1982 Sup. Ct. Rev. 351, 370.

2. As recently as 1972, one authority on the law of eminent domain wrote: "Whether the test is stated as public use or public purpose, there is always one thing about which American courts have always said they were adamant. Eminent domain cannot be used to transfer private property from one private person to another." Stoebuck, A General Theory of Eminent Domain, 47 Wash. L. Rev. 553, 595 (1972). One could not, of course, say such a thing now. In light of the *Berman* case, discussed by the Court in *Midkiff*, how could it be said in 1972?

3. Is there, after *Midkiff*, any practical limit set by the public-use requirement? Is there not "in every case some indirect benefit to the public at large [that] will authorize a forced transfer of property from A to B by state intervention"? Epstein, *supra*, at 366. See also the Notes and Questions beginning at page 1105 of the main text.

NOTE: RECENT (EXTREME) INSTANCES OF "PUBLIC USE"

As *Midkiff* perhaps suggests, the boundaries of public use may exist in theory only, like some subatomic particle one can imagine but not actually see. Two illustrations follow.

Poletown Neighborhood Council v. City of Detroit, 410 Mich. 894, 304 N.W.2d 455 (1981). Detroit planned to condemn a residential neighborhood (not a slum or blighted area), clear the land, and convey it to General Motors as a site for construction of an assembly plant. Residents of the neighborhood sued to enjoin the project on the ground that it would take property for a private not a public use.

"What plaintiffs-appellants . . . challenge is the constitutionality of using the power of eminent domain to condemn one person's property to convey it to another private person in order to bolster the economy. They argue that whatever incidental benefit may accrue to the public, assembling land to General Motors' specifications for conveyance to General Motors for its uncontrolled use in profit making is really a taking for private use and not a public use because General Motors is the primary beneficiary of the condemnation.

"The defendants-appellees contend, on the other hand, that the controlling public purpose in taking this land is to create an industrial site which will be used to alleviate and prevent conditions of unemployment and fiscal distress. The fact that it will be conveyed to and ultimately used by a private manufacturer does not defeat this predominant public purpose.

"There is no dispute about the law. All agree that condemnation for a public use or purpose is permitted. All agree that condemnation for a private use or purpose is forbidden. Similarly, condemnation for a private use cannot be authorized whatever its incidental public benefit and condemnation for a public purpose cannot be forbidden whatever the incidental private gain. The heart of this dispute is whether the proposed condemnation is for the primary benefit of the public or the private user.

"The Legislature has determined that governmental action of the type contemplated here meets a public need and serves an essential public purpose. The Court's role after such a determination is made is limited. . . .

"In the court below, the plaintiffs-appellants challenged the necessity for the taking of the land for the proposed project. In this regard the city presented substantial evidence of the severe economic conditions facing the residents of the city and state, the need for new industrial development to revitalize local industries, the economic boost the proposed project would provide, and the lack of other adequate available sites to implement the project. . . .

"In the instant case the benefit to be received by the municipality invoking the power of eminent domain is a clear and significant one and is sufficient to satisfy this Court that such a project was an intended and a legitimate object of the Legislature when it allowed municipalities to exercise condemnation powers even though a private party will also, ultimately, receive a benefit as an incident thereto.

"The power of eminent domain is to be used in this instance primarily to accomplish the essential public purpose of alleviating unemployment and revitalizing the economic base of the community. The benefit to a private interest is merely incidental.

"Our determination that this project falls within the public purpose, as stated by the Legislature, does not mean that every condemnation proposed by an economic development corporation will meet with similar acceptance simply because it may provide some jobs or add to the industrial or commercial base. If the public benefit was not so clear and significant, we would hesitate to sanction approval of such a project. The power of eminent domain is restricted to furthering public uses and purposes and is not to be exercised without substantial proof that the public is primarily to be benefited. Where, as here, the condemnation power is exercised in a way that benefits specific and identifiable private interests, a court inspects with heightened scrutiny the claim that the public interest is the predominant interest being advanced. Such public benefit cannot be speculative or marginal but must be clear and significant if it is to be within the legitimate purpose as stated by the Legislature. We hold this project is warranted on the basis that its significance for the people of Detroit and the state has been demonstrated. . . ."

There were two dissenting opinions in *Poletown*. One distinguished the slum clearance cases relied on by the city, which upheld condemnation for renewal purposes despite the fact that the property taken was eventually transferred to private parties. "The public purpose that has been found to support the slum clearance cases is the benefit to the public health and welfare that arises from the elimination of existing blight. . . ." In such cases, resale to a private party was not a primary purpose but was, rather, "'incidental and ancillary to the primary and real purpose of clearance.' . . . However, in the present case the transfer of the property to General Motors cannot be considered incidental to the taking. It is only through the acquisition and use of the property by General Motors that the 'public purpose' of promoting employment can be achieved. Thus, it is the economic benefits of the project that are incidental to the private use of the property."

The second dissenting opinion called the case "extraordinary."

"The reverberating clang of its economic, sociological, political, and jurisprudential impact is likely to be heard and felt for generations. By its decision, the Court has altered the law of eminent domain in this state in a most significant way and, in my view, seriously jeopardized the security of all private property ownership. . . .

"The real controversy which underlies this litigation concerns the propriety of condemning private property for conveyance to another private party because the use of it by the new owner promises greater public 'benefit' than the old use. The controversy arises in the context of economic crisis. While unemployment is high throughout the nation, it is of calamitous proportions throughout the state of Michigan, and particularly in the City of Detroit, whose economic lifeblood is the now foundering automobile industry. It is difficult to overstate the magnitude of the crisis. Unemployment in the state of Michigan is at 14.2%. In the City of Detroit it is at 18%, and among black citizens it is almost 30%. The high cost of doing business in Michigan generally has driven many manufacturers out of this state and to the so-called sunbelt states on a continuing basis during the past several years. Nowhere is the exodus more steady or more damaging than from the Metropolitan Detroit area. . . .

Eminent Domain and the Implicit Taking Problem

"A new national administration and a reconstituted Congress are struggling to find acceptable means to assist the American automotive industry to compete with the overseas automobile manufacturing competition which is largely accountable for domestic automobile industry losses. To meet that competition, domestic manufacturers are finding it necessary to construct new manufacturing facilities in order to build redesigned, lighter and more economical cars. That means new factories and new factory locations. . . .

"It was in this economic context, fueled with talk of removal of its long-established Cadillac and Fisher Body manufacturing operations from the Detroit area and the construction of a new 3-million-square-foot plant in a sunbelt state, that in 1980 General Motors made its first overture to the City of Detroit about finding a suitable plant site in the city. . . .

"It was, of course, evident to all interested observers that the removal by General Motors of its Cadillac manufacturing operations to a more favorable economic climate would mean the loss to Detroit of at least 6,000 jobs as well as the concomitant loss of literally thousands of allied and supporting automotive design, manufacture and sales functions. There would necessarily follow, as a result, the loss of millions of dollars in real estate and income tax revenues. The darkening picture was made even bleaker by the operation of other forces best explained by the social sciences, including the city's continuing loss of its industrial base and the decline of its population.

"Thus it was to a city with its economic back to the wall that General Motors presented its highly detailed 'proposal' for construction of a new plant in a 'green field' location in the city of Detroit. In addition to the fact that Detroit had virtually no 'green fields', the requirements of the 'proposal' were such that it was clear that no existing location would be suitable unless the city acquired the requisite land one way or another and did so within the General Motors declared time schedule. . . .

"In a most impressive demonstration of governmental efficiency, the City of Detroit set about its task of meeting General Motors' specifications. . . .

"Behind the frenzy of official activity was the unmistakable guiding and sustaining, indeed controlling, hand of the General Motors Corporation. The city administration and General Motors worked in close contact during the summer and autumn of 1980 negotiating the specifics for the new plant site. . . .

"The evidence is that what General Motors wanted, General Motors got. The corporation conceived the project, determined the cost, allocated the financial burdens, selected the site, established the mode of financing, imposed specific deadlines for clearance of the property and taking title, and even demanded 12 years of tax concessions. . . .

"Stripped of the justifying adornments which have universally attended public description of this controversy, the central jurisprudential issue is the right of government to expropriate property from those who do not wish to sell for the use and benefit of a strictly private corporation."

The *Poletown* case is discussed in Millspaugh, Eminent Domain: Is It Getting Out of Hand?, 11 Real Est. L.J. 99 (1982); Ross, Transferring Land to Private Entities by the Power of Eminent Domain, 51 Geo. Wash. L. Rev. 355 (1983); Note, Public Use, Private Use, and Judicial Review in Eminent Domain, 58 N.Y.U.L. Rev. 409 (1983); 28 Wayne L. Rev. 1975.

With *Poletown* compare In re City of Seattle, 96 Wash. 2d 616, 638 P.2d 549 (1981) (municipal improvement project designed to forestall central city decay by condemning land and using it for retail shopping center, public square, park, museum, and off-street parking held not to be for public use, despite public benefits of project).

City of Oakland v. Oakland Raiders, 31 Cal. 3d 656, 646 P.2d 835, 183 Cal. Rptr. 673 (1982). In 1980 the owners of the Oakland Raiders professional football team decided to move the franchise to Los Angeles. Oakland thereafter sought to keep the team by acquiring it through eminent domain. On the issue of public use, the court said:

"Is it possible for City to prove that its attempt to take and operate the Raiders' football franchise is for a valid public use? We have defined 'public use' as 'a use which concerns the whole community or promotes the general interest in its relation to any legitimate object of government.' (Bauer v. County of Ventura [1955] 45 Cal. 2d 276, 284, 289 P.2d 1.) On the other hand, 'It is not essential that the entire community, or even any considerable portion thereof, shall directly enjoy or participate in an improvement in order to constitute a public use.' (Fallbrook Irrigation District v. Bradley [1896] 164 U.S. 112, 161-162, 17 S. Ct. 56, 64, 41 L. Ed. 369; accord University of So. California v. Robbins [1934] 1 Cal. App. 2d 523, 527-528, 37 P.2d 163.) . . .

"Government Code section 37350.5, for example, authorizes a city to 'acquire by eminent domain any property necessary to carry out any of its powers or functions.' (See also §1240.110.) The legislative comment to this section emphasizes that its 'purpose is to give a city adequate authority to carry out its municipal functions.' (See Cal. Law Revision Com. com. to Gov. Code, §37350.5, Deering's Ann. Gov. Code (1981 pocket supp.) p.111.) Under certain circumstances, the governing body of a city may itself establish by resolution that a proposed taking is necessary for a project which is in the public interest. (See §§1240.030, 1240.040, 1245.250, subd. (a), 1245.255, subd. (b).) While the full effect of these statutes has yet to be construed judicially, the general statutory scheme would appear to afford cities considerable discretion in identifying and implementing public uses. . . .

"No case anywhere of which we are aware has held that a municipality can acquire and operate a professional football team, although we are informed that the City of Visalia owns and operates a professional Class A baseball franchise in the California League; apparently, its right to do so never has been challenged in court. May it do so? In our view, several decisions concerning recreation appear germane. In City of Los Angeles v. Superior Court (1959) 51 Cal. 2d 423, 434, 333 P.2d 745, we noted that a city's acquisition of a baseball field, with recreational facilities to be constructed thereon to be used by the city, was 'obviously for proper public purposes.' Similarly, in County of Alameda v. Meadowlark Dairy Corp. (1964) 227 Cal. App. 2d 80, 84, 38 Cal. Rptr. 474, the court upheld a county's acquisition by eminent domain of lands to be used for a county fair, reasoning that 'Activities which promote recreation of the public constitute a public purpose.' (Id., at p.85, 38 Cal. Rptr. 474.) Considerably earlier, in Egan v. San Francisco (1913) 165 Cal. 576, 582, 133 P. 294, in sustaining a city's power to build an opera house, we declared: 'Generally speaking, anything calculated to promote the education, the recreation or the pleasure of the public is to be included within the legitimate domain of public purposes.'

"The examples of Candlestick Park in San Francisco and Anaheim Stadium in Anaheim, both owned and operated by municipalities, further suggest the acceptance of the general principle that providing access to recreation to its residents in the form of spectator sports is an appropriate function of city government. In connection with the latter stadium, the appellate court upheld the power of the City of Anaheim to condemn land for parking facilities at the stadium on the ground that 'the acquisition, construction, and operation of a stadium by a county or city represents a legitimate public purpose. [Citations.]' (City of Anaheim v. Michel [1968] 259 Cal. App. 2d 835, 839, 66 Cal. Rptr. 543.) . . .

"Is the obvious difference between managing and owning the facility in which the game is played, and managing and owning the team which plays in the facility, legally substantial? To date, respondents have not presented a valid legal basis for concluding that it is, but we do not foreclose the trial court's reaching a different conclusion on a fuller record.

"It has been said that 'The concept of public purpose is a broad one. . . . To be serviceable it must expand when necessary to encompass changing public needs. . . .' (Roe v. Kervick [1964] 42 N.J. 191, 207, 199 A.2d 834, 842.) Stated another way, 'A public use defies absolute definition, for it changes with varying conditions of society, new appliances in the sciences, [and] changing conceptions of the scope and functions of government. . . .' (Barnes v. New Haven [1953] 140 Conn. 8, 15, 98 A.2d 523, 527; see 2A Nichols on Eminent Domain (3d ed. 1980) §§7.2, 7.21, pp.7-18, 7-38 to 7-40.)

"While it is readily apparent that the power of eminent domain formerly may have been exercised only to serve certain traditional and limited public purposes, such as the construction and maintenance of streets, highways and parks, these limitations seem merely to have corresponded to an accepted, but narrower, view of appropriate governmental functions then prevailing. The established limitations were not imposed by either constitutional or statutory fiat. . . .

"From the foregoing we conclude only that the acquisition and, indeed, the operation of a sports franchise may be an appropriate municipal function. If such valid public use can be demonstrated, the statutes discussed herein afford City the power to acquire by eminent domain any property necessary to accomplish that use.

"We caution that we are not concerned with the economic or governmental wisdom of City's acquisition or management of the Raiders' franchise, but only with the legal propriety of the condemnation action. In this period of fiscal constraints, if the city fathers of Oakland in their collective wisdom elect to seek the ownership of a professional football franchise are we to say to them nay? And, if so, on what legal ground? Constitutional? Both federal and state Constitutions permit condemnation requiring only compensation and a public use. Statutory? The applicable statutes authorize a city to take 'any property,' real or personal to carry out appropriate municipal functions. Decisional? Courts have consistently expanded the eminent domain remedy permitting property to be taken for recreational purposes.

"Respondents advance the additional argument that even if it is proper for City to own a sports franchise, it cannot condemn an established team. While some statutes do explicitly prohibit the acquisition of an ongoing enterprise, there is no such provision in present law which would preclude the taking contemplated by City. The Legislature knows how to be specific on the point. Government Code section 37353, subdivision (c), for example, provides that while a municipality may condemn land for use as a golf course, an existing golf course may not be acquired by eminent domain. By necessary implication, this statute would seem to suggest that the Legislature has recognized a municipality's broad eminent domain power to acquire an existing business unless expressly forbidden to do so. Such power, of course, had been exercised under previous law. (See, e.g., Citizens Utilities Co. v. Superior Court [1963] 59 Cal. 2d 805, 31 Cal. Rptr. 316, 382 P.2d 356 [operating public utility taken].) . . .

"Respondents urge, further, that because the NFL constitution bars a city from holding a franchise and being a member, the expenditure of any public monies for acquisition of the Raiders' franchise cannot be deemed in the public interest. On the other hand, an affidavit filed by the NFL commissioner avers that 'a brief interim ownership' by City 'would not be inconsistent with the NFL Constitution. . . .' We, of course, are not bound by such an interpretation. Assuming its validity, however, respondents answer that if City contemplates the prompt transfer to private parties of the property interests which it seeks to condemn, after such brief ownership, that transfer would vitiate any legitimate 'public use' which is a prerequisite to condemnation in the first place. . . . So long as adequate controls are imposed upon any retransfer of the condemned property, there is no reason why the 'public purpose' which justified a taking may not be so served and protected. We envision that the adequacy of any such controls can only be determined within the factual context of a specific retransfer agreement. . . .

"BIRD, Chief Justice, concurring and dissenting.

"The power of eminent domain claimed by the City in this case is not only novel but virtually without limit. This is troubling because the potential for abuse of such a great power is boundless. Although I am forced by the current state of the law to agree with the result reached by the majority, I have not signed their opinion because it endorses this unprecedented application of eminent domain law without even pausing to consider the ultimate consequences of their expansive decision. It should be noted that research both by the parties and by this court has failed to disclose a single case in which the legal propositions relied on here have been combined to reach a result such as that adopted by the majority.

"There are two particularly disturbing questions in this case. First, does a city have the power to condemn a viable, ongoing business and sell it to another private party merely because the original owner has announced his intention to move his business to another city? For example, if a rock concert impresario, after some years of producing concerts in a municipal stadium, decides to move his productions to another city, may the city condemn his business, including his contracts with the rock stars, in order to keep the concerts at the stadium? If a small business that rents a storefront on land originally taken by the city for a redevelopment project decides to move to another city in order to expand, may the city take the business and force it to stay at its original location? May a city condemn *any* business that decides to seek greener pastures elsewhere under the unlimited interpretation of eminent domain law that the majority appear to approve?

"Second, even if a city were legally able to do so, is it proper for a municipality to drastically invade personal property rights to further the policy interests asserted here? . . .

"At what point in the varied and complex business relationships involved herein would this power to condemn end? In my view, this court should proceed most cautiously before placing a constitutional imprimatur upon this aspect of creeping statism. These difficult questions are deserving of more thorough attention than they have yet received in this litigation. . . .

"It strikes me as dangerous and heavy-handed for the government to take over a business, including all of its intangible assets, for the sole purpose of preventing its relocation. The decisional law appears to be silent as to this particular question. It appears that the courts have not yet been confronted with a situation such as that presented by this case. However, a review of the pertinent case law demonstrates that decisions as to the proper scope of the power of eminent domain generally have been considered legislative, rather than judicial, in nature. Therefore, in the absence of a legislative bar to the use of eminent domain in this manner, there appears to be no ground for judicial intervention."

The *Raiders* case is discussed in Comment, Taking the Oakland Raiders: A Theoretical Reconsideration of the Concepts of Public Use and Just Compensation, 32 Emory L.J. 857 (1983); Comment, *City of Oakland v. Oakland Raiders:* Defining the Parameters of Limitless Power, 1983 Utah L. Rev. 397. After the *Raiders* decision, Jim Murray, the sports columnist, wondered whether Brooklyn could reclaim the Dodgers from Los Angeles. L.A. Times, June 24, 1982, Pt. III, at 1.

C. MEASURING JUST COMPENSATION

Page 1124. Before "Notes and Questions," insert:

The Court in *564.54 Acres of Land* reserved the question whether substitute-facilities compensation was available for public condemnees. See the main text at page 1119, footnote 11. That question has now been answered by the following case.

UNITED STATES v. 50 ACRES OF LAND
Supreme Court of the United States, 1984   185 S. Ct. 451

Justice STEVENS delivered the opinion of the Court.

The Fifth Amendment requires that the United States pay "just compensation" — normally measured by fair market value — whenever it takes private property for public use. This case involves the condemnation of property owned by a municipality. The question is whether a public condemnee is entitled to compensation measured by the cost of acquiring a substitute facility if it has a duty to replace the condemned facility. We hold that this measure of compensation is not required when the market value of the condemned property is ascertainable.

I

In 1978, as part of a flood control project, the United States condemned approximately 50 acres of land owned by the city of Duncanville, Texas. The site had been used since 1969 as a sanitary landfill. In order to replace the condemned landfill, the city acquired a 113.7 acre site and developed it into a larger and better facility. In the condemnation proceedings, the city claimed that it was entitled to recover all of the costs incurred in acquiring the substitute site and developing it as a landfill, an amount in excess of $1,276,000. The United States, however, contended that just compensation should be determined by the fair market value of the condemned facility and deposited $199,950 in the registry of the court as its estimation of the amount due....

At trial, both parties submitted evidence on the fair market value of the condemned property and on the cost of the substitute landfill facility.[14a] Responding to special interrogatories, the jury found that the fair market value of the condemned property was $225,000, and that the reasonable cost of a substitute facility was $723,624.01. The District Court entered judgment for the lower amount plus interest on the difference between that amount and the sum already paid. The District Court explained that the city had not met its "burden of establishing what would be a reasonable cost of a substitute facility." In addition, the court was of the view that "substitute facilities compensation should not be awarded in every case where a public condemnee can establish a duty to replace the condemned property, at least where a fair market value can be established." 529 F. Supp. 220, 222 (ND Tex. 1981). The court found no basis for departing from the market value standard in this case, and reasoned that the application of the substitute facilities measure of compensation would necessarily provide the city with a "windfall."

The Court of Appeals reversed and remanded for further proceedings. It reasoned that the city's loss attributable to the condemnation was "the amount of money reasonably spent . . . to create a functionally equivalent facility." 706 F.2d 1356, 1360 (CA5 1983). If the city was required, either as a matter of law or as a matter of practical necessity, to replace the old landfill facility, the Court of Appeals believed that it would receive no windfall. The court, however, held that the amount of compensation should be adjusted to account for any qualitative differences in the substitute site. Finding that the trial judge's instructions had not adequately informed the jury of its duty to discount the costs of the substitute facility in order to account for its increased capacity and superior quality, the Court of Appeals remanded for a new trial. We granted the Government's petition for certiorari . . . and we now reverse with instructions to direct the District Court to enter judgment based on the jury's finding of fair market value.

II

The Court has repeatedly held that just compensation normally is to be measured by "the market value of the property at the time of the taking

---

14a. The city's Director of Public Works admitted on cross-examination that the city had condemnation powers, but did not use them in acquiring the land for the new facility. Nor did the city bargain over the seller's asking price or have the land appraised prior to the acquisition: "This was the price that he had asked for, what we ended up paying for it." The Government's expert witnesses testified that the city paid considerably more than fair market value for the new land.

contemporaneously paid in money." Olson v. United States, 292 U.S. 246, 255, 54 S. Ct. 704, 708, 78 L. Ed. 1236 (1934). "Considerations that may not reasonably be held to affect market value are excluded." *Id.*, at 256, 54 S. Ct., at 709. Deviation from this measure of just compensation has been required only "when market value has been too difficult to find, or when its application would result in manifest injustice to owner or public." United States v. Commodities Trading Corp., 339 U.S. 121, 123, 70 S. Ct. 547, 549, 94 L. Ed. 707 (1950). . . .

This case is not one in which an exception to the normal measure of just compensation is required because fair market value is not ascertainable. Such cases, for the most part, involve properties that are seldom, if ever, sold in the open market. Under those circumstances, "we cannot predict whether the prices previously paid, assuming there have been prior sales, would be repeated in a sale of the condemned property." *Lutheran Synod*, 441 U.S., at 513, 99 S. Ct., at 1858. In this case, however, the testimony at trial established a fairly robust market for sanitary landfill properties, and the jury's determination of the fair market value of the condemned landfill facility is adequately supported by expert testimony concerning the sale prices of comparable property.

The city contends that in this case an award of compensation measured by market value is fundamentally inconsistent with the basic principles of indemnity embodied in the Just Compensation Clause. If the city were a private party rather than a public entity, however, the possibility that the cost of a substitute facility exceeds the market value of the condemned parcel would not justify a departure from the market value measure. *Lutheran Synod*, 441 U.S., at 514-517, 99 S. Ct., at 1858-1860. The question — which we expressly reserved in the *Lutheran Synod* case — is whether a substitute facilities measure of compensation is mandated by the Constitution when the condemnee is a local governmental entity that has a duty to replace the condemned facility.

III

The text of the Fifth Amendment certainly does not mandate a more favorable rule of compensation for public condemnees than for private parties. To the contrary, the language of the Amendment only refers to compensation for "private property," and one might argue that the Framers intended to provide greater protection for the interests of private parties than for public condemnees. That argument would be supported by the observation that many public condemnees have the power of eminent domain, and thus, unlike private parties, need not rely on the availability of property on the market in acquiring substitute facilities.

When the United States condemns a local public facility the loss to the public entity, to the persons served by it, and to the local taxpayers may be no less acute than the loss in a taking of private property. Therefore, it is most reasonable to construe the reference to "private property" in the Takings Clause of the Fifth Amendment as encompassing the property of state and local governments when it is condemned by the United States. Under this construction, the same principles of just compensation presumptively apply to both private and public condemnees.

IV

The Court of Appeals correctly identified a dictum in Brown v. United States, 263 U.S. 78, 44 S. Ct. 92, 68 L. Ed. 171 (1923), as the source of what has become known as the "substitute facilities doctrine." When that passage is read in the context of the Court's decision in that case, it lends no support to the suggestion that a distinction should be drawn between public and private condemnees. Nor does it shed any light on the proper measure of compensation in this case.

The facts of the *Brown* case were, in the Court's word, "peculiar."[14b] The construction of a reservoir on the Snake River flooded approximately three-quarters of the town of American Falls, Idaho, an area of some 640 acres. To compensate both the public and private owners of the flooded acreage, the Government undertook to relocate most of the town to the other side of the river. The owners of a large tract to be included within the limits of the reconstructed town challenged the Government's power to condemn their property, contending that the transfer of their property to other private persons was not a "public use" as required by the Fifth Amendment. Cf. Hawaii Housing Authority v. Midkiff, 104 S. Ct. 2321 (1984).

In rejecting that contention, the Court held that the Government's method of compensating the owners of the flooded property was legitimate. Writing for the Court, Chief Justice Taft observed:

> The usual and ordinary method of condemnation of the lots in the old town, and of the streets and alleys as town property, would be ill adapted to the exigency.... A town is a business center. It is a unit. If three-quarters of it is to be destroyed by appropriating it to an exclusive use like a reservoir, all property

---

14b. "An important town stood in the way of a necessary improvement by the United States. Three-quarters of its streets, alleys and parks and of its buildings, public and private, would have to be abandoned.... American Falls is a large settlement for that sparsely settled country and it was many miles from a town of any size in any direction. It was a natural and proper part of the construction of the dam and reservoir to make provision for a substitute town as near as possible to the old one." 263 U.S., at 81, 44 S. Ct., at 93.

owners, both those ousted and those in the remaining quarter, as well as the State, whose subordinate agency of government is the municipality, are injured. A method of compensation by substitution would seem to be the best means of making the parties whole. *The power of condemnation is necessary to such a substitution.*

263 U.S., at 82-83, 44 S. Ct., at 93-94 (emphasis added). Taken in context, the apparent endorsement of compensation by substitution is made in support of the Government's power to condemn the property in *Brown* and does not state the proper measure of compensation in another case. *Lutheran Synod,* 441 U.S., at 509, n.3, 99 S. Ct., at 1856, n.3.

Brown merely indicates that it would have been constitutionally permissible for the Federal Government to provide the city with a substitute landfill site instead of compensating it in cash. Nothing in *Brown* implies that the Federal Government has a duty to provide the city with anything more than the fair market value of the condemned property.

V

In this case, as in most, the market measure of compensation achieves a fair "balance between the public's need and the claimant's loss." United States v. Toronto, Hamilton & Buffalo Navigation Co., 338 U.S. 396, 402, 70 S. Ct. 217, 221, 94 L. Ed. 195 (1949). This view is consistent with our holding in *Lutheran Synod* that fair market value constitutes "just compensation" for those private citizens who must replace their condemned property with more expensive substitutes and with our prior holdings that the Fifth Amendment does not require any award for consequential damages arising from a condemnation.

The city argues that its responsibility for municipal garbage disposal justifies a departure from the market value measure in this case. This responsibility compelled the city to arrange for a suitable replacement facility or substitute garbage disposal services. This obligation to replace a condemned facility, however, is no more compelling than the obligations assumed by private citizens. Even though most private condemnees are not legally obligated to replace property taken by the Government, economic circumstances often force them to do so. When a home is condemned, for example, its owner must find another place to live. The city's legal obligation to maintain public services that are interrupted by a federal condemnation does not justify a distinction between public and private condemnees for the purpose of measuring "just compensation."

Of course, the decision in *Lutheran Synod* was based, in part, on a fear that a private condemnee might receive a "windfall" if its compensation were measured by the cost of a substitute facility and "substitute facilities were never acquired, or if acquired, were later sold or converted to another use." 441 U.S., at 516, 99 S. Ct., at 1859. The Court of Appeals suggested that the city's obligation to replace the facility avoids this risk, 706 F.2d, at 1360, but we do not agree. If the replacement facility is more costly than the condemned facility, it presumably is more valuable, and any increase in the quality of the facility may be as readily characterized as a "windfall" as the award of cash proceeds for a substitute facility that is never built.

The Court of Appeals, however, believed that the risk of any windfall could be reduced by discounting the cost of the substitute facility to account for its superior quality. *Id.,* at 1362-1363. This approach would add uncertainty and complexity to the valuation proceeding without any necessary improvement in the process. In order to implement the Court of Appeals' approach, the factfinder would have to make at least two determinations: (i) the reasonable (rather than the actual) replacement cost, which would require an inquiry into the fair market value of the second facility; and (ii) the extent to which the new facility is superior to the old, which would require an analysis of the qualitative differences between the new and the old. It would also be necessary to determine the fair market value of the old property in order to provide a basis for comparison. There is a practical risk that the entire added value will not be calculated correctly; moreover, if it is correctly estimated, the entire process may amount to nothing more than a round-about method of arriving at the market value of the condemned facility.

Finally, the substitute facilities doctrine, as applied in this case, diverges from the principle that just compensation must be measured by an objective standard that disregards subjective values which are only of significance to an individual owner. As the Court wrote in Kimball Laundry Co. v. United States, 338 U.S. 1, 5, 69 S. Ct. 1434, 1437, 93 L. Ed. 1765 (1949):

> The value of property springs from subjective needs and attitudes; its value to the owner may therefore differ widely from its value to the taker. Most things, however, have a general demand which gives them a value transferable from one owner to another. As opposed to such personal and variant standards as value to the particular owner whose property has been taken, this transferable value has an external validity which makes it a fair measure of public obligation to compensate the loss incurred by an owner as a result of the taking of his property for public use. In view, however, of the liability of all property to condemnation for the common good, loss to the owner of nontransferable values deriving from his unique need for property or idiosyncratic attachment to it, like loss due to an exercise of the police power, is properly treated as part of the burden of common citizenship.

The subjective elements in the formula for determining the cost of reasonable substitute facilities would enhance the risk of error and prejudice.[14c]

14c. Cf. R. Posner, Economic Analysis of Law 402 (2d Ed. 1977) ("The vogue of cost-benefit analysis has created inflated notions of the effectiveness of analytical techniques in resolving questions of cost and demand").

Since the condemnation contest is between the local community and a national government that may be thought to have unlimited resources, the open-ended character of the substitute facilities standard increases the likelihood that the city would actually derive the windfall that concerned both the District Court and the Court of Appeals. "Particularly is this true where these issues are to be left for jury determination, for juries should not be given sophistical and abstruse formulas as the basis for their findings nor be left to apply even sensible formulas to factors that are too elusive." *Id.*, at 20, 69 S. Ct., at 1445.

The judgment of the Court of Appeals is reversed.

D. EXPLICIT AND IMPLICIT TAKINGS

Page 1146. At the end of the second sentence of Note 1, add:

Just was followed in Graham v. Estuary Properties, Inc., 399 So. 2d 1374 (Fla. 1981), noted in 33 U. Fla. L. Rev. 615 (1981). The court in Graham said (399 So. 2d at 1382):

> As previously stated, the line between the prevention of a public harm and the creation of a public benefit is not often clear. It is a necessary result that the public benefits whenever a harm is prevented. However, it does not necessarily follow that the public is safe from harm when a benefit is created. In this case, the permit was denied because of the determination that the proposed development would pollute the surrounding bays, i.e., cause public harm. It is true that the public benefits in that the bays will remain clean, but that is a benefit in the form of maintaining the status quo. Estuary is not being required to change its development plan so that public waterways will be improved. That would be the creation of a public benefit beyond the scope of the state's police power.

See generally Annot., 19 A.L.R.4th 756 (1983).

Page 1158. Before "3. Diminution in Value," insert:

LORETTO v. TELEPROMPTER MANHATTAN CATV CORP.
Supreme Court of the United States, 1982
458 U.S. 419

Justice MARSHALL delivered the opinion of the court.

This case presents the question whether a minor but permanent physical occupation of an owner's property authorized by government constitutes a "taking" of property for which just compensation is due under the Fifth and Fourteenth Amendments of the Constitution. New York law provides that a landlord must permit a cable television company to install its cable facilities upon his property. N.Y. Exec. Law §828(1) (McKinney Supp. 1981-1982). In this case, the cable installation occupied portions of appellant's roof and the side of her building. The New York Court of Appeals ruled that this appropriation does not amount to a taking. 53 N.Y.2d 124, 423 N.E. 2d 320 (1981). Because we conclude that such a physical occupation of property is a taking, we reverse.

I

Appellant Jean Loretto purchased a five-story apartment building located at 303 West 105th Street, New York City, in 1971. The previous owner had granted appellees Teleprompter Corporation and Teleprompter Manhattan CATV (collectively Teleprompter) permission to install a cable on the building and the exclusive privilege of furnishing cable television (CATV) services to the tenants. The New York Court of Appeals described the installation as follows:

> On June 1, 1970 TelePrompter installed a cable slightly less than one-half inch in diameter and of approximately 30 feet in length along the length of the building about 18 inches above the roof top, and directional taps, approximately 4 inches by 4 inches by 4 inches, on the front and rear of the roof. By June 8, 1970 the cable had been extended another 4 to 6 feet and cable had been run from the directional taps to the adjoining building at 305 West 105th Street.

Id., at 135, 423 N.E.2d, at 324. Teleprompter also installed two large silver boxes along the roof cables. The cables are attached by screws or nails penetrating the masonry at approximately two-foot intervals, and other equipment is installed by bolts.

Initially, Teleprompter's roof cables did not service appellant's building. They were part of what could be described as a cable "highway" circumnavigating the city block, with service cables periodically dropped over the front or back of a building in which a tenant desired service. Crucial to such a network is the use of so-called "crossovers" — cable lines extending from one building to another in order to reach a new group of tenants. Two years after appellant purchased the building, Teleprompter connected a "noncrossover" line — i.e., one that provided CATV service to appellant's own tenants — by dropping a line to the first floor down the front of appellant's building.

Prior to 1973, Teleprompter routinely obtained authorization for its installations from property owners along the cable's route, compensating the owners at the standard rate of 5% of the gross revenues that Teleprompter realized from the particular property. To facilitate tenant access to CATV, the State of New York enacted §828 of the Executive Law, effective January 1, 1973. Section 828 provides that a landlord may not "interfere with the installation of cable television facilities upon his property or premises," and

161

may not demand payment from any tenant for permitting CATV, or demand payment from any CATV company "in excess of any amount which the [State Commission on Cable Television] shall, by regulation, determine to be reasonable." The landlord may, however, require the CATV company or the tenant to bear the cost of installation and to indemnify for any damage caused by the installation. Pursuant to §828(1)(b), the State Commission has ruled that a one-time $1 payment is the normal fee to which a landlord is entitled. In the Matter of Implementation of Section 828 of the Executive Law, No. 90004, Statement of General Policy (New York State Commission on Cable Television, Jan. 15, 1976) (Statement of General Policy), App. 51-52; Clarification of General Policy (Aug. 27, 1976), App. 68-69. The Commission ruled that this nominal fee, which the Commission concluded was equivalent to what the landlord would receive if the property were condemned pursuant to New York's Transportation Corporations Law, satisfied constitutional requirements "in the absence of a special showing of greater damages attributable to the taking." Statement of General Policy, App. 52.

Appellant did not discover the existence of the cable until after she had purchased the building. She brought a class action against Teleprompter in 1976 on behalf of all owners of real property in the State on which Teleprompter has placed CATV components, alleging that Teleprompter's installation was a trespass and, insofar as it relied on §828, a taking without just compensation. She requested damages and injunctive relief. Appellee the City of New York, which has granted Teleprompter an exclusive franchise to provide CATV within certain areas of Manhattan, intervened. The Supreme Court, Special Term, granted summary judgment to Teleprompter and the city, upholding the constitutionality of §828 in both crossover and noncrossover situations. 98 Misc. 2d 944, 415 N.Y.S.2d 180 (1979). The Appellate Division affirmed without opinion. 73 App. Div. 2d 849, 422 N.Y.S.2d 550 (1979).

On appeal, the Court of Appeals, over dissent, upheld the statute. 53 N.Y.2d 124, 423 N.E.2d 320 (1981). The court concluded that the law requires the landlord to allow both crossover and noncrossover installations but permits him to request payment from the CATV company under §828(1)(b), at a level determined by the State Cable Commission, only for noncrossovers. The court then ruled that the law serves a legitimate police power purpose — eliminating landlord fees and conditions that inhibit the development of CATV, which has important educational and community benefits. Rejecting the argument that a physical occupation authorized by government is necessarily a taking, the court stated that the regulation does not have an excessive economic impact upon appellant when measured against her aggregate property rights, and that it does not interfere with any reasonable investment-backed expectations. Accordingly, the court held that §828 does not work a taking of appellant's property. Chief Judge

Cooke dissented, reasoning that the physical appropriation of a portion of appellant's property is a taking without regard to the balancing analysis courts ordinarily employ in evaluating whether a regulation is a taking.

In light of its holding, the Court of Appeals had no occasion to determine whether the $1 fee ordinarily awarded for a noncrossover installation was adequate compensation for the taking. Judge Gabrielli, concurring, agreed with the dissent that the law works a taking but concluded that the $1 presumptive award, together with the procedures permitting a landlord to demonstrate a greater entitlement, affords just compensation. We noted probable jurisdiction. 454 U.S. 938 (1981).

II

The Court of Appeals determined that §828 serves the legitimate public purpose of "rapid development of and maximum penetration by a means of communication which has important educational and community aspects," 53 N.Y.2d, at 143-144, 423 N.E.2d, at 329, and thus is within the State's police power. We have no reason to question that determination. It is a separate question, however, whether an otherwise valid regulation so frustrates property rights that compensation must be paid. See Penn Central Transportation Co. v. New York City, 438 U.S. 104, 127-128 (1978); Delaware, L. & W. R. Co. v. Morristown, 276 U. S. 182, 193 (1928). We conclude that a permanent physical occupation authorized by government is a taking without regard to the public interests that it may serve. Our constitutional history confirms the rule, recent cases do not question it, and the purposes of the Takings Clause compel its retention.

A

In Penn Central Transportation Co. v. New York City, *supra*, the Court surveyed some of the general principles governing the Takings Clause. The Court noted that no "set formula" existed to determine, in all cases, whether compensation is constitutionally due for a government restriction of property. Ordinarily, the Court must engage in "essentially ad hoc, factual inquiries." *Id.*, at 124. But the inquiry is not standardless. The economic impact of the regulation, especially the degree of interference with investment-backed expectations, is of particular significance.

> So, too, is the character of the governmental action. A "taking" may more readily be found when the interference with property can be characterized as a physical invasion by government, than when interference arises from some public program adjusting the benefits and burdens of economic life to promote the common good.

Ibid. (citation omitted).

As *Penn Central* affirms, the Court has often upheld substantial regulation of an owner's use of his own property where deemed necessary to promote the public interest. At the same time, we have long considered a physical intrusion by government to be a property restriction of an unusually serious character for purposes of the Takings Clause. Our cases further establish that when the physical intrusion reaches the extreme form of a permanent physical occupation, a taking has occurred. In such a case, "the character of the government action" not only is an important factor in resolving whether the action works a taking but also is determinative.

When faced with a constitutional challenge to a permanent physical occupation of real property, this Court has invariably found a taking. As early as 1872, in Pumpelly v. Green Bay Co., 13 Wall. 166, this Court held that the defendant's construction, pursuant to state authority, of a dam which permanently flooded plaintiff's property constituted a taking. A unanimous Court stated, without qualification, that "where real estate is actually invaded by superinduced additions of water, earth, sand, or other material, or by having any artificial structure placed on it, so as to effectually destroy or impair its usefulness, it is a taking, within the meaning of the Constitution." *Id.*, at 181. Seven years later, the Court reemphasized the importance of a physical occupation by distinguishing a regulation that merely restricted the use of private property. In Northern Transportation Co. v. Chicago, 99 U.S. 635 (1879), the Court held that the city's construction of a temporary dam in a river to permit construction of a tunnel was not a taking, even though the plaintiffs were thereby denied access to their premises, because the obstruction only impaired the use of plaintiffs' property. The Court distinguished earlier cases in which permanent flooding of private property was regarded as a taking, e.g., *Pumpelly, supra,* as involving "a physical invasion of the real estate of the private owner, and a practical ouster of his possession." In this case, by contrast, "[n]o entry was made upon the plaintiffs' lot." 99 U.S., at 642.

Since these early cases, this Court has consistently distinguished between flooding cases involving a permanent physical occupation, on the one hand, and cases involving a more temporary invasion, or government action outside the owner's property that causes consequential damages within, on the other. A taking has always been found only in the former situation. . . .

More recent cases confirm the distinction between a permanent physical occupation, a physical invasion short of an occupation, and a regulation that merely restricts the use of property. In United States v. Causby, 328 U.S. 256 (1946), the Court ruled that frequent flights immediately above a landowner's property constituted a taking, comparing such overflights to the quintessential form of a taking:

> If, by reason of the frequency and altitude of the flights, respondents could not

use this land for any purpose, their loss would be complete. It would be as complete as if the United States had entered upon the surface of the land and taken exclusive possession of it.

Id., at 261 (footnote omitted). . . .

Although this Court's most recent cases have not addressed the precise issue before us, they have emphasized that physical *invasion* cases are special and have not repudiated the rule that any permanent physical *occupation* is a taking. The cases state or imply that a physical invasion is subject to a balancing process, but they do not suggest that a permanent physical occupation would ever be exempt from the Takings Clause.

Penn Central Transportation Co. v. New York City, as noted above, contains one of the most complete discussions of the Takings Clause. The Court explained that resolving whether public action works a taking is ordinarily an ad hoc inquiry in which several factors are particularly significant — the economic impact of the regulation, the extent to which it interferes with investment-backed expectations, and the character of the governmental action. 438 U.S., at 124. The opinion does not repudiate the rule that a permanent physical occupation is a government action of such a unique character that it is a taking without regard to other factors that a court might ordinarily examine.[27a]

In Kaiser Aetna v. United States, 444 U.S. 164 (1979), the Court held that the Government's imposition of a navigational servitude requiring public access to a pond was a taking where the landowner had reasonably relied on Government consent in connecting the pond to navigable water. The Court emphasized that the servitude took the landowner's right to exclude, "one of the most essential sticks in the bundle of rights that are commonly characterized as property." *Id.*, at 176. The Court explained:

> This is not a case in which the Government is exercising its regulatory power in a manner that will cause an insubstantial devaluation of petitioner's private property; rather, the imposition of the navigational servitude in this context will result in an *actual physical invasion* of the privately owned marina. . . . And even if the Government physically invades only an easement in property, it must nonethe-

---

27a. The City of New York and the opinion of the Court of Appeals place great emphasis on *Penn Central's* reference to a physical invasion "by government," 438 U.S., at 124, and argue that a similar invasion by a private party should be treated differently. We disagree. A permanent physical occupation authorized by state law is a taking without regard to whether the State, or instead a party authorized by the State, is the occupant. See, e.g., Pumpelly v. Green Bay Co., 13 Wall. 166 (1872). *Penn Central* simply holds that in cases of physical invasion short of permanent appropriation, the fact that the government itself commits an invasion from which it directly benefits is one relevant factor in determining whether a taking has occurred. 438 U.S., at 124, 128.

less pay compensation. See United States v. Causby, 328 U.S. 256, 265 (1946); Portsmouth Co. v. United States, 260 U.S. 327 (1922).

Id., at 180 (emphasis added). Although the easement of passage, not being a permanent occupation of land, was not considered a taking per se, *Kaiser Aetna* reemphasizes that a physical invasion is a government intrusion of an unusually serious character.[27b]

Another recent case underscores the constitutional distinction between a permanent occupation and a temporary physical invasion. In PruneYard Shopping Center v. Robins, 447 U.S. 74 (1980), the Court upheld a state constitutional requirement that shopping center owners permit individuals to exercise free speech and petition rights on their property, to which they had already invited the general public. The Court emphasized that the State Constitution does not prevent the owner from restricting expressive activities by imposing reasonable time, place, and manner restrictions to minimize interference with the owner's commercial functions. Since the invasion was temporary and limited in nature, and since the owner had not exhibited an interest in excluding all persons from his property, "the fact that [the solicitors] may have 'physically invaded' [the owners'] property cannot be viewed as determinative." *Id.*, at 84.

In short, when the "character of the governmental action," *Penn Central*, 438 U.S., at 124, is a permanent physical occupation of property, our cases uniformly have found a taking to the extent of the occupation, without regard to whether the action achieves an important public benefit or has only minimal economic impact on the owner.

B

The historical rule that a permanent physical occupation of another's property is a taking has more than tradition to commend it. Such an appropriation is perhaps the most serious form of invasion of an owner's property interests. To borrow a metaphor, cf. Andrus v. Allard, 444 U.S. 51, 65-66 (1979), the government does not simply take a single "strand" from the "bundle" of property rights: it chops through the bundle, taking a slice of every strand.

Property rights in a physical thing have been described as the rights "to possess, use and dispose of it." United States v. General Motors Corp., 323 U.S. 373, 378 (1945). To the extent that the government permanently oc-

---

27b. See also Andrus v. Allard, 444 U.S. 51 (1979). That case held that the prohibition of the sale of eagle feathers was not a taking as applied to traders of bird artifacts. "The regulations challenged here do not compel the surrender of the artifacts, and there is no physical invasion or restraint upon them. . . . In this case, it is crucial that appellees retain the rights to possess and transport their property, and to donate or devise the protected birds. . . . [L]oss of future profits — unaccompanied by any physical property restriction — provides a slender reed upon which to rest a takings claim." *Id.*, at 65-66.

cupies physical property, it effectively destroys *each* of these rights. First, the owner has no right to possess the occupied space himself, and also has no power to exclude the occupier from possession and use of the space. The power to exclude has traditionally been considered one of the most treasured strands in an owner's bundle of property rights.[27c] See *Kaiser Aetna,* 444 U.S., at 179-180; see also Restatement of Property §7 (1936). Second, the permanent physical occupation of property forever denies the owner any power to control the use of the property; he not only cannot exclude others, but can make no nonpossessory use of the property. Although deprivation of the right to use and obtain a profit from property is not, in every case, independently sufficient to establish a taking, see Andrus v. Allard, *supra,* at 66, it is clearly relevant. Finally, even though the owner may retain the bare legal right to dispose of the occupied space by transfer or sale, the permanent occupation of that space by a stranger will ordinarily empty the right of any value, since the purchaser will also be unable to make any use of the property.

Moreover, an owner suffers a special kind of injury when a *stranger* directly invades and occupies the owner's property. As Part II-A, *supra,* indicates, property law has long protected an owner's expectation that he will be relatively undisturbed at least in the possession of his property. To require, as well, that the owner permit another to exercise complete dominion literally adds insult to injury. See Michelman, Property, Utility, and Fairness: Comments on the Ethical Foundations of "Just Compensation" Law, 80 Harv. L. Rev. 1165, 1228, and n.110 (1967). Furthermore, such an occupation is qualitatively more severe than a regulation of the *use* of property, even a regulation that imposes affirmative duties on the owner, since the owner may have no control over the timing, extent, or nature of the invasion. See n.27e, *infra.*

The traditional rule also avoids otherwise difficult line-drawing problems. Few would disagree that if the State required landlords to permit third parties to install swimming pools on the landlords' rooftops for the

---

27c. The permanence and absolute exclusivity of a physical occupation distinguish it from temporary limitations on the right to exclude. Not every physical *invasion* is a taking. As PruneYard Shopping Center v. Robins, 447 U.S. 74 (1980), Kaiser Aetna v. United States, 444 U.S. 164 (1979), and the intermittent flooding cases reveal, such temporary limitations are subject to a more complex balancing process to determine whether they are a taking. The rationale is evident: they do not absolutely dispossess the owner of his rights to use, and exclude others from, his property.

The dissent objects that the distinction between a permanent physical occupation and a temporary invasion will not always be clear. This objection is overstated, and in any event is irrelevant to the critical point that a permanent physical occupation *is* unquestionably a taking. In the antitrust area, similarly, this Court has not declined to apply a per se rule simply because a court must, at the boundary of the rule, apply the rule of reason and engage in a more complex balancing analysis.

convenience of the tenants, the requirement would be a taking. If the cable installation here occupied as much space, again, few would disagree that the occupation would be a taking. But constitutional protection for the rights of private property cannot be made to depend on the size of the area permanently occupied. Indeed, it is possible that in the future, additional cable installations that more significantly restrict a landlord's use of the roof of his building will be made. Section 828 requires a landlord to permit such multiple installations.

Finally, whether a permanent physical occupation has occurred presents relatively few problems of proof. The placement of a fixed structure on land or real property is an obvious fact that will rarely be subject to dispute. Once the fact of occupation is shown, of course, a court should consider the *extent* of the occupation as one relevant factor in determining the compensation due. For that reason, moreover, there is less need to consider the extent of the occupation in determining whether there is a taking in the first instance.

C

Teleprompter's cable installation on appellant's building constitutes a taking under the traditional test. The installation involved a direct physical attachment of plates, boxes, wires, bolts, and screws to the building, completely occupying space immediately above and upon the roof and along the building's exterior wall.[27d]

In light of our analysis, we find no constitutional difference between a crossover and a noncrossover installation. The portions of the installation necessary for both crossovers and noncrossovers permanently appropriate appellant's property. Accordingly, each type of installation is a taking.

Appellees raise a series of objections to application of the traditional rule here. Teleprompter notes that the law applies only to buildings used as rental property, and draws the conclusion that the law is simply a permissible regulation of the use of real property. We fail to see, however, why a physi-

---

27d. It is constitutionally irrelevant whether appellant (or her predecessor in title) had previously occupied this space, since a "landowner owns at least as much of the space above the ground as he can occupy or use in connection with the land." United States v. Causby, *supra*, at 264.

The dissent asserts that a taking of about one-eighth of a cubic foot of space is not of constitutional significance. The assertion appears to be factually incorrect, since it ignores the two large silver boxes that appellant identified as part of the installation. App. 90; Loretto Affidavit in Support of Motion for Summary Judgment (Apr. 21, 1978), Appellants' Appendix in No. 8300/76 (N.Y. App.), p.77. Although the record does not reveal their size, appellant states that they are approximately 18" × 12" × 6", Brief for Appellant 6 n.*, and appellees do not dispute this statement. The displaced volume, then, is in excess of 1½ cubic feet. In any event, these facts are not critical: whether the installation is a taking does not depend on whether the volume of space it occupies is bigger than a breadbox.

cal occupation of one type of property but not another type is any less a physical occupation. Insofar as Teleprompter means to suggest that this is not a permanent physical invasion, we must differ. So long as the property remains residential and a CATV company wishes to retain the installation, the landlord must permit it.

Teleprompter also asserts the related argument that the State has effectively granted a tenant the property right to have a CATV installation placed on the roof of his building, as an appurtenance to the tenant's leasehold. The short answer is that §828(1)(a) does not purport to give the *tenant* any enforceable property rights with respect to CATV installation, and the lower courts did not rest their decisions on this ground. Of course, Teleprompter, not appellant's tenants, actually owns the installation. Moreover, the government does not have unlimited power to redefine property rights. See Webb's Fabulous Pharmacies, Inc. v. Beckwith, 449 U.S. 155, 164 (1980) ("a State, by ipse dixit, may not transform private property into public property without compensation").

Finally, we do not agree with appellees that application of the physical occupation rule will have dire consequences for the government's power to adjust landlord-tenant relationships. This Court has consistently affirmed that States have broad power to regulate housing conditions in general and the landlord-tenant relationship in particular without paying compensation for all economic injuries that such regulation entails. See, e.g., Heart of Atlanta Motel, Inc. v. United States, 379 U.S. 241 (1964) (discrimination in places of public accomodation); Queenside Hills Realty Co. v. Saxl, 328 U.S. 80 (1946) (fire regulation): Bowles v. Willingham, 321 U.S. 503 (1944) (rent control); Home Building & Loan Assn. v. Blaisdell, 290 U.S. 398 (1934) (mortgage moratorium); Edgar A. Levy Leasing Co. v. Siegel, 258 U.S. 242 (1922) (emergency housing law); Block v. Hirsh, 256 U.S. 135 (1921) (rent control). In none of these cases, however, did the government authorize the permanent occupation of the landlord's property by a third party. Consequently, our holding today in no way alters the analysis governing the State's power to require landlords to comply with building codes and provide utility connections, mailboxes, smoke detectors, fire extinguishers, and the like in the common area of a building. So long as these regulations do not require the landlord to suffer the physical occupation of a portion of his building by a third party, they will be analyzed under the multifactor inquiry generally applicable to nonpossessory governmental activity. See Penn Central Transportation Co. v. New York City, 438 U.S. 104 (1978).[27e]

[27e]. If §828 required landlords to provide cable installation if a tenant so desires, the statute might present a different question from the question before us, since the landlord would own the installation. Ownership would give the landlord rights to the placement, manner, use, and possibly the disposition of the installation. The fact of ownership is, contrary to the dissent, not simply "incidental," it would give a landlord (rather than a CATV

III

Our holding today is very narrow. We affirm the traditional rule that a permanent physical occupation of property is a taking. In such a case, the property owner entertains a historically rooted expectation of compensation, and the character of the invasion is qualitatively more intrusive than perhaps any other category of property regulation. We do not, however, question the equally substantial authority upholding a State's broad power to impose appropriate restrictions upon an owner's *use* of his property.

Furthermore, our conclusion that §828 works a taking of a portion of appellant's property does not presuppose that the fee which many landlords had obtained by Teleprompter prior to the law's enactment is a proper measure of the value of the property taken. The issue of the amount of compensation that is due, on which we express no opinion, is a matter for the state courts to consider on remand. . . .

Justice BLACKMUN, with whom Justice BRENNAN and Justice WHITE join, dissenting.

If the Court's decisions construing the Takings Clause state anything clearly, it is that "[t]here is no set formula to determine where regulation ends and taking begins." Goldblatt v. Town of Hempstead, 369 U.S. 590, 594 (1962).

In a curiously anachronistic decision, the Court today acknowledges its historical disavowal of set formulae in almost the same breath as it constructs a rigid per se takings rule: "a permanent physical occupation authorized by government is a taking without regard to the public interests that it may serve." To sustain its rule against our recent precedents, the Court erects a strained and untenable distinction between "temporary physical in-

---

company) full authority over the installation except only as government specifically limited that authority. The *landlord* would decide how to comply with applicable government regulations concerning CATV and therefore could minimize the physical, esthetic, and other effects of the installation. Moreover, if the landlord wished to repair, demolish, or construct in the area of the building where the installation is located, he need not incur the burden of obtaining the CATV company's cooperation in moving the cable.

In this case, by contrast, appellant suffered injury that might have been obviated if she had owned the cable and could exercise control over its installation. The drilling and stapling that accompanied installation apparently caused physical damage to appellant's building. App. 83, 95-96, 104. Appellant, who resides in her building, further testified that the cable installation is "ugly." *Id.*, at 99. Although §828 provides that a landlord may require "reasonable" conditions that are "necessary" to protect the appearance of the premises and may seek indemnity for damage, these provisions are somewhat limited. Even if the provisions are effective, the inconvenience to the landlord of initiating the repairs remains a cognizable burden.

vasions," whose constitutionality concededly "is subject to a balancing process," and "permanent physical occupations," which are "taking[s] without regard to other factors that a court might ordinarily examine."

In my view, the Court's approach "reduces the constitutional issue to a formalistic quibble" over whether property has been "permanently occupied" or "temporarily invaded." Sax, Takings and the Police Power, 74 Yale L.J. 36, 37 (1964). The Court's application of its formula to the facts of this case vividly illustrates that its approach is potentially dangerous as well as misguided. Despite its concession that "States have broad power to regulate . . . the landlord-tenant relationship . . . without paying compensation for all economic injuries that such regulation entails," the Court uses its rule to undercut a carefully considered legislative judgment concerning landlord-tenant relationships. I therefore respectfully dissent.

I

Before examining the Court's new takings rule, it is worth reviewing what was "taken" in this case. At issue are about 36 feet of cable one-half inch in diameter and two 4″ × 4″ × 4″ metal boxes. Jointly, the cable and boxes occupy only about one-eighth of a cubic foot of space on the roof of appellant's Manhattan apartment building. When appellant purchased that building in 1971, the "physical invasion" she now challenges had already occurred.[27f] Appellant did not bring this action until about five years later, demanding 5% of appellee Teleprompter's gross revenues from her building, and claiming that the operation of N.Y. Exec. Law §828 (McKinney Supp. 1981-1982) "took" her property. The New York Supreme Court, the Appellate Division, and the New York Court of Appeals all rejected that claim, upholding §828 as a valid exercise of the State's police power. . . .

The Court of Appeals found, first, that §828 represented a reasoned legislative effort to arbitrate between the interests of tenants and landlords and

---

27f. In January 1968, appellee Teleprompter signed a 5-year installation agreement with the building's previous owner in exchange for a flat fee of $50. Appellee installed both the 30-foot main cable and its 4- to 6-foot "crossover" extension in June 1970. For two years after taking possession of the building and the appurtenant equipment, appellant did not object to the cable's presence. Indeed, despite numerous inspections, appellant had never even noticed the equipment until Teleprompter first began to provide cable television service to one of her tenants. 53 N.Y.2d 124, 134-135, 423 N.W.2d 320, 324 (1981). Nor did appellant thereafter ever specifically ask Teleprompter to remove the components from her building. App. 107, 108, 110.

Although the Court alludes to the presence of "two large silver boxes" on appellant's roof, the New York Court of Appeals' opinion nowhere mentions them, nor are their dimensions stated anywhere in the record.

to encourage development of an important educational and communications medium.[27g] Moreover, under PruneYard Shopping Center v. Robins, 447 U.S., at 83-84, the fact that §828 authorized Teleprompter to make a minor physical intrusion upon appellant's property was in no way determinative of the takings question. 53 N.Y.2d, at 146-147, 423 N. E. 2d, at 331.

Second, the court concluded that the statute's economic impact on appellant was de minimis because §828 did not affect the fair return on her property. 53 N.Y.2d, at 148-150, 423 N.E.2d, at 332-333. Third, the statute did not interfere with appellant's reasonable investment-backed expectations. *Id.*, at 150-151, 423 N.E.2d, at 333-334. When appellant purchased the building, she was unaware of the existence of the cable. Thus, she could not have invested in the building with any reasonable expectation that the one-eighth cubic foot of space occupied by the cable television installment would become income-productive. 53 N.E.2d, at 155, 423 N.W.2d, at 336.

II

Given that the New York Court of Appeals' straightforward application of this Court's balancing test yielded a finding of no taking, it becomes clear why the Court now constructs a per se rule to reverse. The Court can escape the result dictated by our recent takings cases only be resorting to bygone precedents and arguing that "permanent physical occupations" somehow differ qualitatively from all other forms of government regulation.

The Court argues that a per se rule based on "permanent physical occupation" is both historically rooted and jurisprudentially sound. I disagree in both respects. The 19th-century precedents relied on by the Court lack any vitality outside the agrarian context in which they were decided. But if, by chance, they have any lingering vitality, then, in my view, those cases stand for a constitutional rule that is uniquely unsuited to the modern urban age.

27g. The court found that the state legislature had enacted §828 to "prohibit gouging and arbitrary action" by "landlords [who] in many instances have imposed extremely onerous fees and conditions on cable access to their buildings." 53 N.Y.2d, at 141, 423 N.E.2d, at 328, citing testimony of Joseph C. Swidler, Chairman of the Public Service Commission, before the Joint Legislative Committee considering the CATV bill.

Given the growing importance of cable television, the legislature decided that urban tenants' need for access to that medium justified a minor intrusion upon the landlord's interest, which "consists entirely of insisting that some negligible unoccupied space remain unoccupied. The tenant's interest clearly is more substantial, consisting of a right to receive (and perhaps send) communications from and to the outside world. In the electronic age, the landlord should not be able to preclude a tenant from obtaining CATV service (or to exact a surcharge for allowing the service) any more than he could preclude a tenant from receiving mail or telegrams directed to him." *Ibid.*, citing Regulation of Cable Televison by the State of New York, Report to the New York Public Service Commission by Commissioner William K. Jones 207 (1970).

Furthermore, I find logically untenable the Court's assertion that §828 must be analyzed under a per se rule because it "effectively destroys" three of "the most treasured strands in an owner's bundle of property rights."

A

The Court's recent Takings Clause decisions teach that *nonphysical* government intrusions on private property, such as zoning ordinances and other land-use restrictions, have become the rule rather than the exception. Modern government regulation exudes intangible "externalities" that may diminish the value of private property far more than minor physical touchings. Nevertheless, as the Court recognizes, it has "often upheld substantial regulation of an owner's use of his own property where deemed necessary to promote the public interest." . . .

Precisely because the extent to which the government may injure private interests now depends so little on whether or not it has authorized a "physical contact," the Court has avoided per se takings rules resting on outmoded distinctions between physical and nonphysical intrusions. As one commentator has observed, a takings rule based on such a distinction is inherently suspect because "its capacity to distinguish, even crudely, between significant and insignificant losses is too puny to be taken seriously." Michelman, Property, Utility, and Fairness: Comments on the Ethical Foundations of "Just Compensation" Law, 80 Harv. L. Rev. 1165, 1227 (1967).

Surprisingly, the Court draws an even finer distinction today — between "temporary physical invasions" and "permanent physical occupations." When the government authorizes the latter type of intrusion, the Court would find "a taking without regard to the public interests" the regulation may serve. Yet an examination of each of the three words in the Court's "permanent physical occupation" formula illustrates that the newly created distinction is even less substantial than the distinction between physical and nonphysical intrusions that the Court already has rejected.

First, what does the Court mean by "permanent"? Since all "temporary limitations on the right to exclude" remain "subject to a more complex balancing process to determine whether they are a taking," the Court presumably describes a government intrusion that lasts forever. But as the Court itself concedes, §828 does not require appellant to permit the cable installation forever, but only "[s]o long as the property remains residential and a CATV company wishes to retain the installation." This is far from "permanent."

The Court reaffirms that "States have broad power to regulate housing conditions in general and the landlord-tenant relationship in particular without paying compensation for all economic injuries that such regulation entails." Thus, §828 merely defines one of the many statutory responsibilities that a New Yorker accepts when she enters the rental business. If appellant occupies her own building, or converts it into a commercial property, she becomes perfectly free to exclude Teleprompter from her one-eighth cubic foot of roof space. But once appellant chooses to use her property for rental purposes, she must comply with all reasonable government statutes regulating the landlord-tenant relationship. If §828 authorizes a "permanent" occupation, and thus works a taking "without regard to the public interests that it may serve," then all other New York statutes that require a landlord to make physical attachments to his rental property also must constitute takings, even if they serve indisputably valid public interests in tenant protection and safety.[27h]

The Court denies that its theory invalidates these statutes, because they "do not require the landlord to suffer the physical occupation of a portion of his building by a third party." But surely this factor cannot be determinative, since the Court simultaneously recognizes that temporary invasions by third parties are not subject to a per se rule. Nor can the qualitative difference arise from the incidental fact that, under §828, Teleprompter, rather than appellant or her tenants, owns the cable installation. If anything, §828 leaves appellant better off than do other housing statutes, since it ensures that her property will not be damaged esthetically or physically, without burdening her with the cost of buying or maintaining the cable.

In any event, under the Court's test, the "third party" problem would remain even if appellant herself owned the cable. So long as Teleprompter continuously passed its electronic signal though the cable, a litigant could argue that the second element of the Court's formula — a "physical touching" by a stranger — was satisfied and that §828 therefore worked a taking.

27h. See, e.g., N.Y. Mult. Dwell. Law §35 (McKinney 1974) (requiring entrance doors and lights); §36 (windows and skylights for public halls and stairs); §50-a (Supp. 1982) (locks and intercommunication systems); §50-c (lobby attendants); §51-a (peepholes); §51-b (elevator mirrors); §53 (fire escapes); §57 (bells and mail receptacles); §67(3) (fire sprinklers). See also Queenside Hills Realty Co. v. Saxl, 328 U.S. 80 (1946) (upholding constitutionality of New York fire sprinkler provision).

These statutes specify in far greater detail than §828 what types of physical facilities a New York landlord must provide his tenants and where he must provide them. See, e.g., N.Y. Mult. Dwell. Law §75 (McKinney 1974) (owners of multiple dwellings must provide "proper appliances to receive and distribute an adequate supply of water," including "a proper sink with running water and with a two-inch waste and trap"); §35 (owners of multiple dwellings with frontage exceeding 22 feet must provide "at least two lights, one at each side of the entrance way, with an aggregate illumination of one hundred fifty watts or equivalent illumination"); §50-a(2) (Supp. 1981-1982) (owners of Class A multiple dwellings must provide intercommunication system "located at an automatic self-locking door giving public access to the main entrance hall or lobby").

Apartment building rooftops are not exempted. See §62 (landlords must place parapet walls and guardrails on their roofs "three feet six inches or more in height above the level of such area").

Literally read, the Court's test opens the door to endless metaphysical struggles over whether or not an individual's property has been "physically" touched. It was precisely to avoid "permit[ting] technicalities of form to dictate consequences of substance," United States v. Central Eureka Mining Co., 357 U.S. 155, 181 (1958) (Harlan, J., dissenting), that the Court abandoned a "physical contacts" test in the first place.

Third, the Court's talismanic distinction between a continuous "occupation" and a transient "invasion" finds no basis in either economic logic or Takings Clause precedent. In the landlord-tenant context, the Court has upheld against takings challenges rent control statutes permitting "temporary" physical invasions of considerable economic magnitude. See, e.g., Block v. Hirsh, 256 U.S. 135 (1921) (statute permitting tenants to remain in physical possession of their apartments for two years after the termination of their leases). Moreover, precedents record numerous other "temporary" officially authorized invasions by third parties that have intruded into an owner's enjoyment of property far more deeply than did Teleprompter's long-unnoticed cable. See e.g., PruneYard Shopping Center v. Robins, 447 U.S. 74 (1980) (leafletting and demonstrating in busy shopping center); Kaiser Aetna v. United States, 444 U.S. 164 (1979) (public easement of passage to private pond); United States v. Causby, 328 U.S. 256 (1946) (noisy airplane flights over private land). While, under the Court's balancing test, some of these "temporary invasions" have been found to be takings, the Court has subjected none of them to the inflexible per se rule now adapted to analyze the far less obtrusive "occupation" at issue in the present case.

In sum, history teaches that takings claims are properly evaluated under a multifactor balancing test. By directing that all "permanent physical occupations" automatically are compensable, "without regard to whether the action achieves an important public benefit or has only minimal economic impact on the owner," the Court does not further equity so much as it encourages litigants to manipulate their factual allegations to gain the benefit of its per se rule. I do not relish the prospect of distinguishing the inevitable flow of certiorari petitions attempting to shoehorn insubstantial takings claims into today's "set formula."

B

Setting aside history, the Court also states that the permanent physical occupation authorized by §828 is a per se taking because it uniquely impairs appellant's powers to dispose of, use, and exclude others from, her property. In fact, the Court's discussion nowhere demonstrates how §828 impairs these private rights in a manner *qualitatively* different from other garden-variety landlord-tenant legislation.

The Court first contends that the statute impairs appellant's legal right to dispose of cable-occupied space by transfer and sale. But that claim dissolves after a moment's reflection. If someone buys appellant's apartment building, but does not use it for rental purposes, that person can have the cable removed, and use the space as he wishes. In such a case, appellant's right to dispose of the space is worth just as much as if §828 did not exist.

Even if another landlord buys appellant's building for rental purposes, §828 does not render the cable-occupied space valueless. As a practical matter, the regulation ensures that tenants living in the building will have access to cable television for as long as that building is used for rental purposes, and thereby likely increases both the building's resale value and its attractiveness on the rental market.[27i]

In any event, §828 differs little from the numerous other New York statutory provisions that require landlords to install physical facilities "permanently occupying" common spaces in or on their buildings. As the Court acknowledges, the States traditionally — and constitutionally — have exercised their police power "to require landlords to . . . provide utility connections, mailboxes, smoke detectors, fire extinguishers, and the like in the common area of a building." Like §828, these provisions merely ensure tenants access to services the legislature deems important, such as water, electricity, natural light, telephones, intercommunication systems, and mail service. A landlord's dispositional rights are affected no more adversely when he sells a building to another landlord subject to §828, than when he sells that building subject only to these other New York statutory provisions.

The Court also suggests that §828 unconstitutionally alters appellant's right to control the *use* of her one-eighth cubic foot of roof space. But other New York multiple dwelling statutes not only oblige landlords to surrender significantly larger portions of common space for their tenants' use, but also compel the *landlord* — rather than the tenants or the private installers — to pay for and to maintain the equipment. For example, New York landlords are required by law to provide and pay for mailboxes that occupy more than five times the volume that Teleprompter's cable occupies on appellant's building. If the State constitutionally can insist that appellant make this sacrifice so that her tenants may receive mail, it is hard to understand why the State may not require her to surrender less space, *filled at another's expense,* so that those same tenants can receive television signals.

For constitutional purposes, the relevant question cannot be solely *whether* the State has interfered in some minimal way with an owner's use of space on her building. Any intelligible takings inquiry must also ask whether the *extent* of the State's interference is so severe as to constitute a compensable

---

27i. In her pretrial deposition, appellant conceded not only that owners of other apartment buildings thought that the cable's presence had enhanced the market value of their buildings, App. 102-103, but also that her own tenants would have been upset if the cable connection had been removed. *Id.,* at 107, 108, 110.

taking in light of the owner's alternative uses for the property.[27j] Appellant freely admitted that she would have had no other use for the cable-occupied space, were Teleprompter's equipment not on her building.

The Court's third and final argument is that §828 has deprived appellant of her "power to exclude the occupier from possession and use of the space" occupied by the cable. This argument has two flaws. First, it unjustifiably assumes that appellant's tenants have no countervailing property interest in permitting Teleprompter to use that space.[27k] Second, it suggests that the New York Legislature may not exercise its police power to affect appellant's common-law right to exclude Teleprompter even from one-eighth cubic foot of roof space. But this Court long ago recognized that new social circumstances can justify legislative modification of a property owner's common-law rights, without compensation, if the legislative action serves sufficiently important public interests. See Munn v. Illinois, 94 U.S. 113, 134 (1877) ("A person has no property, no vested interest, in any rule of the common law. . . . Indeed, the great office of statutes is to remedy defects in the common law as they are developed, and to adapt it to the changes of time and circumstance"); United States v. Causby, 328 U.S., at 260-261 (In the modern world, "[c]ommon sense revolts at the idea" that legislatures cannot alter common-law ownership rights). . . .

III

In the end, what troubles me most about today's decision is that it represents an archaic judicial response to a modern social problem. Cable televi-

---

27j. For this reason, the Court provides no support for its per se rule by asserting that the State could not require landlords, without compensation, "to permit third parties to install swimming pools," or vending and washing machines, for the convenience of tenants. Presumably, these more intrusive government regulations would create difficult takings problems even under our traditional balancing approach. Depending on the character of the governmental action, its economic impact, and the degree to which it interfered with an owner's reasonable investment-backed expectations, among other things, the Court's hypothetical examples might or might not constitute takings. These examples hardly prove, however, that a permanent physical occupation that works a de minimis interference with a private property interest is a taking per se.

27k. It is far from clear that, under New York law, appellant's tenants would lack all property interests in the few square inches on the exterior of the building to which Teleprompter's cable and hardware attach. Under modern landlord-tenant law, a residential tenancy is not merely a possessory interest in specified space, but also a contract for the provision of a package of services and facilities necessary and appurtenant to that space. See R. Schoshinski, American Law of Landlord and Tenant §3:14 (1980). A modern urban tenant's leasehold often includes not only contractual, but also statutory, rights, including the rights to an implied warranty of habitability, rent control, and such services as the landlord is obliged by statute to provide.

sion is a new and growing, but somewhat controversial, communications medium. See Brief for New York State Cable Television Association as Amicus Curiae 6-7 (about 25% of American homes with televisions — approximately 20 million families — currently subscribe to cable television, with the penetration rate expected to double by 1990). The New York Legislature not only recognized, but also responded to, this technological advance by enacting a statute that sought carefully to balance the interests of all private parties. New York's courts in this litigation, with only one jurist in dissent, unanimously upheld the constitutionality of that considered legislative judgment.

This Court now reaches back in time for a per se rule that disrupts that legislative determination.[271] Like Justice Black, I believe that "the solution of the problems precipitated by... technological advances and new ways of living cannot come about through the application of rigid constitutional restraints formulated and enforced by the courts." United States v. Causby, 328 U.S., at 274 (dissenting opinion). I would affirm the judgment and uphold the reasoning of the New York Court of Appeals.

NOTES AND QUESTIONS

1. The *Loretto* case is discussed in Costonis, Presumptive and Per Se Takings: A Decisional Model for the Taking Issue, 58 N.Y.U.L. Rev. 465 (1983); Epstein, Not Deference, but Doctrine: The Eminent Domain Clause, 1982 Sup. Ct. Rev. 351; 38 U. Miami L. Rev. 165 (1983); 29 Wayne L. Rev. 1245 (1983).

2. *Kaiser Aetna* and *PruneYard*, discussed in the principal case, both suggested that physical invasion does not necessarily result in a taking; rather, a balancing test would be employed. Thus, in *Kaiser Aetna*, where a taking was found, the Court implied that physical invasion would work a taking only in the event of a substantial diminution in the value of the invaded

---

[271]. Happily, the Court leaves open the question whether §828 provides landlords like appellant sufficient compensation for their actual losses. Since the State Cable Television Commission's regulations permit higher than nominal awards if a landlord makes "a special showing of greater damages," App. 52, the concurring opinion in the New York Court of Appeals found that the statute awards just compensation. See 53 N.Y.2d, at 155, 423 N.E.2d, at 336 ("[I]t is obvious that a landlord who actually incurs damage to his property or is restricted in the use to which he might put that property will receive compensation commensurate with the greater injury"). If, after the remand following today's decision, this minor physical invasion is declared to be a taking deserving little or no compensation, the net result will have been a large expenditure of judicial resources on a constitutional claim of little moment.

land. 444 U.S. at 178. *PruneYard* endorsed and refined this approach. There the Court said (447 U.S. at 82-84):

> It is true that one of the essential sticks in the bundle of property rights is the right to exclude others. Kaiser Aetna v. United States, 444 U.S. 164, 179-180 (1979). And here there has literally been a "taking" of that right to the extent that the California Supreme Court has interpreted the State Constitution to entitle its citizens to exercise free expression and petition rights on shopping center property. But it is well established that "not every destruction or injury to property by governmental action has been held to be a 'taking' in the constitutional sense." Armstrong v. United States, 364 U.S. 40, 48 (1960). Rather, the determination whether a state law unlawfully infringes a landowner's property in violation of the Taking Clause requires an examination of whether the restriction on private property "forc[es] some people alone to bear public burdens which, in all fairness and justice, should be borne by the public as a whole." *Id.*, at 49. This examination entails inquiry into such factors as the character of the governmental action, its economic impact, and its interference with reasonable investment-backed expectations. Kaiser Aetna v. United States, *supra*, at 175. When "regulation goes too far it will be recognized as a taking." Pennsylvania Coal Co. v. Mahon, 260 U.S. 393, 415 (1922).
>
> Here the requirement that appellants permit appellees to exercise state-protected rights of free expression and petition on shopping center property clearly does not amount to an unconstitutional infringement of appellants' property rights under the Taking Clause. There is nothing to suggest that preventing appellants from prohibiting this sort of activity will unreasonably impair the value or use of their property as a shopping center. The PruneYard is a large commercial complex that covers several city blocks, contains numerous separate business establishments, and is open to the public at large. The decision of the California Supreme Court makes it clear that the PruneYard may restrict expressive activity by adopting time, place, and manner regulations that will minimize any interference with its commercial functions. Appellees were orderly, and they limited their activity to the common areas of the shopping center. In these circumstances, the fact that they may have "physically invaded" appellants' property cannot be viewed as determinative.
>
> This case is quite different from *Kaiser Aetna* v. *United States, supra. Kaiser Aetna* was a case in which the owners of a private pond had invested substantial amounts of money in dredging the pond, developing it into an exclusive marina, and building a surrounding marina community. The marina was open only to fee-paying members, and the fees were paid in part to "maintain the privacy and security of the pond." *Id.*, at 168. The Federal Government sought to compel free public use of the private marina on the ground that the marina became subject to the federal navigational servitude because the owners had dredged a channel connecting it to "navigable water."
>
> The Government's attempt to create a public right of access to the improved pond interfered with Kaiser Aetna's "reasonable investment backed expectations." We held that it went "so far beyond ordinary regulation or improvement

for navigation as to amount to a taking. . . ." *Id.,* at 178. Nor as a general proposition is the United States, as opposed to the several States, possessed of residual authority that enables it to define "property" in the first instance. A State is, of course, bound by the Just Compensation Clause of the Fifth Amendment, *Chicago, B. & Q. R. Co. v. Chicago,* 166 U. S. 226, 233, 236-237 (1897), but here appellants have failed to demonstrate that the "right to exclude others" is so essential to the use or economic value of their property that the state-authorized limitation of it amounted to a "taking."

Obviously, *Loretto* draws a new line (or perhaps reaffirms an old one) in taking cases involving physical invasions. Where? Does the line make sense?

NOTE: WHAT IS A "PHYSICAL INVASION"?

Fresh Pond Shopping Center, Inc. v. Acheson, 104 S. Ct. 218 (mem. 1983). In this case the Court dismissed for want of a substantial federal question a decision by the Massachusetts Supreme Judicial Court upholding a Cambridge rent control ordinance under which a landlord was denied permission to evict tenants and demolish a rent controlled apartment building. See Fresh Pond Shopping Center, Inc. v. Rent Control Board, 388 Mass. 1051, 446 N.E.2d 1060 (mem. 1983). Justice Rehnquist dissented from the Court's dismissal:

"The primary feature of the Cambridge rent control statute, 1976 Mass. Acts, ch. 36, is to place virtually all residential rental property in Cambridge under control of the Cambridge Rent Control Board, whose members are appellees here. Owners of rent-controlled property are also prohibited from evicting tenants without first obtaining a certificate of eviction from the Rent Control Board. The statute limits issuance of eviction certificates to circumstances where tenants have committed certain improper acts. It preserves the landlord's right to obtain a certificate of eviction to recover possession of the property only for occupancy by the owner or certain of his family members, or if the property is to be removed from the housing market through demolition or otherwise.

"Although the state enabling statute preserves in limited fashion a landlord's traditional right to evict a tenant in order to occupy a rental unit personally, Cambridge City Ordinance 926 eliminated the landlord's right to evict a tenant save when the Rent Control Board first issues a 'removal' permit. Ordinance 926 delegates virtually unfettered discretion to the Board to determine whether to grant a removal permit. The Board may consider the benefits of denying removal to the tenants protected by rent control, the hardship upon existing tenants of the units sought to be removed, and the effect of removal on the proclaimed housing shortage in Cambridge. Nowhere does the ordinance suggest that these considerations be balanced against the landlord's right to put his property to other uses. In short, Ordinance 926 permits denying a 'removal' permit in any situation.

"The combined effect of the limitations imposed by the state enabling statute and Ordinance 926 is to deny appellant use of his property. Appellant, as a corporate entity, simply cannot occupy the remaining apartment for personal use. In effect, then, the Rent Control Board has determined that until the remaining tenant decides to leave, appellant will be unable to vacate and demolish the building. In my view this deprives appellant of the use of its property in a manner closely analogous to a permanent physical invasion, like that involved in Loretto v. Teleprompter Manhattan CATV Corp., 458 U.S. 419, 102 S. Ct. 3164, 73 L.Ed.2d 868 (1982). In *Teleprompter* we were presented with the question whether a New York law that authorized a cable television company to install cable facilities on other persons' property without permission or effective compensation constituted a taking in violation of the Fifth and Fourteenth Amendments. Though the physical invasion was minor, we 'conclude[d] that a permanent physical occupation authorized by government is a taking without regard to the public interests that it may serve.' 102 S. Ct., at 3171. We called a permanent physical occupation of another's property 'the most serious form of invasion of an owner's property interest.' *Id.*, 102 S. Ct., at 3176.

"As the Cambridge ordinance operates in this case, I fail to see how it works anything but a physical occupation of appellant's property. First, appellant's right to evict the tenant was limited by state law to two circumstances: occupation of the rental unit by the owner or certain members of his family, or demolition. The first of these rights is not available to appellant. The second, demolition, is controlled by Cambridge Ordinance 926, and under the administration of that ordinance by the Cambridge Rent Control Board, appellant has been denied the right to remove the unit from the housing market by demolition. It is not certain whether the Rent Control Board would, if the tenant decided to leave, determine that a demolition permit should issue, but it is clear that until the tenant decides to leave of his own volition, appellant is unable to possess the property.

"There is little to distinguish this case from the situation confronting the Court in *Teleprompter*. As in *Teleprompter*, the power to end or terminate the physical invasion is under the control of a private party. As in New York, the Massachusetts legislature can alter the rent control statute to provide appellant with some other means of restoring control of his property. But neither of these factors moved the Court away from its holding in *Teleprompter* that the physical invasion amounted to a taking. I must conclude, as the Court did in *Teleprompter*, that Ordinance 926 has effected a permanent physical invasion of appellant's property.

"It might also be argued that the rent control provisions are justified by the emergency housing shortage in Cambridge, but the very fact that there is no foreseeable end to the emergency takes this case outside the Court's holding in Block v. Hirsh, 256 U.S. 135, 41 S. Ct. 458, 65 L. Ed. 865 (1921). At issue in *Block* was the constitutionality of a rent control statute enacted by Congress to regulate rents and rental practices in the District of Columbia. Like the rent control practices employed in Cambridge, the regulations disputed in *Block* fixed rents and denied the landlord the right to evict a tenant except to allow the owner or a member of his family to occupy the unit. We held the rent control statute constitutional because it was enacted to deal with a wartime emergency housing shortage. We noted that '[a] limit in time, to tide over a passing trouble, may well justify a law that could not be upheld as a permanent change.' *Id.*, at 157, 41 S. Ct., at 460. Thus, although we upheld a regulatory scheme in *Block* that is remarkably similar to that presently in force in the City of Cambridge, we reserved judgment as to whether such a regulatory scheme would be constitutional if it were made part of a permanent scheme. The Cambridge rent control ordinance presents the question thus reserved.

"The provision in the Massachusetts statute ensuring a fair net operating income to the landlord does not change the result that should attend this case. In previous decisions we have recognized that property ownership carries with it a bundle of rights, including the right 'to possess, use and dispose of it.' *Teleprompter, supra,* 102 S. Ct., at 3176, (quoting United States v. General Motors Corp., 323 U.S. 373, 378, 65 S. Ct. 357, 359, 89 L. Ed. 311 (1945)). Though no issue is raised here that the rent paid by the tenant is insufficient, that fact does not end the inquiry. What has taken place is a transfer of control over the reversionary interest retained by appellant. This power to exclude is

> one of the most treasured strands in an owner's bundle of property rights, . . . [because] even though the owner may retain the bare legal right to dispose of the occupied space by transfer or sale, the permanent occupation of that space by a stranger would ordinarily empty the right of any value, since the purchaser will also be unable to make any use of the property.

Teleprompter, supra, 102 S. Ct., at 3176. Cf. Bowles v. Willingham, 321 U.S. 503, 517, 64 S. Ct. 641, 648, 88 L. Ed. 892 (1944) (constitutional wartime rent control did not require owner to offer accommodations for rent). Nothing in the rent control provisions requires the Board to compensate appellant for the loss of control over the use of its property."

See Note, Justice Rehnquist's Theory of Property, 93 Yale L.J. 541 (1984).

The Cambridge rent control litigation and *Loretto* have figured in subsequent attacks against rent control, eviction control, and demolition control ordinances. Two examples follow. Do they suggest any principled application by the state courts of the doctrine announced in *Loretto*? Does Justice

Rehnquist's dissent, set out above, suggest any principled application of that doctrine by the Supreme Court itself? Does *Loretto* draw a line less bright than the majority would have one believe?

Nash v. City of Santa Monica, 37 Cal. 3d 97, 688 P.2d 894, 207 Cal. Rptr. 285 (1984). A Santa Monica ordinance prohibited removal of rental units from the housing market by conversion or demolition, absent a permit from a rent control board. Nash wished to evict his tenants and tear his building down, but was denied permission. The Supreme Court of California, upholding the denial and the ordinance on which it was based, said in part:

"Nash asserts that he is 'not seeking compensation from the City of Santa Monica for being forced to stay in the apartment-rental business, but only the right to go out of that business.' Conceding that there are no decisions precisely in point, and without identifying any particular constitutional provision, Nash contends that there must be limitations upon the power of the state to compel a person to pursue a particular business or occupation against his will.

"We agree. The Thirteenth Amendment to the United States Constitution prohibits involuntary servitude. This court has spoken of the basic liberty to pursue and obtain happiness by engaging in the common occupations of the community. (See Sail'er Inn, Inc. v. Kirby (1971) 5 Cal. 3d 1, 17, 95 Cal. Rptr. 329, 485 P.2d 529.) The exercise of state power to force upon an individual a career chosen by the state would surely raise substantial questions of constitutional dimension.

"The City of Santa Monica has not done that to Nash, however. Rather, it has told him that so long as tenants remain in his apartment units, and so long as he continues to receive a fair rate of return on his investment, he may not evict them and demolish the building. Nash remains free to minimize his personal involvement by delegating responsibility for rent collection and maintenance to a property manager. He remains free under the ordinance to withhold rental units from the market as they become vacant. And, he remains free to sell his property and invest the proceeds elsewhere. The problem arises from the fact that Nash prefers to do none of these things, but to demolish the building and keep the land beneath as an investment. This he claims an absolute right to do, as owner of the property. . . .

". . . [I]n our view the indirect and minimal burden imposed upon Nash's asserted liberty interest by the demolition control provisions of the Santa Monica ordinance does not warrant departure from the traditional tests used to determine the validity of economic regulation. . . .

"Nash is not being called upon to operate a business or engage in a profession unrelated to the property; his landlordly obligations are those which arise out of the ownership of the sort of property which he acquired.

As Justice Holmes said, in rejecting a Thirteenth Amendment attack by a landlord upon an ordinance which made it a misdemeanor to fail to furnish certain services to tenants:

> It is true that the traditions of our law are opposed to compelling a man to perform strictly personal services against his will even when he has contracted to render them. But the services in question ["water, heat, light, elevator, telephone, or other services as may be required by the terms of the lease and necessary to the proper or customary use of the building"] although involving some activities are so far from personal that they constitute the universal and necessary incidents of modern apartment houses. They are analogous to the services that in the old law might issue out of or be attached to the land.

(Marcus Brown Holding Co., Inc. v. Feldman (1921) 256 U.S. 170, 199, 41 S. Ct. 465, 466, 65 L. Ed. 877; accord, Marquam Investment Corp. v. Beers (1980) 47 Or. App. 711, 615 P.2d 1064.)

"Finally, insofar as Nash feels constrained by the ordinance to sell his property rather than undertake other alternatives available to him, he is in no worse position than if the City of Santa Monica were to exercise its power of eminent domain to compel a sale to private parties — a procedure recently upheld in a unanimous decision by the United States Supreme Court. (Hawaii Housing Authority v. Midkiff (1984) 104 S. Ct. 2321.) Indeed, he is in a better position, since he retains the option of continuing to own the property and to operate it at what he concedes to be a fair rate of return. Thus, Nash's argument that the ordinance unconstitutionally impinges upon his right to retain property rather than to sell it simply does not hold water. . . .

"[T]he one reported decision which *does* pass upon antidemolition controls similar to those contained in section 1803, subdivision (t) upholds their constitutionality against both taking and due process challenge. In Fresh Pond Shopping Center, Inc. v. Callahan (1983) 104 S. Ct. 218, . . . the United States Supreme Court left standing the decision of the Massachusetts Supreme Judicial Court, which earlier had affirmed the rent control board's denial of Fresh Pond's applications for removal permits. While the United States Supreme Court dismissed the appeal of Fresh Pond for want of a substantial federal question, the issues presented by the facts of the case were necessarily decided and the judgment has the force of binding precedent. As the sole dissenter from the judgment, Justice Rehnquist, wrote: '[The issues] might be postponed or avoided if the case were here on certiorari, but the case is an appeal; we act on the merits whatever we do.' (104 S. Ct. at p.218.) Thus, while Nash's contentions with respect to the California Constitution are left to this court for response, the United States Supreme Court has addressed the matter and found the assertion of the unconstitutionality of an ordinance nearly identical to Santa Monica's, by one in almost precisely Nash's position, unavailing for purposes of federal constitutional law. The views of Justice Rehnquist — that the Cambridge ordinance represented a 'taking' without just compensation — were apparently rejected by his eight colleagues....

"Turning to the California Constitution, we find no persuasive authority, in precedent or in logic, for a different result....

"Mosk, Justice, dissenting.

"I dissent.

"As Justice Frankfurter wrote in Bay Ridge Co. v. Aaron (1948) 334 U.S. 446, 484, 68 S. Ct. 1186, 1206, 92 L. Ed. 1502 , 'On the question you ask depends the answer you get.'

"In this case if the question is whether a municipality may exercise its police power to reasonably regulate the rental business, the answer is: generally it may do so. But if the question is whether a city may compel a landlord to remain in business against his will, and give him only the alternative of a forced sale, the answer is: not in a democratic society....

"The city suggests that the property owner may avoid its draconian order by the forced sale of his property to another who would in turn be compelled to continue in the rental business. Assuming arguendo that such a person could be found — a doubtful assumption under these circumstances — the city's rationale leaves much to be desired. The city's theory is deceptively simple: 'Once a landlord, always a landlord — or sell the property.' The contention is, in effect, that the property owner has a duty to relieve the municipality of its invalid order by dispossessing himself of his property. Or to put it another way: persons who do not choose to abjectly submit to the city violating their fundamental rights should get out of town.

"If the city forces this owner to involuntarily transfer his property to a third person, the result is no less a taking than if the municipality itself were to assume title to the property. Thus if the city insists upon its asserted public purpose of maintaining these six rental units ad infinitum, it must condemn the building and pay just compensation therefor. Neither the federal nor state Constitutions permit the city to achieve its purpose by impressing this owner and his property into the mold of a public utility bound in perpetuity to provide, maintain, and operate a housing business....

"The majority rely on Fresh Pond Shopping Center v. Callahan (1983) 104 S. Ct. 218, a case that has produced no prevailing written opinion at any level. The trial court published no opinion, the Supreme Court of Massachusetts summarily affirmed the judgment by a tie vote (446 N.E.2d 1060), and the United States Supreme Court summarily dismissed a purported appeal for want of a substantial federal question. That scenario creates no persuasive, let alone binding, authority for anything.

"The majority obtain the facts from the only opinion written in *Fresh Pond:* the dissent of Justice Rehnquist from the dissmissal. But they ignore his conclusion: i.e., that he believes the rent control ordinance is the equivalent of 'a physical occupation of the appellant's property,' which, pursuant to Loretto v. Teleprompter Manhattan CATV Corp. (1982) 458 U.S. 419, 102 S. Ct. 3164, 73 L. Ed. 2d 868, constitutes a taking without just compensation.

"Since the Supreme Court majority declared there is no substantial federal question in *Fresh Pond*, we are free, as was Massachusetts in that case, to decide the present issue entirely on the basis of state authority. I am convinced that although petitioner has not asserted a taking by the city, the implications of [the takings provisions of the] California Constitution . . . cannot be avoided, and are controlling to prevent the arbitrary actions of the city herein. . . .

"After relying on *Fresh Pond*, a case without a prevailing opinion, the majority seem to desperately seek some relevant authority; they therefore cite Hawaii Housing Authority v. Midkiff (1984) 104 S. Ct. 2321. That Hawaiian landowners may have their property taken upon payment of just compensation is small comfort to this plaintiff who must remain a landlord under compulsion and perform the personal services imposed on landlords by case law, or in the alternative involuntarily dispose of his property to someone willing to undertake the required duties of a landlord. *Hawaii Housing Authority* does not purport to approve of such draconian conduct by a public agency."

Gregory v. City of San Juan Capistrano, 142 Cal. App. 3d 72, 191 Cal. Rptr. 47 (4th Dist. 1983). The case involved a rent control ordinance that, among other things, required an owner wishing to sell a mobile home park first to offer it to residents, who had a preemptive right, or right of first refusal, to purchase. In invalidating this portion of the ordinance, the court said:

"[N]o court has ever upheld the naked taking of the preemptive rights involved here. City has unwittingly conceded this point in claiming that the ordinance 'in granting rights to private parties for the public good, is similar to [the] New York statute . . . in Loretto v. Teleprompter Manhattan CATV Corp. (1981) 53 N.Y.2d 124 [440 N.Y.S.2d 843, 423 N.E.2d 320].' After City's opening brief was filed, the United States Supreme Court held the statute at issue in *Loretto* . . . constituted an unconstitutional taking of property without compensation."

Compare Granat v. Keasler, 99 Wash. 2d 564, 663 P.2d 830 (1983). A city ordinance prohibited eviction of floating-home tenants from moorages unless the moorage owner wished to convert the moorage site to personal or noncommercial use, or wished to occupy the site with a floating home to be used as the moorage owner's residence; in any event eviction would be allowed only if the moorage owner located another lawful moorage site within the city for the displaced tenants. The court invalidated the ordinance, finding "the limitations on the use by the moorage owner to be so restrictive as to amount to a taking. . . ." In the court's view, "to require a landlord to locate a nonexistent moorage for a houseboat owner before the residence of the landlord can be moved to the property is not reasonable." If the ordinance "prohibited *everyone* from using the [moorage] in the manner sought by the [moorage owner]" it might be valid, but here "the landlord is prohibited from the intended use of the property, but not the tenant."

See generally Note, Fifth Amendment Takings and Condominium Conversion Regulations that Restrict Owner Occupancy Rights, 62 B.U.L. Rev. 467 (1982).

Page 1168. Before the Note on "Inverse Condemnation," insert:

SAN DIEGO GAS & ELECTRIC CO. v. SAN DIEGO
Supreme Court of the United States, 1981
450 U.S. 621

[The *San Diego* case arose when the city rezoned some of the Gas & Electric Company's land — originally approved for industrial use, and purchased as a possible nuclear power site — in a manner that reduced the industrial acreage and established an open-space plan. The company brought an action alleging a taking and seeking compensation in a so-called inverse condemnation action. (See Note 4, page 1157 of the main text.) Unsuccessful in the state courts, the company appealed to the United States Supreme Court. The majority of the Court, in an opinion not reproduced here, concluded that it lacked jurisdiction because there was no final judgment of the state courts, and dismissed the appeal. Justice Rehnquist concurred in the majority decision, but added that he "would have little difficulty in agreeing with much of what is said in the dissenting opinion of Justice Brennan." Set out below is a portion of that dissent, joined by Justices Stewart, Marshall, and Powell.]

. . . The Just Compensation Clause of the Fifth Amendment, made applicable to the States through the Fourteenth Amendment, Webb's Fabulous Pharmacies, Inc. v. Beckwith, 449 U.S. 155, 160 (1980); see Chicago, B. & Q. R. Co. v. Chicago, 166 U.S. 226, 239, 241 (1897), states in clear and unequivocal terms: "[N]or shall private property be taken for public use, without just compensation." The question presented on the merits in this case is whether a government entity must pay just compensation when a police power regulation has effected a "taking" of "private property" for "public use" within the meaning of that constitutional provision. Implicit in this question is the corollary issue whether a government entity's exercise of its regulatory police power can ever effect a "taking" within the meaning of the Just Compensation Clause.

[T]he California courts have held that a city's exercise of its police power, however arbitrary or excessive, cannot as a matter of federal constitutional law constitute a "taking" within the meaning of the Fifth Amendment. This holding flatly contradicts clear precedents of this Court. For example, in last Term's Agins v. City of Tiburon, 447 U.S. 225, 260 (1980), the Court noted that "[t]he application of a general zoning law to particular property effects a taking if the ordinance does not substantially advance legitimate state interests . . . or [if it] denies an owner economically viable use of his land. . . ." Applying that principle, the Court examined whether the Tiburon zoning ordinance effected a "taking" of the Agins' property, concluding that it did not have such an effect. *Id.*, at 262-263.

In Penn Central Transp. Co. v. New York City, 438 U.S. 104 (1978), the Court analyzed "whether the restrictions imposed by New York City's [Landmarks Preservation] law upon appellants' exploitation of the [Grand Central] Terminal site effect a 'taking' of appellants' property . . . within the meaning of the Fifth Amendment." *Id.*, at 122. Canvassing the appropriate inquiries necessary to determine whether a particular restriction effected a "taking," the Court identified the "economic impact of the regulation on the claimant" and the "character of the governmental action" as particularly relevant considerations. *Id.*, at 124; see *id.*, at 130-131. Although the Court ultimately concluded that application of New York's Landmarks Law did not effect a "taking" of the railroad property, it did so only after deciding that "[t]he restrictions imposed are substantially related to the promotion of the general welfare and not only permit reasonable beneficial use of the landmark site but also afford appellants opportunities further to enhance not only the Terminal site proper but also other properties." *Id.*, at 138 (footnote omitted).

The constitutionality of a local ordinance regulating dredging and pit excavating on a property was addressed in Goldblatt v. Town of Hempstead, 369 U.S. 590 (1962). After observing that an otherwise valid zoning ordinance that deprives the owner of the most beneficial use of his property would not be unconstitutional, *id.*, at 592, the Court cautioned: "That is not to say, however, that governmental action in the form of regulation cannot be so onerous as to constitute a taking which constitutionally requires compensation," *id.*, at 594. On many other occasions, the Court has recognized in passing the vitality of the general principle that a regulation can effect a Fifth Amendment "taking." See, e.g., PruneYard Shopping Center v. Robins, 447 U.S. 74, 83 (1980); Kaiser Aetna v. United States, 444 U.S. 164, 174 (1979); Andrus v. Allard, 444 U.S. 51, 65-66 (1979); United States v. Central Eureka Mining Co., 357 U.S. 155, 168 (1958).

The principle applied in all these cases has its source in Justice Holmes' opinion for the Court in Pennsylvania Coal Co. v. Mahon, 260 U.S. 393, 415 (1922), in which he stated: "The general rule at least is, that while property may be regulated to a certain extent, if regulation goes too far it will be recognized as a taking." The determination of a "taking" is "a question of degree — and therefore cannot be disposed of by general propositions." *Id.,* at 416. While acknowledging that "[g]overnment hardly could go on if to some extent values incident to property could not be diminished without paying for every such change in the general law," *id.,* at 413, the Court rejected the proposition that police power restrictions could never be recognized as a Fifth Amendment "taking." Indeed, the Court concluded that the Pennsylvania statute forbidding the mining of coal that would cause the subsidence of any house effected a "taking." *Id.,* at 414-416.

Not only does the holding of the California Court of Appeal contradict precedents of this Court, but it also fails to recognize the essential similarity of regulatory "takings" and other "takings." The typical "taking" occurs when a government entity formally condemns a landowner's property and obtains the fee simple pursuant to its sovereign power of eminent domain. See, e.g., Berman v. Parker, 348 U.S. 26, 33 (1954). However, a "taking" may also occur without a formal condemnation proceeding or transfer of fee simple. This Court long ago recognized that

> [i]t would be a very curious and unsatisfactory result, if in construing [the Just Compensation Clause] . . . it shall be held that if the government refrains from the absolute conversion of real property to the uses of the public it can destroy its value entirely, can inflict irreparable and permanent injury to any extent, can, in effect, subject it to total destruction without making any compensation, because, in the narrowest sense of that word, it is not *taken* for the public use.

Pumpelly v. Green Bay Co., 13 Wall. 166, 177-178 (1872) (emphasis in original). See Chicago, R. I. & P. R. Co. v. United States, 284 U.S. 80, 96 (1931).

In service of this principle, the Court frequently has found "takings" outside the context of formal condemnation proceedings or transfer of fee simple, in cases where government action benefiting the public resulted in destruction of the use and enjoyment of private property. E.g., Kaiser Aetna v. United States, 444 U.S., at 178-180 (navigational servitude allowing public right of access); United States v. Dickinson, 331 U.S. 745, 750-751 (1947) (property flooded because of Government dam project); United States v. Causby, 328 U.S. 256, 261-262 (1946) (frequent low altitude flights of Army and Navy aircraft over property); Pennsylvania Coal Co. v. Mahon, 260 U.S., at 414-416 (state regulation forbidding mining of coal).

Police power regulations such as zoning ordinances and other land-use restrictions can destroy the use and enjoyment of property in order to promote the public good just as effectively as formal condemnation or physical invasion of property. From the property owner's point of view, it may matter little whether his land is condemned or flooded, or whether it is restricted by regulation to use in its natural state, if the effect in both cases is to deprive him of all beneficial use of it. From the government's point of view, the benefits flowing to the public from preservation of open space through regulation may be equally great as from creating a wildlife refuge through formal condemnation or increasing electricity production through a dam project that floods private property. Appellees implicitly posit the distinction that the government *intends* to take property through condemnation or physical invasion whereas it does not through police power regulations. But "the Constitution measures a taking of property not by what a State says, or by what it intends, but by what it *does*." Hughes v. Washington, 389 U.S. 290, 298 (1967) (Stewart, J., concurring) (emphasis in original); see Davis v. Newton Coal Co., 267 U.S. 292, 301 (1925). It is only logical, then, that government action other than acquisition of title, occupancy, or physical invasion can be a "taking," and therefore a de facto exercise of the power of eminent domain, where the effects completely deprive the owner of all or most of his interest in the property. United States v. Dickinson, *supra,* at 748; United States v. General Motors Corp., 323 U.S. 373, 378 (1945).

Having determined that property may be "taken for public use" by police power regulation within the meaning of the Just Compensation Clause of the Fifth Amendment, the question remains whether a government entity may constitutionally deny payment of just compensation to the property owner and limit his remedy to mere invalidation of the regulation instead. Appellant argues that it is entitled to the full fair market value of the property. Appellees argue that invalidation of the regulation is sufficient without payment of monetary compensation. In my view, once a court establishes that there was a regulatory "taking," the Constitution demands that the government entity pay just compensation for the period commencing on the date the regulation first effected the "taking," and ending on the date the government entity chooses to rescind or otherwise amend[28a] the regulation. This interpretation, I believe, is supported by the express words and purpose of the Just Compensation Clause, as well as by cases of this Court construing it.

The language of the Fifth Amendment prohibits the "tak[ing]" of private property for "public use" without payment of "just compensation." As soon as private property has been taken, whether through formal condemnation proceedings, occupancy, physical invasion, or regulation, the landowner has *already* suffered a constitutional violation, and "'the self-executing character

---

28a. Under this rule, a government entity is entitled to amend the offending regulation so that it no longer effects a "taking." It may also choose formally to condemn the property.

of the constitutional provision with respect to compensation,'" United States v. Clarke, 445 U.S. 253, 257 (1980), quoting 6 J. Sackman, Nichols' Law of Eminent Domain §25.41 (rev. 3d ed. 1980), is triggered. This Court has consistently recognized that the just compensation requirement in the Fifth Amendment is not precatory: once there is a "taking," compensation *must* be awarded. In Jacobs v. United States, 290 U.S. 13 (1933), for example, a Government dam project creating intermittent overflows onto petitioners' property resulted in the "taking" of a servitude. Petitioners brought suit against the Government to recover just compensation for the partial "taking." Commenting on the nature of the landowners' action, the Court observed:

> The suits were based on the right to recover just compensation for property taken by the United States for public use in the exercise of its power of eminent domain. That right was guaranteed by the Constitution. The fact that condemnation proceedings were not instituted and that the right was asserted in suits by the owners did not change the essential nature of the claim. The form of the remedy did not qualify the right. It rested upon the Fifth Amendment. Statutory recognition was not necessary. A promise to pay was not necessary. Such a promise was implied because of the duty to pay imposed by the Amendment.

Id., at 16. See also Griggs v. Allegheny County, 369 U.S. 84, 84-85, 88-90 (1962); United States v. Causby, 328 U.S., at 268. Invalidation unaccompanied by payment of damages would hardly compensate the landowner for any economic loss suffered during the time his property was taken.[28b]

Moreover, mere invalidation would fall far short of fulfilling the funda-

---

28b. The instant litigation is a good case in point. The trial court, on April 9, 1976, found that the city's actions effected a "taking" of appellant's property on June 19, 1973. If true, then appellant has been deprived of all beneficial use of its property in violation of the Just Compensation Clause for the past seven years.

Invalidation hardly prevents enactment of subsequent unconstitutional regulations by the government entity. At the 1974 annual conference of the National Institute of Municipal Law Officers in California, a California City Attorney gave fellow City Attorneys the following advice:

"*IF ALL ELSE FAILS, MERELY AMEND THE REGULATION AND START OVER AGAIN.*

"If legal preventive maintenance does not work, and you still receive a claim attacking the land use regulation, or if you try the case and lose, don't worry about it. All is not lost. One of the extra 'goodies' contained in the recent [California] Supreme Court case of Selby v. City of San Buenaventura, 10 C.3d 110, appears to allow the City to change the regulation in question, even after trial and judgment, make it more reasonable, more restrictive, or whatever, and everybody starts over again. . . .

"See how easy it is to be a City Attorney. Sometimes you can lose the battle and still win the war. Good luck." Longtin, Avoiding and Defending Constitutional Attacks on Land Use Regulations (Including Inverse Condemnation), 38B NIMLO Municipal Law Review 192-193 (1975) (emphasis in original).

mental purpose of the Just Compensation Clause. That guarantee was designed to bar the government from forcing some individuals to bear burdens which, in all fairness, should be borne by the public as a whole. Armstrong v. United States, 364 U.S. 40, 49 (1960). See Agins v. City of Tiburon, 447 U.S., at 260; Andrus v. Allard, 444 U.S., at 65. When one person is asked to assume more than a fair share of the public burden, the payment of just compensation operates to redistribute that economic cost from the individual to the public at large. See United States v. Willow River Co., 324 U.S. 499, 502 (1945); Monongahela Navigation Co. v. United States, 148 U.S. 312, 325 (1893). Because police power regulations must be substantially related to the advancement of the public health, safety, morals, or general welfare, see Village of Euclid v. Ambler Realty Co., 272 U.S. 365, 395 (1926), it is axiomatic that the public receives a benefit while the offending regulation is in effect.[28c] If the regulation denies the private property owner the use and enjoyment of his land and is found to effect a "taking," it is only fair that the public bear the cost of benefits received during the interim period between application of the regulation and the government entity's rescission of it. The payment of just compensation serves to place the landowner in the same position monetarily as he would have occupied if his property had not been taken. Almota Farmers Elevator & Warehouse Co. v. United States, 409 U.S. 470, 473-474 (1973); United States v. Reynolds, 397 U.S. 14, 16 (1970).

The fact that a regulatory "taking" may be temporary, by virtue of the government's power to rescind or amend the regulation, does not make it any less of a constitutional "taking." Nothing in the Just Compensation Clause suggests that "takings" must be permanent and irrevocable. Nor does the temporary reversible quality of a regulatory "taking" render compensation for the time of the "taking" any less obligatory. This Court more than once has recognized that temporary reversible "takings" should be analyzed according to the same constitutional framework applied to permanent irreversible "takings." For example, in United States v. Causby, *supra*, at 258-259, the United States had executed a lease to use an airport for a one-year term "ending June 30, 1942, with a provision for renewals until June 30, 1967, or six months after the end of the national emergency, whichever [was] the earlier." The Court held that the frequent low-level flights of Army and Navy airplanes over respondents' chicken farm, located near the airport, effected a "taking" of an easement on respondents' prop-

---

28c. A different case may arise where a police power regulation is not enacted in furtherance of the public health, safety, morals, or general welfare so that there may be no "public use." Although the government entity may not be forced to pay just compensation under the Fifth Amendment, the landowner may nevertheless have a damages cause of action under 42 U.S.C. §1983 for a Fourteenth Amendment due process violation.

erty. 328 U. S., at 266-267. However, because the flights could be discontinued by the Government at any time, the Court remanded the case to the Court of Claims: "Since on this record *it is not clear whether the easement taken is a permanent or a temporary one,* it would be premature for us to consider whether the amount of the award made by the Court of Claims was proper." *Id.,* at 268 (emphasis added). In other cases where the Government has taken only temporary use of a building, land, or equipment, the Court has not hesitated to determine the appropriate measure of just compensation. See Kimball Laundry Co. v. United States, 338 U.S. 1, 6 (1949); United States v. Petty Motor Co., 327 U.S. 374, 372-375 (1946); United States v. General Motors Corp., 323 U.S., at 374-375.

But contrary to appellant's claim that San Diego must formally condemn its property and pay full fair market value, nothing in the Just Compensation Clause empowers a court to order a government entity to condemn the property and pay its full fair market value, where the "taking" already effected is temporary and reversible and the government wants to halt the "taking." Just as the government may cancel condemnation proceedings before passage of title, see 6 J. Sackman, Nichols' Law of Eminent Domain §24.113, p. 24-21 (rev. 3d ed. 1980), or abandon property it has temporarily occupied or invaded, see United States. v. Dow, 357 U.S. 17, 26 (1958), it must have the same power to rescind a regulatory "taking." As the Court has noted:

> [A]n abandonment does not prejudice the property owner. It merely results in an alteration of the property interest taken — from full ownership to one of temporary use and occupation. . . . In such cases compensation would be measured by the principles normally governing the taking of a right to use property temporarily.

Ibid.; see Danforth v. United States, 308 U. S. 271, 284 (1939).

The constitutional rule I propose requires that, once a court finds that a police power regulation has effected a "taking," the government entity must pay just compensation for the period commencing on the date the regulation first effected the "taking," and ending on the date the government entity chooses to rescind or otherwise amend the regulation. Ordinary principles determining the proper measure of just compensation, regularly applied in cases of permanent and temporary "takings" involving formal condemnation proceedings, occupations, and physical invasions, should provide guidance to the courts in the award of compensation for a regulatory "taking." As a starting point, the value of the property taken may be ascertained as of the date of the "taking." United States v. Clarke, 445 U.S., at 258; Almota Farmers Elevator & Warehouse Co. v. United States, *supra,* at 474; United States v. Miller, 317 U.S. 369, 374 (1943); Olson v. United States, 292 U.S. 246, 255 (1934). The government must inform the court of its intentions vis-à-vis the regulation with sufficient clarity to guarantee a correct assessment of the just compensation award. Should the government decide immediately to revoke or otherwise amend the regulation, it would be liable for payment of compensation only for the interim during which the regulation effected a "taking." Rules of valuation already developed for temporary "takings" may be particularly useful to the courts in their quest for assessing the proper measure of monetary relief in cases of revocation or amendment, see generally Kimball Laundry Co. v. United States, *supra;* United States v. Petty Motor Co., *supra;* United States v. General Motors Corp., *supra,* although additional rules may need to be developed, see Kimball Laundry Co. v. United States, *supra,* at 21-22 (Rutledge, J., concurring); United States v. Miller, *supra,* at 373-374. Alternatively the government may choose formally to condemn the property, or otherwise to continue the offending regulation: in either case the action must be sustained by proper measures of just compensation. See generally United States v. Fuller, 409 U.S. 488, 490-492 (1973); United States ex rel. TVA v. Powelson, 319 U.S. 266, 281-285 (1943).

It should be noted that the Constitution does not embody any specific procedure or form of remedy that the States must adopt: "The Fifth Amendment expresses a principle of fairness and not a technical rule of procedure enshrining old or new niceties regarding 'causes of action' — when they are born, whether they proliferate, and when they die." United States v. Dickinson, 331 U.S., at 748. Cf. United States v. Memphis Cotton Oil Co., 288 U.S. 62, 67-69 (1933). The States should be free to experiment in the implementation of this rule, provided that their chosen procedures and remedies comport with the fundamental constitutional command. See generally Hill, The Bill of Rights and the Supervisory Power, 69 Colum. L. Rev. 181, 191-193 (1969). The only constitutional requirement is that the landowner must be able meaningfully to challenge a regulation that allegedly effects a "taking," and recover just compensation if it does so. He may not be forced to resort to piecemeal litigation or otherwise unfair procedures in order to receive his due. See United States v. Dickinson, *supra,* at 749.

In Agins v. City of Tiburon, 24 Cal. 3d, at 275, 598 P.2d, at 29, the California Supreme Court was "persuaded by various policy considerations to the view that inverse condemnation is an inappropriate and undesirable remedy in cases in which unconstitutional regulation is alleged." In particular, the court cited "the need for preserving a degree of freedom in land-use planning function, and the inhibiting financial force which inheres in the inverse condemnation remedy," in reaching its conclusion. *Id.,* at 276, 598 P.2d, at 31. But the applicability of express constitutional guarantees is not a matter to be determined on the basis of policy judgments made by the legislative, executive, or judicial branches.[28d] Nor can the vindication of those rights depend on the expense in doing so. See Watson v. Memphis, 373 U.S. 526, 537-538 (1963).

Because I believe that the Just Compensation Clause requires the constitutional rule outlined *supra*, I would vacate the judgment of the California Court of Appeal, Fourth District, and remand for further proceedings not inconsistent with this opinion.

NOTES AND QUESTIONS

Consider the following in addition to the matters discussed in the Note on "Inverse Condemnation," pages 1168-1171 of the main text.

1. Several state courts have followed the dissent in the *San Diego* case. See, e.g., Burrows v. City of Keene, 121 N.H. 590, 432 A.2d 15 (1981); Rippley v. City of Lincoln, 330 N.W.2d 505 (N.D. 1983); Zinn v. State, 112 Wis. 2d 417, 334 N.W.2d 67 (1983). Similarly, a few lower federal court decisions have taken the position that Justice Brennan's opinion, given that it was joined in by three other justices and apparently endorsed by Justice Rehnquist, constitutes a majority view in favor of awarding compensation in inverse condemnation for takings effected through overregulation. See, e.g., Martino v. Santa Clara Valley Water District, 703 F.2d 1141 (9th Cir.), *cert. denied*, 104 S. Ct. 151 (1983); Hamilton Bank v. Williamson County Regional Planning Commission, 729 F.2d 402 (6th Cir.), *cert. granted*, 53 U.S.L.W. 3202 (U.S. Oct. 2, 1984). (*Hamilton Bank* may well have been decided by the Court while this supplement was in press.)

2. The arguments for and against inverse condemnation in cases of overregulation are suggested in Justice Brennan's dissenting opinion and in the main text at pages 1168-1171. The *San Diego* case has provoked another round of discussion, but the essential debate remains the same. See, e.g.,

---

28d. Even if I were to concede a role for policy considerations, I am not so sure that they would militate against requiring payment of just compensation. Indeed, land-use planning commentators have suggested that the threat of financial liability for unconstitutional police power regulations would help to produce a more rational basis of decisionmaking that weighs the costs of restrictions against their benefits. Dunham, From Rural Enclosure to Re-Enclosure of Urban Land, 35 N.Y.U.L. Rev. 1238, 1253-1254 (1960). Such liability might also encourage municipalities to err on the constitutional side of police power regulations, and to develop internal rules and operating procedures to minimize overzealous regulatory attempts. Cf. Owen v. City of Independence, 445 U.S. 622, 651-652 (1980). After all, if a policeman must know the Constitution, then why not a planner? In any event, one may wonder as an empirical matter whether the threat of just compensation will greatly impede the efforts of planners. Cf. *id.*, at 656.

Bauman, The Supreme Court, Inverse Condemnation and the Fifth Amendment: Justice Brennan Confronts the Inevitable in Land Use Controls, 15 Rutgers L.J. 15 (1983); Girard, Constitutional "Takings Clauses" and the Regulation of Private Property, Pts. I & II, 34 Zoning Digest No. 10, at 4, id. No. 11, at 4 (Oct. & Nov. 1982); Johnson, Compensation for Invalid Land-Use Regulation, 15 Ga. L. Rev. 559 (1981); Krier, The Regulation Machine, 1 Sup. Ct. Econ. Rev. 1 (1982); Mandelker, Land Use Takings: The Compensation Issue, 8 Hastings Const. L.Q. 491 (1981); Cunningham, Inverse Condemnation as a Remedy for "Regulatory Takings," *id.* at 517; Comment, Just Compensation or Just Invalidation: The Availability of a Damage Remedy in Challenging Land Use Regulations, 29 U.C.L.A.L. Rev. 711 (1982).

3. An alternative to compensation on a theory of inverse condemnation for a taking is a civil rights suit for damages for deprivation of constitutional rights under color of state law. See the main text at page 1169, footnote 29. Among other things, the alternative theory avoids the conceptual problems that obviously arise in awarding Fifth Amendment "just compensation" for losses caused by state activities that do not involve a public use, or that are carried out by public entities that lack the power of eminent domain. See footnote 28c of Justice Brennan's dissent in *San Diego* and Hernandez v. City of Lafayette, 643 F.2d 1188, 1200 n.26 (5th Cir. 1981), *cert. denied*, 455 U.S. 907 (1982). On the alternative theories and possible differences between them, see Rockwell, Constitutional Violations in Zoning: The Emerging Section 1983 Damages Remedy, 33 U. Fla. L. Rev. 168 (1981); Wright, Damages or Compensation for Unconstitutional Land Use Regulation, 37 Ark. L. Rev. 612 (1983).

Chapter Eleven
Zoning Processes, Practices, and Problems

B. THE NONCONFORMING USE

Page 1243. At the end of line 4, add:

The Supreme Court of Indiana recently confronted the amortization issue for the first time in Ailes v. Decatur County Area Planning Comm., 448 N.E.2d 1057 (Ind. 1983). The court held "that an ordinance prohibiting any continuation of an existing lawful use within a zoned area regardless of the length of time given to amortize that use is unconstitutional. . . ." 448 N.E.2d at 1060.

C. ACHIEVING FLEXIBILITY IN ZONING

Page 1285. At the end of Note 5, add:

The role assigned the comprehensive plan by the court in *Fasano* is criticized in two recent articles. See Krasnowiecki, Abolish Zoning, 31 Syracuse L. Rev. 719 (1980); Rose, Planning and Dealing: Piecemeal Land Controls as a Problem of Local Legitimacy, 71 Calif. L. Rev. 839 (1983).

Page 1292. At the end of "Note: Zoning through Popular Consent," add:

A recent thorough overview of the subject may be found in Rosenberg, Referendum Zoning: Legal Doctrine and Practice, 53 Cinn. L. Rev. 381 (1983).

D. THE OBJECTIVES OF ZONING (LEGITIMATE AND OTHERWISE)

Page 1338. At the end of the first full paragraph, add:

For a significant recent re-examination of the problems of aesthetic regulation, see Costonis, Law and Aesthetics: A Critique and a Reformulation of the Dilemmas, 80 Mich. L. Rev. 355 (1982).

Page 1338. In Note 5, add the following to the references on historic preservation:

Rose, Preservation and Community: New Directions in the Law of Historic Preservation, 33 Stan. L. Rev. 473 (1981).

Page 1339. The *Metromedia* case has been reversed by the United States Supreme Court. Delete the case and substitute the following (the Note beginning on page 1350 may be retained):

METROMEDIA, INC. v. SAN DIEGO
Supreme Court of the United States, 1981
453 U.S. 490

Justice WHITE announced the judgment of the Court and delivered an opinion, in which Justice STEWART, Justice MARSHALL, and Justice POWELL joined....

Billboards are a well-established medium of communication, used to convey a broad range of different kinds of messages....

But whatever its communicative function, the billboard remains a "large, immobile, and permanent structure which like other structures is subject to ... regulation." Moreover, because it is designed to stand out and apart from its surroundings, the billboard creates a unique set of problems for land-use planning and development.

Billboards, then, like other media of communication, combine communicative and noncommunicative aspects. As with other media, the government has legitimate interests in controlling the noncommunicative aspects of the medium, but the First and Fourteenth Amendments foreclose a similar interest in controlling the communicative aspects. Because regulation of the noncommunicative aspects of a medium often impinges to some degree on the communicative aspects, it has been necessary for the courts to reconcile the government's regulatory interests with the individual's right to expression....

As construed by the California Supreme Court, the ordinance restricts the use of certain kinds of outdoor signs. . . .

Thus, under the ordinance (1) a sign advertising goods or services available on the property where the sign is located is allowed; (2) a sign on a building or other property advertising goods or services produced or offered elsewhere is barred; (3) noncommercial advertising, unless within one of the specific exceptions, is everywhere prohibited. The occupant of property may advertise his own goods or services; he may not advertise the goods or services of others, nor may he display most noncommercial messages.

Appellants' principal submission is that enforcement of the ordinance will eliminate the outdoor advertising business in San Diego and that the First and Fourteenth Amendments prohibit the elimination of this medium of communication. Appellants contend that the city may bar neither all offsite commercial signs nor all noncommercial advertisements and that even if it may bar the former, it may not bar the latter. Appellants may raise both arguments in their own right because, although the bulk of their business consists of offsite signs carrying commercial advertisements, their billboards also convey a substantial amount of noncommercial advertising. Because our cases have consistently distinguished between the constitutional protection afforded commercial as opposed to noncommercial speech, in evaluating appellants' contention we consider separately the effect of the ordinance on commercial and noncommercial speech. . . .

[I]n Central Hudson Gas & Electric Corp. v. Public Service Comm'n, 447 U.S. 557 (1980), we held: "The Constitution . . . accords a lesser protection to commercial speech than to other constitutionally guaranteed expression. The protection available for a particular commercial expression turns on the nature both of the expression and of the governmental interests served by its regulation." *Id.*, at 562-563 (citation omitted). We then adopted a four-part test for determining the validity of government restrictions on commercial speech as distinguished from more fully protected speech. (1) The First Amendment protects commercial speech only if that speech concerns lawful activity and is not misleading. A restriction on otherwise protected commercial speech is valid only if it (2) seeks to implement a substantial governmental interest, (3) directly advances that interest, and (4) reaches no further than necessary to accomplish the given objective. *Id.*, at 563-566.

Appellants agree that the proper approach to be taken in determining the validity of the restrictions on commercial speech is that which was articulated in *Central Hudson,* but assert that the San Diego ordinance fails that test. We do not agree.

There can be little controversy over the application of the first, second, and fourth criteria. There is no suggestion that the commercial advertising at issue here involves unlawful activity or is misleading. Nor can there be substantial doubt that the twin goals that the ordinance seeks to further — traffic safety and the appearance of the city — are substantial governmental goals. It is far too late to contend otherwise with respect to either traffic safety, Railway Express Agency, Inc. v. New York, 336 U.S. 106 (1949), or esthetics, see Penn Central Transportation Co. v. New York City, 438 U.S. 104 (1978); Village of Belle Terre v. Boraas, 416 U.S. 1 (1974); Berman v. Parker, 348 U.S. 26, 33 (1954). Similarly, we reject appellants' claim that the ordinance is broader than necessary and, therefore, fails the fourth part of the *Central Hudson* test. If the city has a sufficient basis for believing that billboards are traffic hazards and are unattractive, then obviously the most direct and perhaps the only effective approach to solving the problems they create is to prohibit them. The city has gone no further than necessary in seeking to meet its ends. Indeed, it has stopped short of fully accomplishing its ends: It has not prohibited all billboards, but allows onsite advertising and some other specifically exempted signs.

The more serious question, then, concerns the third of the *Central Hudson* criteria: Does the ordinance "directly advance" governmental interests in traffic safety and in the appearance of the city? . . .

It is . . . argued that the city denigrates its interests in traffic safety and beauty and defeats its own case by permitting onsite advertising and other specified signs. Appellants question whether the distinction between onsite and offsite advertising on the same property is justifiable in terms of either esthetics or traffic safety. The ordinance permits the occupant of property to use billboards located on that property to advertise goods and services offered at that location; identical billboards, equally distracting and unattractive, that advertise goods or services available elsewhere are prohibited even if permitting the latter would not multiply the number of billboards. Despite the apparent incongruity, this argument has been rejected, at least implicitly, in all of the cases sustaining the distinction between offsite and onsite commercial advertising. . . .

. . . San Diego has obviously chosen to value one kind of commercial speech — onsite advertising — more than another kind of commercial speech — offsite advertising. The ordinance reflects a decision by the city that the former interest, but not the latter, is stronger than the city's interests in traffic safety and esthetics. The city has decided that in a limited instance — onsite commercial advertising — its interests should yield. We do not reject that judgment. As we see it, the city could reasonably conclude that a commercial enterprise — as well as the interested public — has a stronger interest in identifying its place of business and advertising the products or services available there than it has in using or leasing its available space for the purpose of advertising commercial enterprises located elsewhere. See *Railway Express, supra*, at 116 (Jackson, J., concurring); Bradley v. Public Utilities Comm'n, 289 U.S. 92, 97 (1933). It does not follow from the fact that the city has concluded that some commercial interests outweigh its mu-

Zoning Processes, Practices, and Problems

nicipal interests in this context that it must give similar weight to all other commercial advertising. Thus, offsite commercial billboards may be prohibited while onsite commercial billboards are permitted.

The constitutional problem in this area requires resolution of the conflict between the city's land-use interests and the commercial interests of those seeking to purvey goods and services within the city. In light of the above analysis, we cannot conclude that the city has drawn an ordinance broader than is necessary to meet its interests, or that it fails directly to advance substantial government interests. In sum, insofar as it regulates commercial speech the San Diego ordinance meets the constitutional requirements of *Central Hudson, supra.*

It does not follow, however, that San Diego's general ban on signs carrying noncommercial advertising is also valid under the First and Fourteenth Amendments. The fact that the city may value commercial messages relating to onsite goods and services more than it values commercial communications relating to offsite goods and services does not justify prohibiting an occupant from displaying its own ideas or those of others.

As indicated above, our recent commercial speech cases have consistently accorded noncommercial speech a greater degree of protection than commercial speech. San Diego effectively inverts this judgment, by affording a greater degree of protection to commercial than to noncommercial speech. There is a broad exception for onsite commercial advertisements, but there is no similar exception for noncommercial speech. The use of onsite billboards to carry commercial messages related to the commercial use of the premises is freely permitted, but the use of otherwise identical billboards to carry noncommercial messages is generally prohibited. The city does not explain how or why noncommercial billboards located in places where commercial billboards are permitted would be more threatening to safe driving or would detract more from the beauty of the city. Insofar as the city tolerates billboards at all, it cannot choose to limit their content to commercial messages; the city may not conclude that the communication of commercial information concerning goods and services connected with a particular site is of greater value than the communication of noncommercial messages.

Furthermore, the ordinance contains exceptions that permit various kinds of noncommercial signs, whether on property where goods and services are offered or not, that would otherwise be within the general ban. A fixed sign may be used to identify any piece of property and its owner. Any piece of property may carry or display religious symbols, commemorative plaques of recognized historical societies and organizations, signs carrying news items or telling the time or temperature, signs erected in discharge of any governmental function, or temporary political campaign signs. No other noncommercial or ideological signs meeting the structural definition are permitted, regardless of their effect on traffic safety or esthetics.

Although the city may distinguish between the relative value of different categories of commercial speech, the city does not have the same range of choice in the area of noncommercial speech to evaluate the strength of, or distinguish between, various communicative interests. See Carey v. Brown, 447 U.S., at 462; Police Dept of Chicago v. Mosley, 408 U.S. 92, 96 (1972). With respect to noncommercial speech, the city may not choose the appropriate subjects for public discourse: "To allow a government the choice of permissible subjects for public debate would be to allow that government control over the search for political truth." . . . Because some noncommercial messages may be conveyed on billboards throughout the commercial and industrial zones, San Diego must similarly allow billboards conveying other noncommercial messages throughout those zones.[35a]

Finally, we reject appellees' suggestion that the ordinance may be appropriately characterized as a reasonable "time, place, and manner" restriction. The ordinance does not generally ban billboard advertising as an unacceptable "manner" of communicating information or ideas; rather, it permits various kinds of signs. Signs that are banned are banned everywhere and at all times. We have observed that time, place, and manner restrictions are permissible if "they are justified without reference to the content of the regulated speech, . . . serve a significant governmental interest, and . . . leave open ample alternative channels for communication of the information." Virginia Pharmacy Board v. Virginia Citizens Consumer Council, 425 U.S., at 771. Here, it cannot be assumed that "alternative channels" are available, for the parties stipulated to just the opposite: "Many businesses and politicians and other persons rely upon outdoor advertising because other forms of advertising are insufficient, inappropriate and prohibitively expensive."[35b] . . .

Because the San Diego ordinance reaches too far into the realm of protected speech, we conclude that it is unconstitutional on its face. The judgment of the California Supreme Court is reversed, and the case is remanded to that court.[35c]

Justice BRENNAN, with whom Justice BLACKMUN joins, concurring in the judgment. . . .

Let me first state the common ground that I share with the plurality. The

---

[35a]. Because a total prohibition of outdoor advertising is not before us, we do not indicate whether such a ban would be consistent with the First Amendment. But see Schad v. Mount Ephraim, 452 U.S. 61 (1981), on the constitutional problems created by a total prohibition of a particular expressive forum, live entertainment in that case.

[35b]. See Joint Stipulation of Facts No. 28, App. 48a.

[35c]. . . . Since our judgment is based essentially on the inclusion of noncommercial speech within the prohibitions of the ordinance, the California courts may sustain the ordinance by limiting its reach to commercial speech, assuming the ordinance is susceptible to this treatment.

plurality and I agree that billboards are a medium of communication warranting First Amendment protection. The plurality observes that "[b]illboards are a well-established medium of communication, used to convey a broad range of different kinds of messages." . . .

. . . Although there are alternative channels for communication of messages appearing on billboards, such as newspapers, television, and radio, these alternatives have never dissuaded active and continued use of billboards as a medium of expression and appear to be less satisfactory. . . .

Where the plurality and I disagree is in the characterization of the San Diego ordinance and thus in the appropriate analytical framework to apply. The plurality believes that the question of a total ban is not presented in this case, because the ordinance contains exceptions to its general prohibition. In contrast, my view is that the *practical* effect of the San Diego ordinance is to eliminate the billboard as an effective medium of communication. . . . None of the exceptions provides a practical alternative for the general commercial or noncommercial billboard advertiser. Indeed, unless the advertiser chooses to buy or lease premises in the city, or unless his message falls within one of the narrow exempted categories, he is foreclosed from announcing either commercial or noncommercial ideas through a billboard.

The characterization of the San Diego regulation as a total ban of a medium of communication has more than semantic implications, for it suggests a First Amendment analysis quite different from the plurality's. Instead of relying on the exceptions to the ban to invalidate the ordinance, I would apply the tests this Court has developed to analyze content-neutral prohibitions of particular media of communication. Most recently, in Schad v. Mount Ephraim, 452 U.S. 61 (1981), this Court assessed "the substantiality of the governmental interests asserted" and "whether those interests could be served by means that would be less intrusive on activity protected by the First Amendment," in striking down the borough's total ban on live commercial entertainment. *Id.*, at 70. *Schad* merely articulated an analysis applied in previous cases concerning total bans of media of expression. . . . In the case of billboards, I would hold that a city may totally ban them if it can show that a sufficiently substantial governmental interest is directly furthered by the total ban, and that any more narrowly drawn restriction, i.e., anything less than a total ban, would promote less well the achievement of that goal.

Applying that test to the instant case, I would invalidate the San Diego ordinance. The city has failed to provide adequate justification for its substantial restriction on protected activity. See Schad v. Mount Ephraim, *supra*, at 72. First, although I have no quarrel with the substantiality of the city's interest in traffic safety, the city has failed to come forward with evidence demonstrating that billboards actually impair traffic safety in San Diego. Indeed, the joint stipulation of facts is completely silent on this issue. . . .

Second, I think that the city has failed to show that its asserted interest in aesthetics is sufficiently substantial in the commercial and industrial areas of San Diego. I do not doubt that "[i]t is within the power of the [city] to determine that the community should be beautiful," Berman v. Parker, 348 U.S. 26, 33 (1954), but that power may not be exercised in contravention of the First Amendment. . . .

It is no doubt true that the appearance of certain areas of the city would be enhanced by the elimination of billboards, but "it is not immediately apparent as a matter of experience" that their elimination in all other areas as well would have more than a negligible impact on aesthetics. . . . A billboard is not *necessarily* inconsistent with oil storage tanks, blighted areas, or strip development. Of course, it is not for a court to impose its own notion of beauty on San Diego. But before deferring to a city's judgment, a court must be convinced that the city is seriously and comprehensively addressing aesthetic concerns with respect to its environment. Here, San Diego has failed to demonstrate a comprehensive coordinated effort in its commercial and industrial areas to address other obvious contributors to an unattractive environment. In this sense the ordinance is underinclusive. . . . Of course, this is not to say that the city must address all aesthetic problems at the same time, or none at all. Indeed, from a planning point of view, attacking the problem incrementally and sequentially may represent the most sensible solution. On the other hand, if billboards alone are banned and no further steps are contemplated or likely, the commitment of the city to improving its physical environment is placed in doubt. By showing a comprehensive commitment to making its physical environment in commercial and industrial areas more attractive, and by allowing only narrowly tailored exceptions, if any, San Diego could demonstrate that its interest in creating an aesthetically pleasing environment is genuine and substantial. This is a requirement where, as here, there is an infringement of important constitutional consequences.

I have little doubt that some jurisdictions will easily carry the burden of proving the substantiality of their interest in aesthetics. For example, the parties acknowledge that a historical community such as Williamsburg, Va., should be able to prove that its interests in aesthetics and historical authenticity are sufficiently important that the First Amendment value attached to billboards must yield. And I would be surprised if the Federal Government had much trouble making the argument that billboards could be entirely banned in Yellowstone National Park, where their very existence would so obviously be inconsistent with the surrounding landscape. . . . But San Diego failed to do so here, and for that reason I would strike down its ordinance.

The plurality's treatment of the commercial-noncommercial distinction in this case is mistaken in its factual analysis of the San Diego ordinance, and departs from this Court's precedents. . . . [T]he plurality concludes that the San Diego ordinance is constitutional insofar as it regulates commercial speech. . . .

. . . I cannot agree with the plurality's view that an ordinance totally banning commercial billboards but allowing noncommercial billboards would be constitutional. For me, such an ordinance raises First Amendment problems at least as serious as those raised by a total ban, for it gives city officials the right — before approving a billboard — to determine whether the proposed message is "commercial" or "noncommercial." . . .

It is one thing for a court to classify in specific cases whether commercial or noncommercial speech is involved, but quite another — and for me dispositively so — for a city to do so regularly for the purpose of deciding what messages may be communicated by way of billboards. . . . I would be unhappy to see city officials dealing with the following series of billboards and deciding which ones to permit: the first billboard contains the message "Visit Joe's Ice Cream Shoppe"; the second, "Joe's Ice Cream Shoppe uses only the highest quality dairy products"; the third, "Because Joe thinks that dairy products are good for you, please shop at Joe's Shoppe"; and the fourth, "Joe says to support dairy price supports: they mean lower prices for you at his Shoppe." Or how about some San Diego Padres baseball fans — with no connection to the team — who together rent a billboard and communicate the message "Support the San Diego Padres, a great baseball team." May the city decide that a United Automobile Workers billboard with the message "Be a patriot — do not buy Japanese-manufactured cars" is "commercial" and therefore forbid it? What if the same sign is placed by Chrysler?

I do not read our recent line of commercial cases as authorizing this sort of regular and immediate line-drawing by governmental entities. . . .

Accordingly, I would reverse the decision of the California Supreme Court upholding the San Diego billboard ordinance.

Justice STEVENS, dissenting in part. If enforced as written, the ordinance at issue in this case will eliminate the outdoor advertising business in the city of San Diego.[35d] The principal question presented is, therefore, whether a city may prohibit this medium of communication. Instead of answering that question, the plurality focuses its attention on the exceptions from the total ban and, somewhat ironically, concludes that the ordinance is an unconstitutional abridgment of speech because it does not abridge enough speech. . . .

Although it is possible that some future applications of the San Diego ordinance may violate the First Amendment, I am satisfied that the ordinance survives the challenges that these appellants have standing to raise.

35d. The parties so stipulated.

Unlike the plurality, I do not believe that this case requires us to decide any question concerning the kind of signs a property owner may display on his own premises. I do, however, believe that it is necessary to confront the important question, reserved by the plurality, whether a city may entirely ban one medium of communication. My affirmative answer to that question leads me to the conclusion that the San Diego ordinance should be upheld. . . .

Because the legitimacy of the interests supporting a citywide zoning plan designed to improve the entire municipality are beyond dispute, in my judgment the constitutionality of the prohibition of outdoor advertising involves two separate questions. First, is there any reason to believe that the regulation is biased in favor of one point of view or another, or that it is a subtle method of regulating the controversial subjects that may be placed on the agenda for public debate? Second, is it fair to conclude that the market which remains open for the communication of both popular and unpopular ideas is ample and not threatened with gradually increasing restraints?

In this case, there is not even a hint of bias or censorship in the city's actions. Nor is there any reason to believe that the overall communications market in San Diego is inadequate. . . .

If one is persuaded, as I am, that a wholly impartial total ban on billboards would be permissible, it is difficult to understand why the exceptions in San Diego's ordinance present any additional threat to the interests protected by the First Amendment. . . .

The essential concern embodied in the First Amendment is that government not impose its viewpoint on the public or select the topics on which public debate is permissible. The San Diego ordinance simply does not implicate this concern. . . .

To the extent that the exceptions relate to subject matter at all, I can find no suggestion on the face of the ordinance that San Diego is attempting to influence public opinion or to limit public debate on particular issues. . . .

CHIEF JUSTICE BURGER, dissenting. Today the Court takes an extraordinary — even a bizarre — step by severely limiting the power of a city to act on risks it perceives to traffic safety and the environment posed by large, permanent billboards. Those joining the plurality opinion invalidate a city's effort to minimize these traffic hazards and eyesores simply because, in exercising rational legislative judgment, it has chosen to permit a narrow class of signs that serve special needs.

Relying on simplistic platitudes about content, subject matter, and the dearth of other means to communicate, the billboard industry attempts to escape the real and growing problems every municipality faces in protecting safety and preserving the environment in an urban area. The Court's disposition of the serious issues involved exhibits insensitivity to the impact of these billboards on those who must live with them and the delicacy of the legislative judgments involved in regulating them. American cities desiring to mitigate the dangers mentioned must, as a matter of *federal constitutional law*, elect between two unsatisfactory options: (a) allowing all "noncommercial" signs, no matter how many, how dangerous, or how damaging to the environment; or (b) forbidding signs altogether. Indeed, lurking in the recesses of today's opinions is a not-so-veiled threat that the second option, too, may soon be withdrawn. This is the long arm and voracious appetite of federal power — this time judicial power — with a vengeance, reaching and absorbing traditional concepts of local authority. . . .

It is not really relevant whether the San Diego ordinance is viewed as a regulation regarding time, place, and manner, or as a total prohibition on a medium with some exceptions defined, in part, by content. Regardless of the label we give it, we are discussing a very simple and basic question: the authority of local government to protect its citizens' legitimate interests in traffic safety and the environment by eliminating distracting and ugly structures from its buildings and roadways, to define which billboards actually pose that danger, and to decide whether, in certain instances, the public's need for information outweighs the dangers perceived. The billboard industry's superficial sloganeering is no substitute for analysis, and the plurality opinion and the opinion concurring in the judgment adopt much of that approach uncritically. . . .

In the process of eradicating . . . perceived harms, the ordinance here in no sense suppresses freedom of expression, either by discriminating among ideas or topics or by supressing discussion generally. San Diego has not attempted to suppress any particular point of view or any category of messages; it has not censored any information; it has not banned any thought. . . .

The messages conveyed on San Diego billboards — whether commercial, political, social, or religious — are not inseparable from the billboards that carry them. These same messages can reach an equally large audience through a variety of other media: newspapers, televison, radio, magazines, direct mail, pamphlets, etc. True, these other methods may not be so "eye-catching" — or so cheap — as billboards, but there has been no suggestion that billboards heretofore have advanced any particular viewpoint or issue disproportionately to advertising generally. Thus, the ideas billboard advertisers have been presenting are not *relatively* disadvantaged vis-à-vis the messages of those who heretofore have chosen other methods of spreading their views. . . . It borders on the frivolous to suggest that the San Diego ordinance infringes on freedom of expression, given the wide range of alternative means available. . . .

San Diego simply is exercising its police power to provide an environment of tranquility, safety, and as much residual beauty as a modern metropolitan area can achieve. A city's simultaneous recognition of the need for certain exceptions permitting limited forms of communication, purely factual in nature and neutral as to the speaker, should not wholly deprive the city of its ability to address the balance of the problem....

The fatal flaw in the plurality's logic comes when it concludes that San Diego, by exempting onsite commercial signs, thereby has "afford[ed] a greater degree of protection to commercial than to noncommercial speech." The "greater degree of protection" our cases have given noncommercial speech establishes a narrower range of constitutionally permissible regulation. To say noncommercial speech receives a greater degree of *constitutional* protection, however, does not mean that a legislature is forbidden to afford differing degrees of *statutory* protection when the restrictions on each form of speech — commercial and noncommercial — otherwise pass constitutional muster under the standards respectively applicable....

By allowing communication of certain commercial ideas via billboards, but forbidding noncommercial signs altogether, a city does not necessarily place a greater "value" on commercial speech. In these situations, the city is simply recognizing that it has greater latitude to distinguish among various forms of commercial communication when the same distinctions would be impermissible if undertaken with regard to noncommercial speech. Indeed, when adequate alternative channels of communication are readily available so that the message may be freely conveyed through other means, a city arguably is more faithful to the Constitution by treating all noncommercial speech the same than by attempting to impose the same classifications in noncommercial as it has in commercial areas. To undertake the same kind of balancing and content judgment with noncommercial speech that is permitted with commercial speech is far more likely to run afoul of the First Amendment.

Thus, we may, consistent with the First Amendment, hold that a city may — and perhaps must — take an all-or-nothing approach with noncommercial speech yet remain free to adopt selective exceptions for commercial speech, as long as the latter advance legitimate governmental interests....

Justice REHNQUIST, dissenting. I agree substantially with the views expressed in the dissenting opinions of THE CHIEF JUSTICE and Justice STEVENS and make only these two additional observations: (1) In a case where city planning commissions and zoning boards must regularly confront constitutional claims of this sort, it is a genuine misfortune to have the Court's treatment of the subject be a virtual Tower of Babel, from which no definitive principles can be clearly drawn; and (2) I regret even more keenly my contribution to this judicial clangor, but find that none of the views expressed in the other opinions written in the case come close enough to mine to warrant the necessary compromise to obtain a Court opinion.

In my view, the aesthetic justification alone is sufficient to sustain a total prohibition of billboards within a community, see Berman v. Parker, 348 U.S. 26, 32-33 (1954), regardless of whether the particular community is "a historical community such as Williamsburg" or one as unsightly as the older parts of many of our major metropolitan areas. Such areas should not be prevented from taking steps to correct, as best they may, mistakes of their predecessors. Nor do I believe that the limited exceptions contained in the San Diego ordinance are the type which render this statute unconstitutional. The closest one is the exception permitting billboards during political campaigns, but I would treat this as a virtually self-limiting exception which will have an effect on the aesthetics of the city only during the periods immediately prior to a campaign. As such, it seems to me a reasonable outlet, limited as to time, for the free expression which the First and Fourteenth Amendments were designed to protect.

Unlike Justice BRENNAN, I do not think a city should be put to the task of convincing a local judge that the elimination of billboards would have more than a negligible impact on aesthetics. Nothing in my experience on the bench has led me to believe that a judge is in any better position than a city or county commission to make decisions in an area such as aesthetics. Therefore, little can be gained in the area of constitutional law, and much lost in the process of democratic decisionmaking, by allowing individual judges in city after city to second-guess such legislative or administrative determinations.

NOTES

1. Subsequent to the Court's remand in *Metromedia,* the California Supreme Court concluded that the San Diego ordinance could not reasonably be construed in a manner that would preserve its constitutionality. Metromedia, Inc. v. City of San Diego, 32 Cal. 3d 180, 649 P.2d 902, 185 Cal. Rptr. 260 (1982).

2. Members of City Council of Los Angeles v. Taxpayers for Vincent, 104 S. Ct. 2118 (1984), confronted the Court with an ordinance prohibiting the posting of signs on public property. The Court upheld the constitutionality of the ordinance as applied to the campaign activities of a group supporting a political candidate; it said in part (104 S. Ct. at 2128-2132):

> The ordinance prohibits appellees from communicating with the public in a certain manner, and presumably diminishes the total quantity of their communication in the City. The application of the ordinance to appellees' expressive activities surely raises the question whether the ordinance abridges their "freedom of speech" within the meaning of the First Amendment, and appellees certainly have standing to challenge the application of the ordinance to their own expressive activities. "But to say the ordinance presents a First Amendment *issue*

is not necessarily to say that it constitutes a First Amendment *violation.*" Metromedia, Inc. v. San Diego, 453 U.S. 490, 561, 101 S. Ct. 2882, 2920, 69 L.Ed.2d 800 (1981) (BURGER, C.J., dissenting). It has been clear since this Court's earliest decisions concerning the freedom of speech that the state may sometimes curtail speech when necessary to advance a significant and legitimate state interest. . . . The general principle that has emerged from this line of cases is that the First Amendment forbids the government from regulating speech in ways that favor some viewpoints or ideas at the expense of others. . . .

That general rule has no application to this case. For there is not even a hint of bias or censorship in the City's enactment or enforcement of this ordinance. There is no claim that the ordinance was designed to suppress certain ideas that the City finds distasteful or that it has been applied to appellees because of the views that they express. The text of the ordinance is neutral — indeed it is silent — concerning any speaker's point of view and the District Court's findings indicate that it has been applied to appellees and others in an evenhanded manner. . . .

It is well settled that the state may legitimately exercise its police powers to advance esthetic values. . . .

In this case, [there is no] dispute that it is within the constitutional power of the City to attempt to improve its appearance, or that this interest is basically unrelated to the suppression of ideas. Therefore the critical inquiries are whether that interest is sufficiently substantial to justify the effect of the ordinance on appellees' expression, and whether that effect is no greater than necessary to accomplish the City's purpose. . . .

Metromedia, Inc. v. City of San Diego, 453 U.S. 490, 101 S. Ct. 2882, 69 L. Ed. 2d 800 (1981), dealt with San Diego's prohibition of certain forms of outdoor billboards. There the Court considered the city's interest in avoiding visual clutter, and seven Justices explicitly concluded that this interest was sufficient to justify a prohibition of billboards, see *id.,* at 507-508, 510, 101 S. Ct., at 2892-2893, 2894 (opinion of White, J., joined by Stewart, Marshall & Powell, JJ.); *id.,* at 552, 101 S. Ct., at 2915 (Stevens, J., dissenting in part); *id.;* at 559-561, 101 S. Ct., at 2919-2921 (Burger, C.J., dissenting); *id.,* at 570, 101 S. Ct., at 2924-2925 (Rehnquist, J., dissenting).[35e] Justice White, writing for the plurality, expressly conclud-

---

35e. The Court of Appeals relied on Justice BRENNAN's opinion concurring in the judgment in *Metromedia* to support its conclusion that the City's interest in esthetics was not sufficiently substantial to outweigh the constitutional interest in free expression unless the City proved that it had undertaken a comprehensive and coordinated effort to remove other elements of visual clutter within San Diego. This reliance was misplaced because Justice BRENNAN's analysis was expressly rejected by a majority of the Court. Moreover, Justice BRENNAN was concerned that the San Diego ordinance might not in fact have a substantial salutary effect on the appearance of the city because it did not ameliorate other types of visual clutter beside billboards, thus suggesting that in fact it had been applied to areas where it did not advance the interest in esthetics sufficiently to justify an abridgment of speech.

ed that the city's esthetic interests were sufficiently substantial to provide an acceptable justification for a content neutral prohibition against the use of billboards; San Diego's interest in its appearance was undoubtedly a substantial governmental goal.

We reaffirm the conclusion of the majority in *Metromedia*. The problem addressed by this ordinance — the visual assault on the citizens of Los Angeles presented by an accumulation of signs posted on public property — constitutes a significant substantive evil within the City's power to prohibit....

We turn to the question whether the scope of the restriction on appellees' expressive activity is substantially broader than necessary to protect the City's interest in eliminating visual clutter. The incidental restriction on expression which results from the City's attempt to accomplish such a purpose is considered justified as a reasonable regulation of the time, place, or manner of expression if it is narrowly tailored to serve that interest.... The District Court found that the signs prohibited by the ordinance do constitute visual clutter and blight. By banning these signs, the City did no more than eliminate the exact source of the evil it sought to remedy. The plurality wrote in *Metromedia:* "It is not speculative to recognize that billboards by their very nature, wherever located and however constructed, can be perceived as an 'esthetic harm.'" 453 U.S., at 510, 101 S. Ct., at 2893-2894. The same is true of posted signs.

It is true that the esthetic interest in preventing the kind of litter that may result from the distribution of leaflets on the public streets and sidewalks cannot support a prophylactic prohibition against the citizens' exercise of that method of expressing his views. In Schneider v. State, 308 U.S. 147, 60 S. Ct. 146, 84 L. Ed. 155 (1939), the Court held that ordinances that absolutely prohibited handbilling on the streets were invalid....

With respect to signs posted by appellees, however, it is the tangible medium of expressing the message that has the adverse impact on the appearance of the landscape. In *Schneider,* an anti-littering statute could have addressed the substantive evil without prohibiting expressive activity, whereas application of the prophylactic rule actually employed gratuitously infringed upon the right of an individual to communicate directly with a willing listener. Here, the substantive evil — visual blight — is not merely a possible by-product of the activity, but is created by the medium of expression itself. In contrast to *Schneider,* therefore, the application of ordinance in this case responds precisely to the substantive problem which legitimately concerns the City. The ordinance curtails no more speech than is necessary to accomplish its purpose....

The Court of Appeals accepted the argument that a prohibition against the use of unattractive signs cannot be justified on esthetic grounds if it fails to apply to all equally unattractive signs wherever they might be located. A comparable argument was categorically rejected in *Metromedia*. In that case it was argued that the city could not simultaneously permit billboards to be used for on-site advertising and also justify the prohibition against offsite advertising on esthetic grounds, since both types of advertising were equally unattractive. The Court held, however, that the city could reasonably conclude that the esthetic interest was outweighed by the countervailing interest in one kind of advertising even though it was not outweighed by the other. So here, the validity of the esthetic interest in the elimination of signs on public property is not compromised by failing to extend the ban to private property. The private citizen's interest in controlling the use of his own property justifies the disparate treatment. Moreover, by not extending the ban to all locations, a significant opportunity to communicate by means of temporary signs is preserved, and private property owners' esthetic concerns will keep the posting of signs on their property within reasonable bounds. Even if some visual blight remains, a partial, content-neutral ban may nevertheless enhance the City's appearance. . . .

Page 1353. After line 3, add:

In Schad v. Mount Ephraim, 452 U.S. 61 (1981), the appellants were operators of an adult bookstore and movie arcade located in a commercial zone. When the appellants added to their business coin-operated machines that permitted customers to watch live nude dancers, they were convicted under an ordinance that excluded live entertainment throughout the Borough of Mount Ephraim. On appeal, the Court overturned the convictions. Live entertainment, the Court held, falls within the protective reach of the First Amendment, and cannot be excluded absent sufficient justification. The *Mini Theatres* case was not controlling because the zoning ordinance upheld there merely dispersed adult movie theaters, it did not exclude them. "The Court did not imply that a municipality could ban all adult theaters — much less all live entertainment or all nude dancing — from its commercial districts citywide." 452 U.S. at 71. The ordinance in *Mini Theatres* aimed at a substantial problem — neighborhood deterioration caused by concentration of adult theaters — and put only the incidental burden of dispersal on First Amendment interests. "In this case, however, Mount Ephraim has not adequately justified its substantial restriction of protected activity." *Id.* at 72.

Page 1367. After "3. Exclusionary Zoning," insert:

The opinion in *Mount Laurel*, which appears in the main text beginning at page 1367, has now been updated by *Mount Laurel II*, reproduced below. A quick reading of *Mount Laurel I*, especially the facts, is recommended; so too regarding the Notes and Questions following the case (beginning at page 1385 of the main text). *Mount Laurel II* is a leviathan of sorts. The case was argued in late 1980 but not decided until early 1983, and the report (in the Atlantic Reporter) runs 120 pages in length. The version that follows has been subjected to drastic surgery.

SOUTHERN BURLINGTON COUNTY NAACP v. TOWNSHIP OF MOUNT LAUREL [MOUNT LAUREL II]

Supreme Court of New Jersey, 1983
92 N.J. 158, 456 A.2d 390

WILENTZ, C.J. This is the return, eight years later, of . . . *Mount Laurel I*. We set forth in that case, for the first time, the doctrine requiring that municipalities' land use regulations provide a realistic opportunity for low and moderate income housing. The doctrine has become famous. The *Mount Laurel* case itself threatens to become infamous. After all this time, ten years after the trial court's initial order invalidating its zoning ordinance, Mount Laurel remains afflicted with a blatantly exclusionary ordinance. Papered over with studies, rationalized by hired experts, the ordinance at its core is true to nothing but Mount Laurel's determination to exclude the poor. Mount Laurel is not alone; we believe that there is widespread non-compliance with the constitutional mandate of our original opinion in this case.

To the best of our ability, we shall not allow it to continue. This Court is more firmly committed to the original *Mount Laurel* doctrine than ever, and we are determined, within appropriate judicial bounds, to make it work. The obligation is to provide a realistic opportunity for housing, not litigation. We have learned from experience, however, that unless a strong judicial hand is used, *Mount Laurel* will not result in housing, but in paper, process, witnesses, trials and appeals. We intend by this decision to strengthen it, clarify it, and make it easier for public officials, including judges, to apply it.

This case is accompanied by five others, heard together and decided in this opinion. All involve questions arising from the *Mount Laurel* doctrine. They demonstrate the need to put some steel into that doctrine. The deficiencies in its application range from uncertainty and inconsistency at the trial level to inflexible review criteria at the appellate level. The waste of judicial energy involved at every level is substantial and is matched only by the often needless expenditure of talent on the part of lawyers and experts. The length and complexity of trials is often outrageous, and the expense of litigation is so high that a real question develops whether the municipality can afford to defend or the plaintiffs can afford to sue.

There is another side to the story. We believe, both through the representations of counsel and from our own research and experience, that the doctrine has done some good, indeed, perhaps substantial good. We have tried to make the doctrine clearer for we believe that most municipal officials will in good faith strive to fulfill their constitutional duty. There are a number of municipalities around the State that have responded to our decisions by amending their zoning ordinances to provide realistic opportunities for the construction of low and moderate income housing. Further, many other municipalities have at least recognized their obligation to provide such opportunities in their ordinances and master plans. Finally, state and county government agencies have responded by preparing regional housing plans that help both the courts and municipalities themselves carry out the *Mount Laurel* mandate. Still, we are far from where we had hoped to be and nowhere near where we should be with regard to the administration of the doctrine in our courts.

These six cases not only afford the opportunity for, but demonstrate the necessity of reexamining the *Mount Laurel* doctrine. We do so here. The doctrine is right but its administration has been ineffective.

A brief statement of the cases may be helpful at this point. *Mount Laurel II* results from the remand by this Court of the original *Mount Laurel* case. The municipality rezoned, purportedly pursuant to our instructions, a plenary trial was held, and the trial court found that the rezoning constituted a bona fide attempt by Mount Laurel to provide a realistic opportunity for the construction of its fair share of the regional lower income housing need. Reading our cases at that time (1978) as requiring no more, the trial court dismissed the complaint of the N.A.A.C.P. and other plaintiffs but granted relief in the form of a builder's remedy, to a developer-intervenor who had attacked the total prohibition against mobile homes. Plaintiffs' appeal of the trial court's ruling sustaining the ordinance in all other respects was directly certified by this Court, as ultimately was defendant's appeal from the grant of a builder's remedy allowing construction of mobile homes. We reverse and remand to determine Mount Laurel's fair share of the regional need and for further proceedings to revise its ordinance; we affirm the grant of the builder's remedy. . . .

[The five other cases involved local governments other than Mount Laurel. Three were actions brought by landowners seeking a builder's remedy. In the remaining two cases local chapters of the Urban League were asking the court to order certain municipalities to revise their ordinances to comply with their fair-share obligations.]

I. Background

B. CONSTITUTIONAL BASIS FOR MOUNT LAUREL AND THE JUDICIAL ROLE

. . . The basis for the constitutional obligation is simple: the State controls the use of land, *all* of the land. In exercising that control it cannot favor rich over poor. It cannot legislatively set aside dilapidated housing in urban ghettos for the poor and decent housing elsewhere for everyone else. The government that controls this land represents everyone. While the State may not have the ability to eliminate poverty, it cannot use that condition as the basis for imposing further disadvantages. And the same applies to the municipality, to which this control over land has been constitutionally delegated.

The clarity of the constitutional obligation is seen most simply by imagining what this state could be like were this claim never to be recognized and enforced: poor people forever zoned out of substantial areas of the state, not because housing could not be built for them but because they are not wanted; poor people forced to live in urban slums forever not because suburbia, developing rural areas, fully developed residential sections, seashore resorts, and other attractive locations could not accommodate them, but simply because they are not wanted. It is a vision not only at variance with the requirement that the zoning power be used for the general welfare but with all concepts of fundamental fairness and decency that underpin many constitutional obligations.

Subject to the clear obligation to preserve open space and prime agricultural land, a builder in New Jersey who finds it economically feasible to provide decent housing for lower income groups will no longer find it governmentally impossible. Builders may not be able to build just where they want — our parks, farms, and conservation areas are not a land bank for housing speculators. But if sound planning of an area allows the rich and middle class to live there, it must also realistically and practically allow the poor. And if the area will accommodate factories, it must also find space for workers. The specific location of such housing will of course continue to depend on sound municipal land use planning.

While *Mount Laurel I* discussed the need for "an appropriate variety and choice of housing," 67 N.J. 179, 336 A.2d 713, the specific constitutional obligation addressed there, as well as in our opinion here, is that relating to low and moderate income housing. *Id.* All that we say here concerns that category alone; the doctrine as we interpret it has no present applicability to other kinds of housing. See *Pascack*, 74 N.J. at 480, 379 A.2d 6. It is obvious that eight years after *Mount Laurel I* the need for satisfaction of this doctrine is greater than ever. Upper and middle income groups may search with increasing difficulty for housing within their means; for low and moderate income people, there is nothing to search for.

No one has challenged the *Mount Laurel* doctrine on these appeals. Nevertheless, a brief reminder of the judicial role in this sensitive area is appropriate, since powerful reasons suggest, and we agree, that the matter is better left to the Legislature. We act first and foremost because the Constitution of our State requires protection of the interests involved and because the Legislature has not protected them. We recognize the social and economic controversy (and its political consequences) that has resulted in relatively little legislative action in this field. We understand the enormous difficulty of achieving a political consensus that might lead to significant legislation enforcing the constitutional mandate better than we can, legislation that might completely remove this Court from those controversies. But enforcement of constitutional rights cannot await a supporting political consensus. So while we have always preferred legislative to judicial action in this field, we shall continue — until the Legislature acts — to do our best to uphold the constitutional obligation that underlies the *Mount Laurel* doctrine. That is our duty. We may not build houses, but we do enforce the Constitution.

We note that there has been some legislative initiative in this field. We look forward to more. The new Municipal Land Use Law explicitly recognizes the obligation of municipalities to zone with regional consequences in mind, N.J.S.A. 40:55D-28(d); it also recognizes the work of the Division of State and Regional Planning in the Department of Community Affairs (DCA), in creating the State Development Guide Plan (1980) (SDGP), which plays an important part in our decisions today. Our deference to these legislative and executive initiatives can be regarded as a clear signal of our readiness to defer further to more substantial actions.

The judicial role, however, which could decrease as a result of legislative and executive action, necessarily will expand to the extent that we remain virtually alone in this field. In the absence of adequate legislative and executive help, we must give meaning to the constitutional doctrine in the cases before us through our own devices, even if they are relatively less suitable. That is the basic explanation of our decisions today.

C. SUMMARY OF RULINGS

Our rulings today have several purposes. First, we intend to encourage voluntary compliance with the constitutional obligation by defining it more clearly. We believe that the use of the State Development Guide Plan and the confinement of all *Mount Laurel* litigation to a small group of judges, selected by the Chief Justice with the approval of the Court, will tend to serve that purpose. Second, we hope to simplify litigation in this area. While we are not overly optimistic, we think that the remedial use of the SDGP may achieve that purpose, given the significance accorded it in this opinion. Third, the decisions are intended to increase substantially the effectiveness of the judicial remedy. In most cases, upon determination that the municipality has not fulfilled its constitutional obligation, the trial court will retain jurisdiction, order an immediate revision of the ordinance (including, if necessary, supervision of the revision through a court appointed master), and require the use of effective affirmative planning and zoning devices. The long delays of interminable appellate review will be discouraged, if not completely ended, and the opportunity for low and moderate income housing found in the new ordinance will be as realistic as judicial remedies can make it. We hope to achieve all of these purposes while preserving the fundamental legitimate control of municipalities over their own zoning and, indeed, their destiny.

The following is a summary of the more significant rulings of these cases:

(1) *Every* municipality's land use regulations should provide a realistic opportunity for decent housing for at least some part of its resident poor who now occupy dilapidated housing. The zoning power is no more abused by keeping out the region's poor than by forcing out the resident poor. In other words, each municipality must provide a realistic opportunity for decent housing for its indigenous poor except where they represent a disproportionately large segment of the population as compared with the rest of the region. This is the case in many of our urban areas.

(2) The existence of a municipal obligation to provide a realistic opportunity for a fair share of the region's present and prospective low and moderate income housing need will no longer be determined by whether or not a municipality is "developing." The obligation extends, instead, to every municipality, any portion of which is designated by the State, through the SDGP as a "growth area." This obligation, imposed as a remedial measure, does not extend to those areas where the SDGP discourages growth — namely, open spaces, rural areas, prime farmland, conservation areas, limited growth areas, parts of the Pinelands and certain Coastal Zone areas. The SDGP represents the conscious determination of the State, through the executive and legislative branches, on how best to plan its future. It appropriately serves as a judicial remedial tool. The obligation to encourage lower income housing, therefore, will hereafter depend on rational long-range land use planning (incorporated into the SDGP) rather than upon the sheer economic forces that have dictated whether a municipality is "developing." Moreover, the fact that a municipality is fully developed does not eliminate this obligation although, obviously, it may affect the extent of the obligation and the timing of its satisfaction. The remedial obligation of municipalities that consist of both "growth areas" and other areas may be reduced, based on many factors, as compared to a municipality completely within a "growth area."

There shall be a heavy burden on any party seeking to vary the foregoing remedial consequences of the SDGP designations.

(3) *Mount Laurel* litigation will ordinarily include proof of the municipality's fair share of low and moderate income housing in terms of the number of units needed immediately, as well as the number needed for a reasonable period of time in the future. "Numberless" resolution of the issue based upon a conclusion that the ordinance provides a realistic opportunity for *some* low and moderate income housing will be insufficient. Plaintiffs, however, will still be able to prove a prima facie case, without proving the precise fair share of the municipality, by proving that the zoning ordinance is substantially affected by restrictive devices, that proof creating a presumption that the ordinance is invalid.

The municipal obligation to provide a realistic opportunity for low and moderate income housing is not satisfied by a good faith attempt. The housing opportunity provided must, in fact, be the substantial equivalent of the fair share.

(4) Any future *Mount Laurel* litigation shall be assigned only to those judges selected by the Chief Justice with the approval of the Supreme Court. The initial group shall consist of three judges, the number to be increased or decreased hereafter by the Chief Justice with the Court's approval. The Chief Justice shall define the area of the State for which each of the three judges is responsible: any *Mount Laurel* case challenging the land use ordinance of a municipality included in that area shall be assigned to that judge. . . .

(5) The municipal obligation to provide a realistic opportunity for the construction of its fair share of low and moderate income housing may require more than the elimination of unnecessary cost-producing requirements and restrictions. Affirmative governmental devices should be used to make that opportunity realistic, including lower-income density bonuses and mandatory set-asides. Furthermore the municipality should cooperate with the developer's attempts to obtain federal subsidies. For instance, where federal subsidies depend on the municipality providing certain municipal tax treatment allowed by state statutes for lower income housing, the municipality should make a good faith effort to provide it. Mobile homes may not be prohibited, unless there is solid proof that sound planning in a particular municipality requires such prohibition.

(6) The lower income regional housing need is comprised of both low and moderate income housing. A municipality's fair share should include both in such proportion as reflects consideration of all relevant factors, including the proportion of low and moderate income housing that make up the regional need.

(7) Providing a realistic opportunity for the construction of least-cost housing will satisfy a municipality's *Mount Laurel* obligation if, and only if, it cannot otherwise be satisfied. In other words, it is only after *all* alternatives have been explored, *all* affirmative devices considered, including, where appropriate, a reasonable period of time to determine whether low and moderate income housing is produced, only when everything has been considered and tried in order to produce a realistic opportunity for low and moderate income housing that least-cost housing will provide an adequate substitute. Least-cost housing means what it says, namely, housing that can be produced at the lowest possible price consistent with minimal standards of health and safety.

(8) Builder's remedies will be afforded to plaintiffs in *Mount Laurel* litigation where appropriate, on a case-by-case basis. Where the plaintiff has acted in good faith, attempted to obtain relief without litigation, and thereafter vindicates the constitutional obligation in *Mount Laurel*-type litigation, ordinarily a builder's remedy will be granted, provided that the proposed proj-

ect includes an appropriate portion of low and moderate income housing, and provided further that it is located and designed in accordance with sound zoning and planning concepts, including its environmental impact.

(9) The judiciary should manage *Mount Laurel* litigation to dispose of a case in all of its aspects with one trial and one appeal, unless substantial considerations indicate some other course. . . . The trial court will appoint a master to assist in formulating and implementing a proper remedy whenever that course seems desirable.

(10) The *Mount Laurel* obligation to meet the prospective lower income housing need of the region is, by definition, one that is met year after year in the future, throughout the years of the particular projection used in calculating prospective need. In this sense the affirmative obligation to provide a realistic opportunity to construct a fair share of lower income housing is met by a "phase-in" over those years; it need not be provided immediately. Nevertheless, there may be circumstances in which the obligation requires zoning that will provide an immediate opportunity — for instance, zoning to meet the region's present lower income housing need. In some cases, the provision of such a realistic opportunity might result in the immediate construction of lower income housing in such quantity as would radically transform the municipality overnight. Trial courts shall have the discretion, under those circumstances, to moderate the impact of such housing by allowing even the present need to be phased in over a period of years. Such power, however, should be exercised sparingly. The same power may be exercised in the satisfaction of prospective need, equally sparingly, and with special care to assure that such further postponement will not significantly dilute the *Mount Laurel* obligation.

We reassure all concerned that *Mount Laurel* is not designed to sweep away all land use restrictions or leave our open spaces and natural resources prey to speculators. Municipalities consisting largely of conservation, agricultural, or environmentally sensitive areas will not be required to grow because of *Mount Laurel*. No forests or small towns need be paved over and covered with high-rise apartments as a result of today's decision.

As for those municipalities that may have to make adjustments in their lifestyles to provide for their fair share of low and moderate income housing, they should remember that they are not being required to provide more than their *fair* share. No one community need be concerned that it will be radically transformed by a deluge of low and moderate income developments. Nor should any community conclude that its residents will move to other suburbs as a result of this decision, for those "other suburbs" may very well be required to do their part to provide the same housing. Finally, once a community has satisfied its fair share obligation, the *Mount Laurel* doctrine will not restrict other measures, including large-lot and open area zoning, that would maintain its beauty and communal character.

[In the *Chester Township* case, one of the five consolidated with the *Mount Laurel II* litigation, the court held that five-acre lot minimums do not invariably violate the *Mount Laurel* doctrine.]

... Our scenic and rural areas will remain essentially scenic and rural, and our suburban communities will retain their basic suburban character. But there will be *some* change, as there must be if the constitutional rights of our lower income citizens are ever to be protected. That change will be much less painful for us than the status quo has been for them.

II. Resolution of the Issues

B. DETERMINING THE MOUNT LAUREL OBLIGATION: USE OF THE STATE DEVELOPMENT GUIDE PLAN

... By using proven sound planning concepts the Division of State and Regional Planning, statutorily charged with the obligation (N.J.S.A. 13:1B-15.52), developed a master plan (the SDGP and the Concept Map) for the purpose of guiding the future growth and development of this state.

The SDGP divides the state into six basic areas: growth, limited growth, agriculture, conservation, pinelands and coastal zones (the pinelands and coastal zones actually being the product of other protective legislation). While it does not purport to draw its lines so finely as to delineate actual municipal boundaries or specific parcels of land, the concept map, through the county maps, makes it quite clear how every municipality in the state should be classified. . . . By clearly setting forth the state's policy as to where growth should be encouraged and discouraged, these maps effectively serve as a blueprint for the implementation of the *Mount Laurel* doctrine. Pursuant to the concept map, development (including residential development) is targeted for areas characterized as "growth." . . .

The lessons of history are clear, even if rarely learned. One of those lessons is that unplanned growth has a price: natural resources are destroyed, open spaces are despoiled, agricultural land is rendered forever unproductive, and people settle without regard to the enormous cost of the public facilities needed to support them. Cities decay; established infrastructures deteriorate for lack of funds; and taxpayers shudder under a financial burden of public expenditures resulting in part from uncontrolled migration to anywhere anyone wants to settle, roads leading to places they should never be — a pattern of total neglect of sensible conservation of resources, funds, prior public investment, and just plain common sense. These costs in New Jersey, the most highly urbanized state in the nation, are staggering, and our knowledge of our limited ability to support them has become acute. More than money is involved, for natural and man-made physical resources are irreversibly damaged. Statewide comprehensive planning is no longer simply desirable, it is a necessity recognized by both the federal and state governments.

Based on all of the foregoing, we are able to fashion judicial relief through means not available to us when we established the "developing municipality" remedial doctrine. These considerations, founded in sound public policy relating to comprehensive planning, are compelling in favor of a remedial solution that imposes the *Mount Laurel* obligation only in those areas designated as "growth areas" by the SDGP [, except in those unusual cases where a party persuades the trial court that the SDGP should not govern whether the *Mount Laurel* doctrine applies to a particular municipality.] . . .

. . . In non-growth areas, however (limited growth, conservation, and agricultural), no municipality will have to provide for more than the present need generated within the municipality, for to require more than that would be to induce growth in that municipality in conflict with the SDGP.

It is our intention by this decision generally to channel the *entire* prospective lower income housing need in New Jersey into "growth areas." It is clear that that is what the SDGP intends and there is nothing to indicate that those areas are not more than sufficient to accommodate such growth for the foreseeable future. . . .

Our use of the State Development Guide Plan for the purpose of determining where *Mount Laurel* applies does not, of course, guarantee that lower income housing will be constructed in the future solely pursuant to this comprehensive rational plan for the development of New Jersey. . . . [N]othing . . . prevents municipalities from encouraging growth, including residential growth, in areas designated by the SDGP as limited growth, agricultural or conservation areas. . . . Except for protective legislation (such as that pertaining to the Pinelands and certain coastal areas) limited to particular ecologically sensitive areas, the state has imposed no proscriptions against development. . . .

C. CALCULATING FAIR SHARE

The most troublesome issue in *Mount Laurel* litigation is the determination of fair share. It takes the most time, produces the greatest variety of opinions, and engenders doubt as to the meaning and wisdom of *Mount Laurel*. Determination of fair share has required resolution of three separate issues: identifying the relevant region, determining its present and prospective housing needs, and allocating those needs to the municipality or municipalities involved. Each of these issues produces a morass of facts, statistics, projections, theories and opinions sufficient to discourage even the staunchest supporters of *Mount Laurel*. The problem is capable of monopolizing counsel's time for years, overwhelming trial courts and inundating reviewing courts with a record on review of superhuman dimensions. . . .

The restriction of *Mount Laurel* litigation to three judges should simplify and perhaps, in time, substantially eliminate the issues of "region" and "regional need" from litigation. Of the three major issues in this area, their determination is most susceptible to judicial treatment. . . .

The determination of region and regional need by any of these judges shall be presumptively valid as to all municipalities included in the region unless the judge hearing the matter indicates otherwise for reasons stated in his or her decision. Given the importance of these determinations, municipalities not named as parties may attempt to intervene or the court may require their joinder if, all things considered, it is thought advisable that such a municipality be bound by the determination even though such joinder may complicate the litigation. . . .

In short we foresee that within several years . . . the only issue (other than the adequacy of the housing opportunity provided by the ordinance) that may require serious litigation is a particular municipality's fair share of [regional] need. . . .

[On that issue,] we offer some suggestions. Formulas that accord substantial weight to employment opportunities in the municipality, especially new employment accompanied by substantial ratables, shall be favored; formulas that have the effect of tying prospective lower income housing needs to the present proportion of lower income residents to the total population of a municipality shall be disfavored; formulas that have the effect of unreasonably diminishing the share because of a municipality's successful exclusion of lower income housing in the past shall be disfavored.

In determining fair share, the court should decide the proportion between low and moderate income housing unless there are substantial reasons not to do so. The provisions and devices needed to produce moderate income housing may fall short of those needed for lower. Since there are two fairly distinct lower income housing needs, an effort must be made to meet both.

The proportion between the two is, inevitably, a matter for expert testimony. It will depend, as does the fair share itself, on a complex mix of factors. . . .

We recognize that the tools for calculating present and prospective need and its allocation are imprecise and further that it is impossible to predict with precision how many units of housing will result from specific ordinances. What is required is the precision of a specific area and specific numbers. They are required not because we think scientific accuracy is possible, but because we believe the requirement is most likely to achieve the goals of *Mount Laurel*. . . .

D. MEETING THE MOUNT LAUREL OBLIGATION

1. Removing Excessive Restrictions and Exactions

In order to meet their *Mount Laurel* obligations, municipalities, at the very least, must remove all municipally created barriers to the construction of their fair share of lower income housing. Thus, to the extent necessary to meet their prospective fair share and provide for their indigenous poor (and, in some cases, a portion of the region's poor), municipalities must remove zoning and subdivision restrictions and exactions that are not necessary to protect health and safety. . . .

It may be difficult for a municipality to determine how to balance the need to reduce the costs of its regulations against the need to adequately protect health and safety, just as it may be difficult for a court to determine when a municipality has reduced these costs enough. There are, however, relatively objective guides that can help both the municipality and the court. Particularly helpful, though in no way conclusive as to what the minimum standards should be in a particular community, are the Department of Housing and Urban Development's Minimum Property Standards and the suggestions as to minimum zoning and subdivision standards made by the Rutgers Center for Urban Policy Research in [S. Seidel, Housing Costs and Government Regulations (1978)]. With these and other such guides, plus specific evidence submitted by the parties, we believe that a court can determine whether municipally-imposed housing costs have been sufficiently reduced.

Once a municipality has revised its land use regulations and taken other steps affirmatively to provide a realistic opportunity for the construction of its fair share of lower income housing, the *Mount Laurel* doctrine requires it to do no more. For instance, a municipality having thus complied, the fact that its land use regulations contain restrictive provisions incompatible with lower income housing, such as bedroom restrictions, large lot zoning, prohibition against mobile homes, and the like, does not render those provisions invalid under *Mount Laurel*. Obviously, if they are otherwise invalid — for instance if they bear no reasonable relationship to any legitimate governmental goal — they may be declared void on those other grounds. But they are not void because of *Mount Laurel* under those circumstances. *Mount Laurel* is not an indiscriminate broom designed to sweep away all distinctions in the use of land. Municipalities may continue to reserve areas for upper income housing, may continue to require certain community amenities in certain areas, may continue to zone with some regard to their fiscal obligations: they may do all of this, provided that they have otherwise complied with their *Mount Laurel* obligations.

2. *Using Affirmative Measures*

. . . Satisfaction of the *Mount Laurel* doctrine cannot depend on the inclination of developers to help the poor. It has to depend on affirmative inducements to make the opportunity real. . . .

Therefore, unless removal of restrictive barriers will, without more, afford a realistic opportunity for the construction of the municipality's fair share of the region's lower income housing need, affirmative measures will be required.

There are two basic types of affirmative measures that a municipality can use to make the opportunity for lower income housing realistic: (1) encouraging or requiring the use of available state or federal housing subsidies, and (2) providing incentives for or requiring private developers to set aside a portion of their developments for lower income housing. Which, if either, of these devices will be necessary in any particular municipality to assure compliance with the constitutional mandate will be initially up to the municipality itself. Where necessary, the trial court overseeing compliance may require their use. We note again that least-cost housing will not ordinarily satisfy a municipality's fair share obligation to provide low and moderate income housing unless and until it has attempted the inclusionary devices outlined below or otherwise has proven the futility of the attempt.

a. Subsidies

Because the kinds of lower income housing subsidies available are subject to change — and have in fact changed often — it is more important to establish the municipality's general *Mount Laurel* obligation concerning subsidies than its required role as to any particular existing subsidy. The importance of defining that obligation may depend at any particular time on the then extent and impact of available subsidies; if anything, the quantity of housing subsidies varies even more than the kind. For example, the amount of lower income housing subsidies now available is substantially less than several years ago, and there is no indication that subsidies for lower income housing construction are likely to increase in the near future. They are, nevertheless, apparently a permanent part of the housing scene; the long-term importance of defining the municipality's *Mount Laurel* obligation in relation to such subsidies is that the construction of lower income housing is practically impossible without some kind of governmental subsidy. . . .

On occasion, what is needed to obtain a subsidy may be as simple as a "resolution of need" stating that "there is a need for moderate income housing" in the municipality. N.J.S.A. 55:14J-6(b). In addition to the "resolution of need," the most important federal program for providing lower income housing subsidies (the section 8 low and moderate income housing program; 42 U.S.C. §1437F (1982 Supp.)) requires in New Jersey, as a practical matter, that the municipality grant tax abatements to developers. See N.J.S.A. 55:14J-8(f).

. . . The trial court in a *Mount Laurel* case, therefore, shall have the power to require a municipality to cooperate in good faith with a developer's attempt to obtain a subsidy and to require that a tax abatement be granted for that purpose pursuant to applicable New Jersey statutes where that abatement does not conflict with other municipal interests of greater importance.

b. Inclusionary Zoning Devices

There are several inclusionary zoning techniques that municipalities must use if they cannot otherwise assure the construction of their fair share of lower income housing. Although we will discuss some of them here, we in no way intend our list to be exhaustive; municipalities and trial courts are encouraged to create other devices and methods for meeting fair share obligations.[45a]

The most commonly used inclusionary zoning techniques are incentive zoning and mandatory set-asides. The former involves offering economic incentives to a developer through the relaxation of various restrictions of an ordinance (typically density limits) in exchange for the construction of certain amounts of low and moderate income units. The latter, a mandatory set-aside, is basically a requirement that developers include a minimum amount of lower income housing in their projects.

(i) Incentive Zoning

Incentive zoning is usually accomplished either through a sliding scale density bonus that increases the permitted density as the amount of lower income housing provided is increased, or through a set bonus for participation in a lower income housing program. See Fox & Davis, 3 Hastings Const. L.Q. 1015, 1060-62 (1977).

Incentive zoning leaves a developer free to build only upper income housing if it so chooses. Fox and Davis, in their survey of municipalities using inclusionary devices, found that while developers sometimes profited through density bonuses, they were usually reluctant to cooperate with incentive zoning programs; and that therefore those municipalities that relied exclusively on such programs were not very successful in actually providing lower income housing. *Id.* at 1067.

Sole reliance on "incentive" techniques (or, indeed, reliance exclusively on any one affirmative device) may prove in a particular case to be insufficient to achieve compliance with the constitutional mandate.

(ii) Mandatory Set-Asides

A more effective inclusionary device that municipalities must use if they cannot otherwise meet their fair share obligations is the mandatory set-aside.[45b] According to the Department of Community Affairs, as of 1976

45a. For useful discussions of how inclusionary techniques have been utilized [see] Fox & Davis, "Density Bonus Zoning to Provide Low and Moderate Cost Housing," 3 Hastings Const. L.Q. 1015 (1977); Kleven, "Inclusionary Ordinances — Policy and Legal Issues in Requiring Private Developers to Build Low Cost Housing," 21 U.C.L.A.L. Rev. 1432 (1974); H. Franklin, D. Falk, A. Levin, In-Zoning: A Guide for Policy Makers on Inclusionary Land Use Programs (1974).

45b. Mandatory set-asides do not give rise to the legal issues treated in Property Owners Ass'n of N. Bergen v. Twp. of N. Bergen, 74 N.J. 327, 378 A.2d 25 (1977). We held in that case that rent control ordinances that exempted units occupied by senior citizens from future rent increases were confiscatory as to the landlord. . . . [T]he builder who undertakes a project that includes a mandatory set-aside voluntarily assumes the financial burden, if there is any, of that condition. There may very well be no "subsidy" in the sense of either the landlord or other tenants bearing some burden for the benefit of the lower income there were six municipalities in New Jersey with mandatory set-aside programs, which varied from a requirement that 5 percent of developments in a certain zone be composed of low and moderate income units (Cherry Hill, Camden County) to a requirement that between 15 and 25 percent of all PUDs be reserved for low and moderate income housing (East Windsor, Mercer County). Apparently, judging from the Handbook itself and from responses to our inquiries at oral argument, lower income housing is in fact being built pursuant to these mandatory requirements.

The use of mandatory set-asides is not without its problems: dealing with the scarcity of federal subsidies, maintaining the rent or sales price of lower income units at lower income levels over time, and assuring developers an adequate return on their investments. Fox and Davis found that the scarcity of federal subsidies has greatly undermined the effectiveness of mandatory set-asides where they are triggered only when a developer is able to obtain such subsidies. Fox & Davis, *supra*, 3 Hastings Const. L.Q. at 1065-66. Where practical, a municipality should use mandatory set-asides even where subsidies are not available.[45c]

As several commentators have noted, the problem of keeping lower income units available for lower income people over time can be a difficult one. Because a mandatory set-aside program usually requires a developer to sell or rent units at below their full value so that the units can be affordable to lower income people, the owner of the development or the initial tenant or purchaser of the unit may be induced to re-rent or re-sell the unit at its full value.

This problem, which municipalities *must* address in order to assure that they continue to meet their fair share obligations, can be dealt with in two ways. First, the developer can meet its mandatory quota of lower income units with lower cost housing, such as mobile homes or "no-frills" apartments, which may be affordable by lower income families at close to the units' market value. The other, apparently more common, approach for dealing with the re-sale or re-rent problem is for the municipality to require that re-sale or re-rent prices be kept at lower income levels. For example, the Cherry Hill ordinance requires that there be "regulations which reasonably assure that the dwelling units be occupied by [lower income persons]." . . .

In addition to the mechanisms we have just described, municipalities and

---

units: those units may be priced low not because someone else is subsidizing the price, but because of realistic considerations of cost, amenities, and therefore underlying values.

45c. Where set-asides are used, courts, municipalities, and developers should attempt to assure that lower income units are integrated into larger developments in a manner that both provides adequate access and services for the lower income residents and at the same time protects as much as possible the value and integrity of the project as a whole. For a helpful discussion of how this can be done see O. Newman, Community of Interest (1980).

trial courts must consider such other affirmative devices as zoning substantial areas for mobile homes and for other types of low cost housing and establishing maximum square footage zones, i.e., zones where developers cannot build units with *more* than a certain footage or build anything other than lower income housing or housing that includes a specified portion of lower income housing. In some cases, a realistic opportunity to provide the municipality's fair share may require over-zoning, i.e., zoning to allow for *more* than the fair share if it is likely, as it usually is, that not all of the property made available for lower income housing will actually result in such housing.

Although several of the defendants concede that simply removing restrictions and exactions is unlikely to result in the construction of lower income housing, they maintain that requiring the municipality to use affirmative measures is beyond the scope of the court's authority. We disagree....

The specific contentions are that inclusionary measures amount to a taking without just compensation and an impermissible socio-economic use of the zoning power, one not substantially related to the use of land. Reliance is placed to some extent on Board of Supervisors v. DeGroff Enterprises, Inc., 214 Va. 235, 198 S.E.2d 600 (1973), to that effect. We disagree with that decision.... We hold that where the *Mount Laurel* obligation cannot be satisfied by removal of restrictive barriers, inclusionary devices such as density bonuses and mandatory set-asides keyed to the construction of lower income housing, are constitutional and within the zoning power of a municipality....

We find the distinction between the exercise of the zoning power that is "directly tied to the physical use of the property," *Madison*, 72 N.J. at 517, 371 A.2d 1192, and its exercise tied to the income level of those who use the property artificial in connection with the *Mount Laurel* obligation, although it obviously troubled us in *Madison*. The prohibition of this kind of affirmative device seems unfair when we have for so long allowed large lot single family residence districts, a form of zoning keyed, in effect, to income levels. The constitutional obligation itself is not to build three bedroom units, or single family residences on very small lots, or high-rise multifamily apartments, but rather to provide through the zoning ordinance a realistic opportunity to construct *lower income housing*. All of the physical uses are simply a means to this end. We see no reason why the municipality cannot exercise its zoning power to achieve that end directly rather than through a mass of detailed regulations governing the "physical use" of land, the sole purpose of which is to provide housing within the reach of lower income families. We know of no governmental purpose relating to zoning that is served by requiring a municipality to ingeniously design detailed land use regulations, purporting to be "directly tied to the physical use of the property," but actually aimed at accommodating lower income families, while not allowing it directly to require developers to construct lower income units. Indirection of this kind has no more virtue where its goal is to achieve that which is permitted — indeed, constitutionally mandated — than it has in achieving that which is prohibited.

3. Zoning for Mobile Homes

As the cost of ordinary housing skyrockets for purchasers and renters, mobile homes become increasingly important as a source of low cost housing.... Therefore, subject to the qualifications noted hereafter, we rule that municipalities that cannot otherwise meet their fair share obligations must provide zoning for low-cost mobile homes as an affirmative device in their zoning ordinances.

Townships such as Mount Laurel that now ban mobile homes do so in reliance upon Vickers v. Gloucester, 37 N.J. 232, 181 A.2d (1962), in which this court upheld such bans. *Vickers,* however, explicitly recognized that changed circumstances could require a different result. *Id.* at 250, 181 A.2d 129. We find that such changed circumstances now exist. As Judge Wood found in *Mount Laurel II,* mobile homes have since 1962 become "structurally sound [and] attractive in appearance." 161 N.J. Super. at 357, 391 A.2d 935. Further, since 1974, the safety and soundness of mobile homes have been regulated by the National Mobile Home Construction and Safety Standards Act, 42 U.S.C. 5401 (1974). *Vickers,* therefore, is overruled; absolute bans of mobile homes are no longer permissible on the grounds stated in that case....

Lest we be misunderstood, we do *not* hold that every municipality must allow the use of mobile homes as an affirmative device to meet its *Mount Laurel* obligation, or that any ordinance that totally excludes mobile homes is per se invalid. Insofar as the *Mount Laurel* doctrine is concerned, whether mobile homes must be permitted as an affirmative device will depend upon the overall effectiveness of the municipality's attempts to comply: if compliance can be just as effectively assured without allowing mobile homes, *Mount Laurel* does not command them; if not, then assuming a suitable site is available, they must be allowed....

4. Providing "Least Cost" Housing

... [In most cases,] middle income housing will not satisfy the *Mount Laurel* obligation. This is so despite claims by some defendant-municipalities that the provisions of such middle income housing will allow less expensive housing to "filter down" to lower income families. The problem with this theory is that the housing that has been built and is now being built in suburbs such as Mount Laurel is rapidly *appreciating* in value so that none of *it* will "filter down" to poor people. Instead, if the only housing constructed in municipalities like Mount Laurel continues to be middle and upper income. the only "filter down" effect that will occur will be that housing on the fringes of our inner cities will "filter down" to the poor as more of the middle class leave for suburbs, thereby exacerbating the economic segregation of our cities and suburbs. See A. Downs, [Opening up the Suburbs 9-12 (1973)]. Only if municipalities like Mount Laurel begin now to build lower income or least cost housing will some part of *their* housing stock ever "filter down" to New Jersey's poorer families.

E. JUDICIAL REMEDIES. . .

1. Builder's Remedy

Builder's remedies have been one of many controversial aspects of the *Mount Laurel* doctrine. Plaintiffs, particularly plaintiff-developers, maintain that these remedies are (i) essential to maintain a significant level of *Mount Laurel* litigation, and the only effective method to date of enforcing compliance; (ii) required by principles of fairness to compensate developers who have invested substantial time and resources in pursuing such litigation; and (iii) the most likely means of ensuring that lower income housing is actually built. . . .

. . . We hold that where a developer succeeds in *Mount Laurel* litigation and proposes a project providing a substantial amount of lower income housing,[45d] a builder's remedy should be granted unless the municipality establishes that because of environmental or other substantial planning concerns, the plaintiff's proposed project is clearly contrary to sound land use planning. We emphasize that the builder's remedy should not be denied solely because the municipality prefers some other location for lower income housing, even if it is in fact a better site. Nor is it essential that considerable funds be invested or that the litigation be intensive. . . .

. . . Trial courts should guard the public interest carefully to be sure that plaintiff-developers do not abuse the *Mount Laurel* doctrine. Where builder's remedies are awarded, the remedy should be carefully conditioned to assure that in fact the plaintiff-developer *constructs* a substantial amount of lower income housing. Various devices can be used for that purpose, including prohibiting construction of more than a certain percentage of the non-lower income housing until a certain amount of the lower income housing is completed.

2. Revision of the Zoning Ordinance: the Master

If the trial court determines that a municipality's zoning ordinance does

---

45d. What is "substantial" in a particular case will be for the trial court to decide. The court should consider such factors as the size of the plaintiff's proposed project, the percentage of the project to be devoted to lower income housing (20 percent appears to us to be a reasonable minimum), what proportion of the defendant municipality's fair share allocation would be provided by the project, and the extent to which the remaining housing in the project can be categorized as "least cost." . . .

not satisfy its *Mount Laurel* obligation, it shall order the defendant to revise it. Unless it is clear that the requisite realistic opportunity can be otherwise provided, the trial court should direct the municipality to incorporate in that new ordinance the affirmative devices discussed above most likely to lead to the construction of lower income housing. The trial court shall order the revision to be completed within 90 days of its original judgment against the municipality. For good cause shown, a municipality may be granted an extension of that time period.

To facilitate this revision, the trial court may appoint a special master to assist municipal officials in developing constitutional zoning and land use regulations. . . .

III. Resolution of the Cases

A. MOUNT LAUREL II

1. The 1976 Revised Zoning Ordinance . . .

. . . Instead of attempting to amend [its] specific deficiencies, Mount Laurel simply added three new zones to meet its fair share obligation, presumably assuming that such action would conform to the underlying intent of our ruling.

We find that the amended ordinance falls far short of what was required, that it neither corrects the particular deficiencies of the prior ordinance nor otherwise affirmatively provides a realistic opportunity for Mount Laurel's fair share of lower income housing. It is little more than a smoke screen that attempts to hide the Township's persistent intention to exclude housing for the poor. . . .

Nothing has really changed since the date of our first opinion, either in Mount Laurel or in its land use regulations. The record indicates that the Township continues to thrive with added industry, some new businesses, and continued growth of middle, upper middle, and upper income housing.[45e] As far as lower income housing is concerned, from the date of that opinion to today (as far as the record before us shows) no one has yet constructed one unit of lower income housing — nor has anyone even tried

---

45e. Between 1970 and 1977, Mount Laurel added 1,300,000 square feet to its industrial floor space and 700,000 square feet to its office space. Between 1970 and 1980, 2,784 new housing units were built in Mount Laurel, *all* of them under the restrictive conditions that this Court held in *Mount Laurel I* could not produce lower income housing. The total population of Mount Laurel has increased tremendously, from 11,221 in 1970 to 17,614 in 1980, a 57 percent increase during a decade when the total population of the state increased by less than 5 percent and the total population of Burlington County increased by only 12 percent.

Zoning Processes, Practices, and Problems

to.[45f] Mount Laurel's lower income housing effort has been either a total failure or a total success — depending on its intention.

We realize that given today's economy, especially as it affects housing, the failure of developers to build lower income housing does not necessarily prove that a town's zoning ordinances are unduly restrictive. One might have expected, however, that in the eight years that have elapsed since our decision, Mount Laurel would have something to show other than this utter cipher — that is, unless one looked at the amended ordinance.

Mount Laurel's notion of providing a realistic opportunity to build lower income housing has led to the rezoning of less than one-fourth of one percent of its land (about 20 out of 14,700 acres). This miniscule acreage consists of three zones, R-5, -6, and -7, each one owned by a different individual (apparently not residential developers in the cases of R-5 and R-6) who may very well elect never to take "advantage" of the alleged opportunity to build lower income housing.

The zone designated R-5, consisting of 13 acres, allows the construction of townhouses and garden apartments with a maximum of 10 units per acre. It is owned by an industrial developer, is totally surrounded by industrially zoned land, virtually isolated from residential uses, has no present access to other parts of the community, no water or sewer connections nearby, is in the path of a proposed high speed railroad line, and is subject to possible flooding. It would be hard to find (other than R-6) a less suitable parcel for lower income or indeed any kind of housing. Furthermore, as one of plaintiffs' experts pointed out, no experienced industrial developer would allow this parcel to become a pocket of protesting residents objecting to his planned industrial uses surrounding them.

The R-6 zone is for detached single family residences on 6,000 square foot lots, which is an effort to comply with the *Mount Laurel I* requirement that there be some residential development permitted on "very small lots." *Mount Laurel I*, 67 N.J. at 187, 336 A.2d 713. It includes, however, only 7.45 acres. It has an extremely serious drainage problem, lying so low compared to the surrounding area that it would cost $10,000 per acre, according to plaintiffs' experts, to raise it so as to minimize that problem. In addition, there are no water or sewer connections nearby. There are cost-generating

---

45f. There has been a continuing application for construction of mobile homes, but no applications of any kind other than this and certainly none pursuant to the new ordinance.

If this continues, and no new lower income housing is built in Mount Laurel to the year 2000, then by that year the percentage of lower income families in the Township will have dropped to 7.7 percent, from 25.5 percent in 1970 and 41.4 percent in 1960. The percentage of lower income families in the Burlington, Gloucester, Camden region has been, and will, it is assumed, continue to be through 2000, roughly 40 percent.

requirements concerning parking, street widths, and others, that will subsequently affect the price of homes, if they are ever to be built. The size of the zone itself is so small that it is highly unlikely that any developer would consider building low and moderate income housing there, for the necessary economies of scale could never be achieved. Defendant's planner estimated that only 30 units could be built in this zone, and conceded that under no circumstances would *anything* be built for five to six years since there would be no sewer or water access available until then. Lower income housing on this tract is a phantom.

The R-7 zone is somewhat more complex. It does not consist of any specific land but rather is defined as being a maximum of 10 percent of the units to be built in Section VII of an existing approved PUD known as Larchmont. . . .

R-7 is really not a zone at all, but rather a waiver by Mount Laurel of certain restrictions and requirements that would otherwise have been imposed on the Larchmont Section VII units. . . .

Unless something changes radically, it is certain that no builder will construct lower income housing in R-7. There is no evidence that the present developer has any intention to do so, especially in light of the benefits available to him when he builds upper and middle income housing in the R-7 zone. . . .

[Although Mount Laurel asserted that these zones satisfied its fair share obligation, Wilentz, C.J., found the township's analysis of its obligation to be "blatantly self-serving." The Delaware Valley Regional Planning Commission estimated Burlington County's need for lower income housing through the year 2000 at 22,900 dwelling units.] The sole factor used by Mount Laurel's planners in allocating this regional need . . . was "developable land." Its studies indicated that Mount Laurel had 5,936 acres of such land, and Burlington County 263,282 acres, and concluded that this 2.25 percent ratio, when applied to the county need of 22,900 units through the year 2000, meant that Mount Laurel's fair share was 515 units. Vacant developable land, at this point, may be regarded as land not legally committed to other uses. The formula, therefore, assigns the same share to 100 acres located 100 miles from Camden, totally unsuitable for lower income housing and totally devoid of any demand for such use, as it does to 100 acres 10 miles from the center of Camden, near shopping centers, transportation facilities, and highly suited for lower income housing and subject to intensive demand for such use. In fact Mount Laurel's formula equates the highly desirable vacant acreage of Mount Laurel with that of the Pine Barrens. . . .

In sum, we find that Mount Laurel's 1976 revised zoning ordinance fails completely to comply with the mandate of *Mount Laurel I*. . . .

We therefore remand this matter to the trial court for further proceedings to determine Mount Laurel's fair share, and upon such determination to require further actions by the municipality to assure the expeditious revision of Mount Laurel's land use regulations (and other actions) all in accordance with this opinion. While we have held that the bona fides of Mount Laurel is irrelevant in determining its compliance with the underlying constitutional obligation, it is not irrelevant in determining the remedy adopted herein. Where, as here, there is evidence of lack of municipal good faith and/or interminable delay, trial courts must closely supervise orders designed to compel compliance. Here that supervison must include the appointment of a master.

2. *The Builder's Remedy*

Davis Enterprises was permitted to intervene as plaintiff in this case after *Mount Laurel I* was decided. Davis proposed a 535 unit, 107 acre mobile home park for the Township. Davis committed itself to securing federal Section 8 subsidies for 20 percent of the units. Mount Laurel originally rejected the Davis project because its zoning ordinance barred all mobile homes. Although this rationale for excluding Davis is no longer tenable after our overturning of *Vickers*, we must still decide whether Davis is entitled to the builder's remedy it seeks.

The trial court granted the builder's remedy, ordering the Mount Laurel Planning Board to consider the Davis application and review it in a "manner consistent with the least-cost housing principles enunciated in Oakwood v. Madison," 161 N.J. Super. at 359, 391 A.2d 935. We affirm the grant of a builder's remedy. It is clearly appropriate in this case under the new standard enunciated in this opinion. First, the Davis project *will* provide lower income housing for Mount Laurel. Beside the fact that mobile homes are generally much less costly than site-built housing, the trial court's decision requires that Davis construct *at least* 20 percent of its units for lower income persons. In addition, the site chosen by Davis is plainly suited for mobile home development and Mount Laurel has presented no real evidence to the contrary. Finally, we feel that after ten years of litigation it is time that *something* be built for the resident and non-resident lower income plaintiffs in this case who have borne the brunt of Mount Laurel's unconstitutional policy of exclusion.

... On December 2, 1980, the trial court ... ordered Mount Laurel to grant Davis a building permit on condition that Davis apply to HUD for Section 8 subsidies for 20 percent of its units.... We now affirm the December 2, 1980, order with the added condition that if Davis is not able to obtain the Section 8 subsidies being sought, the developer must use whatever other means are available to make certain that *at least* 20 percent of the units built are affordable by lower income households, with *at least* half of these being affordable by low income households....

NOTES AND QUESTIONS

1. For a summary of exclusionary zoning developments since 1980 in other states active in the area (New York, Pennsylvania, Michigan, and California), see R. Ellickson & A. D. Tarlock, Land-Use Controls, 1984 Supplement 129-138 (1984).

2. Between the time of *Mount Laurel I* (reproduced in the main text beginning at page 1367) and *Mount Laurel II*, a chief concern of the New Jersey Supreme Court was the removal of obstacles to the construction of new least-cost housing that, though it might be too expensive for low-income families, would let used housing trickle down to them. *Mount Laurel II*, in contrast, calls for measures to ensure production of new housing affordable for low-income families. Could the idea backfire? See Ellickson, The Irony of "Inclusionary Zoning," 54 S. Cal. L. Rev. 1167 (1981). See also Rose, The *Mount Laurel II* Decision: Is it Based on Wishful Thinking?, 12 Real Est. L.J. 115, 124-125, 136 (1983):

> There is an underlying assumption of the *Mount Laurel* decisions that may prove to be incorrect. That assumption is that it is *economically* feasible to build *new* housing for lower-income persons. The major thrust of the *Mount Laurel* decisions is to eliminate the *political* obstacle to new housing for low-income persons in the suburbs. Having determined that exclusionary zoning laws are unconstitutional, the court is now faced with the question whether its underlying assumption is correct (i.e., that it is economically feasible to build new housing for lower-income persons when seeking to provide a remedy for that unconstitutional act). If it is not possible to build new housing for lower-income persons (because the lowest possible cost of such housing is still beyond their reach) then the only housing to be built in the suburbs as a result of the *Mount Laurel* decisions will be least-cost/trickle-down housing. If the court's assumption that municipalities can in fact fulfill their primary obligation to build low-income housing turns out to be incorrect then the net effect of *Mount Laurel II* will be to build least-cost housing in the suburbs. This will further accelerate the flight of the middle class from the cities, where their presence and resources are needed if there is to be any hope of preserving and improving the cities where most poor people live. Thus, the justice and the wisdom of the *Mount Laurel* decisions may be evaluated in the future by two standards: (1) whether any significant amount of new housing for low-income persons is in fact built in the suburbs and (2) whether the interests of low-income persons in the cities would be better served by a policy that seeks to redirect people and resources into (rather than away from) the cities where the greatest concentrations of low-income people now live and can be expected to continue to live in the forseeable future. . . .
>
> The *Mount Laurel II* decision is a strong and determined statement by the New Jersey Supreme Court of its belief in the fundamental principle protected by the state constitution, that every person has the right to move freely within the state and to live where he believes opportunities of employment, safety, and the pursuit of happiness exist. This constitutionally protected right may not be frustrat-

ed by land-use regulations that make housing prohibitively expensive or by the failure of municipalities to take affirmative measures to make housing available for low-income persons.

These are noble ideals and cannot be faulted. The weakness of the decision may emerge in time, not from its ethical principles, but from the economic and political assumptions on which it rests. It remains to be seen whether *new* housing can be built that meets minimum standards of safety and health, and is affordable by low-income persons; it remains to be seen whether there is any realistic prospect of a sufficient commitment by the American people of a portion of our national resources for anything more than a token amount of subsidized low-income housing; it remains to be seen whether the net effect of the decision will result in anything more than an acceleration of the movement of upwardly mobile middle-income families from the central cities to suburbs, creating an even greater exacerbation of the problem of the deteriorating central cities; it remains to be seen whether municipal officials representing embattled suburban citizens seeking to protect their own quest for safety, security, and happiness will accede to the authority of the three judges and their appointed "masters"; it remains to be seen whether the principles of sound state land-use planning will prevail against the political forces directed by a fearful and threatened suburban citizenry. Until these questions can be answered with some certainty, it may be fair to continue to ask whether the underlying goals and remedial measures of the *Mount Laurel II* decision are presently achievable or whether they are "based upon the wistful hopes of an idealistic but credulous court."

3. See generally *Mount Laurel II* Symposium, 14 Seton Hall L. Rev. 829 (1984).